D0992251

HERE IN THIS ISLAND WE ARRIVED

Here in This Island
We Arrived

Shakespeare and Belonging in Immigrant New York

ELISABETH H. KINSLEY

The Pennsylvania State University Press
University Park, Pennsylvania

Library of Congress Cataloging-in-Publication Data

Names: Kinsley, Elisabeth H., 1983– author.
Title: Here in this island we arrived : Shakespeare and belonging
    in immigrant New York / Elisabeth H. Kinsley.
Description: University Park, Pennsylvania : The Pennsylvania State
    University Press, [2019] | Includes bibliographical references and index.
Summary: "Explores the uses of Shakespeare in Manhattan's Lower
    East Side as part of a cultural exchange among non-Anglo and
    Anglo-identified groups from the 1890s to 1920s. Examines these groups'
    ideas about what Shakespeare, race, and national belonging should and
    could mean for Americans"—Provided by publisher.
Identifiers: LCCN 2018055872 | ISBN 9780271083223 (cloth : alk. paper)
Subjects: LCSH: Shakespeare, William, 1564–1616—Stage
    history—New York (State)—New York. | Shakespeare, William,
    1564–1616—Stage History—1800–1950. | Shakespeare, William,
    1564–1616—Influence. | Immigrants—New York (State)—New
    York—History—19th century. | Immigrants—New York (State)—
    New York—History—20th century. | Theater—New York
    (State)—New York—History—19th century. | Theater—New York
    (State)—New York—History—20th century. | Lower East Side
    (New York, N.Y.)—History—19th century. | Lower East Side (New
    York, N.Y.)—History—20th century.
Classification: LCC PR3105.K56 2019 | DDC 792.09747/1—dc23
LC record available at https://lccn.loc.gov/2018055872

Chapter 3 first appeared as "This Island's Mine: Mapping the Borders of
Shakespeare, Whiteness, and National Belonging in Manhattan's Ethnic
Theaters, 1890–1910" in *Text and Performance Quarterly*, volume 34, issue 1,
2014, pages 52–71.

Chapter 4 copyright © The Johns Hopkins University Press. This article
first appeared as "'The Jew That Shakespeare Drew, at Least in Outlines':
Renderings of a Yiddish-Speaking Shylock in New York, circa 1900" in
Theatre Journal, volume 68, issue 1, 2016, pages 17–36.

Copyright © 2019 Elisabeth H. Kinsley
All rights reserved
Printed in the United States of America
Published by The Pennsylvania State University Press,
University Park, PA 16802-1003

The Pennsylvania State University Press is a member of the Association of
University Presses.

It is the policy of The Pennsylvania State University Press to use acid-free
paper. Publications on uncoated stock satisfy the minimum requirements
of American National Standard for Information Sciences—Permanence of
Paper for Printed Library Material, ANSI Z39.48–1992.

*For my Grandma Mary Romani Kinsley,
who passed peacefully at age ninety on the
four-hundredth anniversary of Shakespeare's
death—and who extended an open heart, a
curious mind, and unconditional kindness to
everyone she met, no matter who they were,
where they came from, or what they believed.*

CONTENTS

ILLUSTRATIONS

ACKNOWLEDGMENTS

I owe warm thanks to a number of institutions, organizations, communities, and individuals for supporting me throughout the process of researching and writing this book. Of course, I am thankful to Penn State University Press for taking interest in my project and seeing the manuscript through to publication. Series editors Leah Ceccarelli and Michael Bernard-Donals provided valuable input after reviewing an initial book proposal, and editor-in-chief Kendra Boileau has been a wonderful collaborator and perceptive commentator throughout the revising process. The book has also benefited from the insights of peer reviewers, as well as careful attention from the press's faculty reviewers and staff.

Here in This Island We Arrived traces all the way back to a course paper I wrote for Angela G. Ray's rhetorical criticism seminar at Northwestern University, and it is a gift that Angela has remained a central influence on this work—and in my life—ever since. One could not hope for a more generous, dedicated, astute, and encouraging academic mentor and friend. Along with Angela, I was lucky to have Tracy C. Davis and Janice A. Radway as advisors; these three are mind-blowingly careful, considerate, and challenging readers, and the honor of naming them among those whose teaching and intellectual input most informed this book is not lost on me.

I am thankful, too, for a number of other Northwestern community members and academic colleagues. Among the faculty who shaped my thinking and research along the way are Linda Austern, Kate Baldwin, Henry Binford, Paul Edwards, Jessica Greenberg (now at the University of Illinois), Robert Hariman, Jeffrey Masten, Carl Smith, C. Riley Snorton (now at Cornell University), and Wendy Wall. My Yiddish instructor, Khane-Faygl Turtletaub, is tops as a teacher and translator and gave me crucial tools for research and analysis. My students have kept me on my toes, pushed me to clarify ideas, and inspired new connections along the way. And I feel special gratitude for the ideas, humor, love, and support that my Ph.D. cohort shared from day one, and continues to share in the years since graduation. Historian George W. Pierson once described a "company of scholars and society of friends," and I am lucky to have found this best-case scenario in my own academic settings. This book has been touched by too many scholar-friends to name, but Robert E. Mills and Robert Topinka gave feedback that undoubtedly ushered early versions of my arguments toward more compelling iterations. And Andy Horowitz and Ruth Martin also deserve special mention: conversations with these two always reaffirm the human in "humanities," and I owe much of my confidence and joy in this project to the enthusiasm each has shown along the way.

Material from chapters 3 and 4 saw initial publication in the January 2014 issue of *Text and Performance Quarterly* (34, no. 1) and the March 2016 issue of *Theatre Journal* (68, no. 1), respectively. I thank both journals for the opportunity to share this material again here, and for choosing editorial staff so wisely, as I received formative input from Dustin Goltz, Mindy Fenske, and Jennifer Parker-Starbuck, as well as other editors and reviewers affiliated with these publications. Many of the ideas in this book likewise evolved through various conference papers over the years, and I am grateful to those who responded to my work, both formally and informally, with thoughtful questions and feedback.

A good deal of archival research went into this project. Thanks to the wonderful archivists and library staff at Yale University's Beinecke Rare Book and Manuscript Library, the Folger Shakespeare Library, the Harvard Theatre Collection, the New York Public Library's Dorot Jewish Division and Manuscripts and Archives Division, the New York Public Library for the Performing Arts's Billy Rose Theater Division, the University of Minnesota's Immigration History Research Center Archives, and the YIVO Institute for Jewish Research. Thanks, too, to fellow Folger researcher Monika Smialkowska for sharing materials relevant to the 1916 Shakespeare Tercentennial. I also acknowledge the critical resources at Northwestern University Libraries, as well as the wonderful network of friends who energized and encouraged me at home in Chicago. Fellowship and grant funding from the American Society for Theatre Research, Northwestern's Department of Communication Studies, and The Graduate School at Northwestern made my travels to these archives possible, as did the hospitality of friends and family who hosted me in New Haven, Washington, D.C., Boston, and New York.

My parents and sister were among those generous hosts, but they merit singling out here. Books are inevitably reflections of one's personal values and experiences, and no three people have more directly shaped my values and experiences than my sister Johanna, my father, Dominic Kinsley, and my mother Judy Hoberman. My dad introduced me to Shakespeare and the importance of topic sentences, and my mom instilled in me a strong identification with New York's Ashkenazic Jewish culture and an orientation toward matters of social equity. Writing this made me feel close to my family, surely a sustaining force in a lengthy and patience-trying process.

Finally, to my most loving collaborator (and superlative spouse), Dave: your unflagging and effusive faith in my ability to get this done, your willingness to read various drafts, your patience with my impatience, and your inspiring dedication to your own creative undertakings have pushed me toward each next deadline. Your partnership, like Angela's mentorship, puts the "us" in generous—I am deeply grateful.

All translations throughout this book are my own unless otherwise credited. For several instances of Yiddish translation, I relied on the assistance
of Dr. Khane-Faygl Turtletaub. I have transliterated Yiddish characters into
English characters by way of the YIVO system of transliteration, which can
be found on the website of the Max Weinreich Center for Advanced Jewish
Studies of the YIVO Institute for Jewish Research in New York (https://
www.yivo.org/Yiddish-Alphabet).

———

Per this system, vowels are generally sounded as follows:
    a = *ah* as in *wand*
    ay = *aye* as in *Aye, aye, Captain*
    e = *eh* as in *gem*
    ey = long *a* as in *wave*
    i = in some cases, short *i* as in *bit*; in other cases, *ee* as in *beet*
    o = a dark *aw*, as in the first syllable of *daughter*
    oy = *oy* as in *boy*
    u = in some cases *oo* as in *look*, in other cases *oo* as in *goop*
    y = hard *y* as in *yum*
The following consonant clusters are sounded as follows:
    dzj = *j* as in *judge*
    kh = a guttural *ch* as in *Chanukah*
    tsh = *ch* as in *cherry*
    sch (preceded by a vowel) = *sh* as in *fish*
    zh = *j* as in *beige*
Names of well-known Yiddish figures, such as Jacob P. Adler, Bertha Kalich,
and Bores Thomashefsky, are rendered according to the Library of Congress Name Authority File.

Introduction

Shakespeare and American Culture

In 1932, Shakespeare scholar Joseph Quincy Adams—a South Carolina–born Baptist minister's son with no close ties to the political Adamses—delivered a lecture titled "Shakespeare and American Culture" at the official opening of the Folger Shakespeare Library.[1] The library, located about a block from the U.S. Capitol building in Washington, D.C. (where it still stands), was built to house the vast Shakespeariana collection of former Standard Oil president Henry Clay Folger and his wife, Emily Jordan Folger. Today, it continues to hold the world's largest Shakespeare collection, as well as major collections of other early modern books, manuscripts, and art.[2] The library's dedication ceremony took place in its small east-end theatre before an intimate but high-powered audience: President Herbert Hoover was there, as were several ambassadors, military and navy personnel, university officers and presidents, and stage luminaries Ben Greet and Edith Matthison.[3] It was a group that made very clear Shakespeare's great national significance.

As the library's first director of research, Adams spoke with authority about Shakespeare's role in sustaining what he called the "bonds of a common Anglo-Saxon culture" over the course of the nation's history. Voicing an unquestioned belief in the country's Anglo-Saxon essence, Adams implicitly endorsed the Anglocentric ideal of U.S. national (and racial) belonging that historian Nell Irvin Painter has termed "American whiteness." His narrative culminated in praise of Shakespeare's influence during the unprecedented surge of American immigration that began in the 1880s and continued into the following decades, peaking in 1907, ebbing during World War I, and definitively subsiding around 1920, when the U.S. Congress passed a series of legislative acts that curbed further growth of the country's foreign-born population.[4] Compared to earlier currents of immigration, this enormous late nineteenth-century wave, largely comprising Jews and Italians from Eastern and Southern Europe, was, by Adams's measure, "far more threatening in kind. . . . A menace to the preservation of our long-established English civilization." To him, these new immigrants were "[f]oreign in their background and alien in their outlook upon life," and "America seemed destined to become a babel of tongues and cultures." "Fortunately," he advised, Shakespeare's place in the nation's schoolrooms proved an antidote to this dire destiny. Instead of a babel of tongues, American immigrant children voiced the language of Shakespeare. In Adams's words, "Everywhere pupils were set to the task of memorizing his lines . . . reciting on platforms his more eloquent passages." For Adams, then, Shakespeare fostered a spirit of racial coherence—or, as he put it, "something like homogeneity"—in the face of a rapidly expanding and diversifying American populace.[5]

Today's Folger collection houses certain records of how U.S. immigrant groups engaged Shakespeare during this same turn-of-the-century period that muddy Adams's account of Shakespeare and American culture. Take, for one, playwright Samuel Mencher's Yiddish version of Macbeth, translated and arranged for performance by a Yiddish-speaking company in New York City in the early 1900s.[6] Mencher was one among many writers and translators producing material for Manhattan's Yiddish-speaking actors at this time, and Macbeth was one among several Shakespearean dramas staged by the handful of Yiddish theatres clustered on the Lower East Side—a section of the city that changed dramatically in the decades flanking 1900, as an extraordinary number of new U.S. residents settled in this relatively contained urban area. The neighborhood's fast-growing immigrant populations meant larger theatre audiences, and the Yiddish playhouses thrived along with nearby Italian and German venues, where Shakespearean repertoire likewise frequently appeared on the program. Two cases in point: the Folger also houses a broadside advertisement for Antonio Maiori and Pasquale Rapone's Italian-language production of *Amleto: Principe di Danimarca* (*Hamlet: Prince of Denmark*), performed in 1901 at the Teatro Italiano, about a five-minute walk from the Thalia Theatre leased by Mencher's collaborators. And if the library's curators can be persuaded to pull from the vault a fragile 1894 album created in memory of renowned American Shakespearean Edwin Booth (brother of Abraham Lincoln's notorious assassin, John Wilkes Booth), one will find a playful affirmation of the German American theatre's claim to Shakespeare in New York at that time: among the clippings preserved in the album's final pages is a newspaper caricature titled "Two great Hamlets—Booth and Sonnenthal," depicting Booth, who was born in Maryland to English American parents, hand-in-hand with German tragedian Adolf von Sonnenthal. The Folger catalog traces this cartoon to an issue of the *New York Evening Telegram* printed in 1885, the year that Sonnenthal made his U.S. debut at the very same Thalia Theatre, which stood as the city's leading German-language venue prior to its coming under a Yiddish troupe's management in the 1890s. In this sketch, the two actors are practically mirror images of one another, each turned toward the man next to him, stepping forward past identical skulls that lie at either side of their feet (fig. 1).[7] As such, the clipping portrays Anglo-American and German American Shakespeare performances on quite literally equal footing in the late 1800s.

As Adams remembered the period, non-Anglo immigrants gained social mobility and racial acceptance at the turn of the century through Shakespeare, treating the Bard's English lines as a script for American identity, at the behest of the Progressive Era's U.S. educational system. But Mencher's script, the Teatro Italiano playbill, and the sketch of Booth and Sonnenthal suggest that immigrants adapted Shakespeare to their own lives and localities in turn-of-the-twentieth-century New York. Taken together as extant traces of the era's vibrant Lower East Side immigrant theatre communities, these ephemera evidence how Shakespeare played alternative roles in American culture that looked and sounded very different from that which Adams set forth at the Folger's opening ceremony.

Had Adams (who was born in 1880) traveled to lower Manhattan around 1900, what might he have said about the Yiddish-, Italian-, and German-language Shakespeare performances that regularly took place in New York at the same historic moment that the city's schoolchildren obediently took to platforms to recite the Bard's "more eloquent passages"? That is, how might Adams have reconciled these concurrent Shakespeare scenes? Moreover, how might the lived experiences of the producers, performers,

TWO   GREAT   HAMLETS.

BOOTH   AND   SONNENTHAL

FIGURE 1 "Two great Hamlets, Booth and Sonnenthal." By permission of the Folger Shakespeare Library.

and audiences who staged or saw Mencher's *Macbeth*, Maiori and Rapone's *Amleto*, or Sonnenthal's *Hamlet* have confounded the ideological correlations between Shakespeare, race, and American belonging that the school exercises and Adams's later encomium to them took for granted? Certainly, actors' and spectators' experiences of Shakespeare-in-translation, adapted to the conditions and tastes of lower Manhattan's largely working-class immigrant audiences, stood apart from, and perhaps ran counter to, Adams's vision of Shakespearean verse that steeled the country against the imminent possibility of becoming a polyglot and polyracial babel. Given this, would Adams have acknowledged or disavowed these immigrant performances as Shakespearean? As American? And how might a performance of *Macbeth* in Yiddish or *Hamlet* in Italian or German have proved instructive to Adams, expanding his perception of the types of bodies and voices that could viably enact cultural categories like "Shakespearean" and "American"? Finally, in what ways might a young person's evening outing to a Shakespeare play at the Yiddish, Italian, or German theatre have mutually informed—even complicated—her or his daytime study of Shakespeare in English (a learning process well outside any schoolteacher's control)?

Here in This Island We Arrived explores the types of questions raised by Adams's hypothetical visit to the Lower East Side by studying documented scenarios in which Anglo-identified people, perspectives, and experiences intersected with non-Anglo people, perspectives, and experiences via Shakespeare in Progressive Era New York, the entry city for most American immigrant groups and the vanguard of American stage culture at this time. Throughout the book, I show how public discourse about these Shakespearean intersections shaped their social meaning for audiences in New York (and beyond, in cases where newspapers or magazines circulated outside of the city). I also aim my analysis beneath the surface of preserved materials to imagine unscripted human experiences not explicitly chronicled in formal accounts of the past—experiences that often complicate conventional narratives of social power.[8]

Although several scholars have tracked instances like Adams's Folger Library lecture to show how American elites used Shakespeare at the turn of the twentieth century to shape and secure American whiteness, fewer have studied the ways in which Shakespeare—both the popular *idea* of "Shakespeare," and "Shakespeare" as a performance repertoire—formed a prime social arena for group intersections and interactions in the country's fast-diversifying cities during this period.[9] Literature scholar Alexander C. Y. Huang has flagged the "[s]elective attentiveness, if not valorization, [that] has routinely been given to the most dominant and the most resistant readings of Shakespeare, highlighting a linear relationship of either assimilation or opposition between Shakespeare and world cultures."[10] Mindful of this pattern (and aspiring to dodge it), I reveal how Shakespeare was not simply a source of cultural capital, cultural authority, or cultural resistance for Americans in the late 1800s and early 1900s but was also a site of cultural exchange, where historical actors negotiated the vicissitudes of national belonging. As such, Shakespeare spurred nuanced and improvisatory social encounters between New York's empowered and marginalized groups—encounters that intermingled different communities' ideas about what Shakespeare, race, and national belonging should and could mean for Americans at this time. The cartoon of Booth and Sonnenthal, for one, is a marvelous instance of actual intermingling, as American and German tragedians clasped hands before the *New York Evening Telegram*'s readership. At the broadest level, then, *Here in This Island We Arrived* treats Shakespeare, whiteness, and Americanness as a trio of inter-influential, unstable categories—merely masquerading as fixed conceptions of culture, race, and nation—and demonstrates how groups' printed representations and/ or lived experiences of Shakespeare performance in Manhattan's immigrant communities formed, performed, circulated, and reconfigured associations between these categories at the turn of the twentieth century.

RACE AND SHAKESPEARE IN NEW YORK

The island of Manhattan was itself a geographic hotbed of group intersections and exchanges in the decades of peak immigration and major industrial development that neighbored 1900. Of the 23 million immigrants who came to the United States between 1880 and 1920, 17 million passed through the Port of New York, with Eastern Europeans, Italians, and Germans consistently among the largest incoming groups. By 1900, roughly 250,000 Italians, almost 300,000 Germans, and nearly as many Eastern European Jews resided in the city, and these numbers increased exponentially over the next decade. Between the turn of the century and World War I, for example, another 1.5 million Jews came to the United States from Eastern Europe; by 1910, over 540,000 had settled on the Lower East Side.[11] Indeed, this southeast corner of Manhattan staged the period's immigration trends in a particularly concentrated manner, forming a dense cross section of groups whose members arrived in droves, packed into tenement buildings, settled into lives as Americans, and—in remarkably close proximity to one another—went about their everyday activities, some of which strengthened intragroup ties and others of which fostered diverse intergroup connections.

For these incoming populations, this "New World experience was . . . decisively stamped by their entering an arena where race was the prevailing idiom for discussing citizenship and the relative merits of a given people," as American studies scholar Matthew Frye Jacobson observes. As free white persons, members of these groups were eligible for political citizenship under the United States' 1790 naturalization law, but these same individuals were not necessarily viewed, at least initially, as white Americans, and they therefore faced social and cultural exclusions. The period was thus marked by a "profound ideological tension between established codes of whiteness as inclusive of all Europeans, and new, racialist revisions" that, according to Jacobson, mounted in American public consciousness as immigration numbers rose throughout the late 1800s and early 1900s. After all, race is "an idea, not a fact," to quote Painter; it is a "public fiction" that, as Jacobson asserts, is a "[matter] of both conception and perception," residing "not in nature but in politics and culture," and profoundly influenced by its time and place.[12] So while a contemporary U.S. outlook would likely attribute certain practices, affiliations, languages, and physical traits to ethnic heritage, many turn-of-the-twentieth-century Americans—Adams, for one—would have associated these ethnic markers with racial and, by extension, national differ- ence. Such a worldview meant that the relationship of non-Anglo whiteness to U.S. national belonging was pointedly ambiguous during this period, especially on the Lower East Side, where the expanding size and increasing density of multiple immigrant communities cast a continuous spotlight on the country's precipitous population growth and change.

It was here, in Lower Manhattan at the turn of the twentieth century, that Shakespeare fostered exchanges between Anglo-identified and non-Anglo New Yorkers. Archived records tell of social reformers who brought Shake- speare in English to immigrant audiences as part of Americanization efforts, and extant theatre commentary indicates that Anglo-identified playgoers and critics attended German, Yiddish, and Italian Shakespeare productions, able to follow the stage action despite language barriers. Press coverage and memoirs likewise reveal that Lower East Siders ventured north to main- stream venues along Broadway. Packed into vast theatres seating as many as 3,000 people, individuals who hailed from different neighborhoods, spanned different social classes, and spoke different languages collectively hushed as the curtain rose and, together, took in a play.

This New York network of Shakespearean exchanges poses a departure from histories that trace the stratification of highbrow and lowbrow culture to this very same period, with Shakespeare strictly linked to high culture, and the Lower East Side's immigrant populations generally assigned lowbrow tastes. As historian Lawrence W. Levine and others have shown, the nineteenth century cemented Shakespeare's popularity among American audiences, and by the late 1800s, the playwright was considered a sort of national author, despite biographical evidence to the contrary.[13] But whereas Levine contends that Shakespeare's amplified symbolic status attached him to privileged culture, *Here in This Island We Arrived* demonstrates that his plays' widespread appeal and perceived universality served to initiate interactions among different social groups in Manhattan. A *New York Tribune* review of Sonnenthal's aforementioned 1885 appearance as Hamlet invites this point: "There was a great crowd at the Thalia Theatre last night, and the assemblage included many Americans as well as many Germans," a critic wrote on March 20. (Of course, the "Germans" in this case were in large part German Americans, but such was the parlance of the day.) He continues, "The engagement of Herr Sonnenthal at the Thalia Theatre began on March 9. . . . It was not until last evening, however, when he came forward as *Hamlet*, that [he] directly addressed himself to the American public. His performances all along have been in Teutonic pieces and for an audience of his own countrymen . . . but they have not displayed him in a universal light."[14]

Such intersections between non-Anglo and Anglo-identified experiences are largely overlooked across studies of American Shakespeare culture in the long nineteenth century. Scholars rarely analyze non-Anglo alongside Anglo-identified perspectives, and even more rarely treat non-Anglo theatre histories in sufficient depth, instead isolating marginalized stage traditions or looking primarily at dominant trends, often with a focus on mainstream Broadway venues. Across such studies, Shakespeare history yields U.S. history, as researchers read Americans' various interactions with the Bard as meaningful instances of national identity formation in the 1800s and early 1900s.[15] But if narratives of nineteenth-century American Shakespeare performance are to double as narratives of nineteenth-century U.S. identity building, then we must better account for Shakespeare performances staged by and for the country's non-Anglo immigrant communities during this period. And so this book turns to the Lower East Side for a more complete history.

Shakespeare also precipitated interactions and affiliations among different non-Anglo groups in lower Manhattan. As the opening examples of Mencher's *Macbeth*, Maiori and Rapone's *Amleto*, and Sonnenthal's *Hamlet* let on, the neighborhood's German, Yiddish, and Italian theatre troupes and their patrons thrived in extremely close quarters. The venues where these troupes rehearsed and performed were just blocks if not steps from one another, and records such as newspaper ads and editorials suggest that members of different groups (whose first languages—and customary onstage languages—were not the same) occasionally attended one another's productions, shared one another's stages, and even cast the same actors in the case of German and Yiddish companies.[16] Nightly, immigrant audiences emerged from separate side streets—this one designated the Italian quarter, that one the Hebrew, and the German several blocks north—and poured onto the Bowery (the neighborhood's main thoroughfare), brushing past one another en route to their respective destinations. Because all of these immigrant venues staged Shakespeare, the Bard offered a special point of common ground that enabled and enriched cross-group exchanges. Actors critiqued one another's interpretations of Shakespearean roles. Theatre marquees and posters hailed a sea of polyglot passersby, walking to work or a bar or a bank, who may not have been able to make out the advertisements' meaning but recognized the name Shakespeare in all its permutations. Schoolchildren, fluent in their parents' native tongues as well as in English, may have swapped impressions of two concurrent *Hamlet* productions seen the evening prior, one performed in German at the Irving Place theatre and the other in Yiddish at the People's Theatre.

Most studies of New York's immigrant theatres chronicle a single group's stage history, too often neglecting the daily routes and routines that brought different communities and their theatre activities into contact, as well as the cultural exchanges and shifts in perspective that resulted from these intersections. *Here in This Island We Arrived* wagers a more comprehensive scope in order to build on earlier feats of deep-dive research.[17] Indeed, this book not only recognizes the diversity of Shakespeare traditions that thrived within a short walk of one another in this small section of lower Manhattan, but it also takes their proximity as an injunction to study the group interactions that ensued. By focusing on the intersections, tensions, and exchanges between different non-Anglo groups, as well as those between non-Anglo and Anglo-identified perspectives, I keep in view the complex social dimensions of New York's larger turn-of-the-twentieth-century Shakespeare scene.

To be sure, New York offers a particular time and place where these intersections, tensions, and exchanges make for particularly rich analysis; but the effects of this localized activity also had a wider geographic reach. The Lower East Side stage where U.S. immigration trends (and the racial and social complexities thereof) became so acutely visible during this period had a spectatorship that extended beyond Manhattan. American studies scholar David Scobey has stressed that the city, as the "headquarters of American capitalism and public culture" and "the emerging center of American publishing, taste-making, and commercial culture," was "scrutinized obsessively" in the last quarter of the nineteenth century. Scobey positions New York as not merely representative but *formative* of national identity. "Beginning in the early 1850s," he explains, "the city and its environment were invested with meaning as a figure or microcosm for the nation—'a symbol, an intensification of the country,' as one popular journalist put it." He further explains how discussions and images of New York circulated widely in magazines and newspapers, serving as an imagined as well as a material urban space in which to become and/or feel American. James Fenimore Cooper captured this dynamic well in the 1860s when he wrote, "New York is essentially national in interests, position, and pursuits.... No one thinks of the place as belonging to a particular State, but to the United States."[18]

New York was also the nexus of American theatre culture at the turn of the twentieth century. Shakespeare scholar Charles H. Shattuck put it this way: "ultimately whatever set the style of Shakespearean playing and production in America [in the nineteenth century] came into or came out of the theatrical capital of the country." Sabine Haenni, an expert in U.S. urban and media history, emphasizes the "portability" of the New York stage as a symbol and influence that exceeded the city's boundaries at the turn of the twentieth century—a portability illustrated by newspapers outside the city that frequently reported on Manhattan's Shakespeare productions.[19] Historical records of Shakespeare in New York thus offer insight into widespread currents of American performance culture as well as the ideas about class, race, and national belonging that traveled the country by way of those currents.

Just as immigration trends, cultural and racial attitudes, and geographic forces inflected the period's Shakespeare scene, so too did public ideas about Shakespeare and his works shape and reflect the period's complex social landscape. Indeed, Shakespeare—as fluid a concept as "white" or "American"—proved a flashpoint for the "racialist revisions" that brought non-Anglo whiteness under scrutiny in the late 1800s and early 1900s. Like New York, Shakespeare was turf that Anglo-identified Americans, operating under what theatre scholar Dennis Kennedy calls "the myth of cultural ownership," took for granted as theirs. "Here in this island we arrived," the title of this book and a line from Shakespeare's *The Tempest*, in part gestures toward this claim to the island of Manhattan and to Shakespearean ground.[20] And just as immigrants crossing the U.S. border into New York entered a geographic space (as well as an imagined community) where privileged groups set certain terms of racial and national belonging, so too did immigrant Shakespeareans cross into cultural territory where bourgeois whites felt empowered to enact—in the sense of legislate—certain modes and manners of performance.[21]

But "Here in this island we arrived" asserts the presence and promise of newcomers just as surely as it marks the spot of those who came before. Inevitably, immigrants' experiences of adapting to their New York surroundings changed those surroundings, and likewise did immigrant groups' adaptations and translations of Shakespeare reshape the playwright's repertoire, along with its value and meaning for particular communities of Americans. Italian and English literature scholar Anne Paolucci describes the "immigrant experience [as] a constant oscillation from past to present, a spiraling toward a new identity." In a similar vein, literary scholars Craig Dionne and Parmita Kapadia call Shakespeare "the center of [a] process" whereby marginalized and/or postcolonial groups seeking a mode of address "reshap[e] the new through the old."[22]

A key premise of this book, then, is that a study of Shakespeare performance by and for Lower East Side immigrant communities at the turn of the twentieth century is a study of multiple and entangled processes of assimilation: immigrant groups' adaptations *to* and *of* U.S. forms of whiteness and national belonging, and immigrant groups' adaptations *to* and *of* Shakespeare. In her contribution to a volume on "world-wide Shakespeares," Sonia Massai suggests that non-Anglo groups' Shakespeare performances "stretch, challenge, and modify our sense of what 'Shakespeare' is"; likewise, immigrants' claims to whiteness and American identity stretched, challenged, and modified the possible meanings of these social categories in Progressive Era New York.[23] In doing so, immigrant groups made Manhattan theirs by enacting—in the sense of performing—Shake-speare, race, and U.S. belonging.

CULTURAL PERSPECTIVES

"What does it mean to be American now?" muses a *Washington Post* head-line. Another published days later asks, "Who's worthy of immigrating here? We may never decide." Two among many such sound bites in their time, these news fragments boil down to its essence Americans' deep anx-iety over the terms of U.S. identity (terms both legal and cultural) at the turn of the twentieth century.

Except these headlines do not date back to the decades of mass immi-gration surrounding 1900. They date to January 2018.[24] Over a century later, questions about what makes a good American still swirl in the public imag-inary. Official statements conflating race and civic identity still circulate to an ever-more-global audience. (Donald Trump's alleged degradation of immigrants from Haiti, El Salvador, and African nations in contrast to his favoring newcomers from Norway is an infamous case in point that also—and not coincidentally—dates to January 2018.) Struggles over who can claim national belonging still rage, from the chambers of U.S. Congress to small-town bars. And symbolic cultural terrain like Shakespeare remains deeply significant to these questions about, conflations of, and struggles over race and nation.

Indeed, the stories about Shakespeare told in this book cannot help but lay bare the structures of power that enabled and inhibited claims to cultural ownership in Progressive Era New York, and they may well conjure for readers connections to similar dynamics in their own present day. But *Here in This Island We Arrived* is not ultimately about pointing up power structures. Instead, these stories offer an even more complex and far less conclusive history lesson, inviting us to notice the quotidian cultural goings-on that shaped, sustained, and shifted social attitudes and behaviors. By tracing the ways in which everyday cultural production and participa-tion link to lofty questions like "What does it mean to be American now?" we can begin to answer the central question driving this book: *How do* ideas about cultural belonging form within human communities?

To me, this is a fundamentally rhetorical question, and not in the col-loquial sense of the phrase. I mean rhetorical in the persuasive sense. For if we can recognize the forces that *influence* public thought—the publications, performances, proclamations, posters (print and social media posters, alike), conversations, all of the collective and individual experiences that shape our views of ourselves and each other—then we can begin to understand how ideas about cultural belonging form. And, in turn, how they transform.

For our present purposes, the public perceptions and expressions of Shakespeare, race, and national belonging that conditioned life on the Lower East Side around 1900 come into view via popular books, social reform guides, press clippings, photographs, theatre broadsides, sheet music, and other texts and images that reached sizable populations. Materials like these appealed to particular audiences, in particular contexts, at a particular time in history. And as such, they lend considerable insight into the makeup—and the mak*ing* up—of these audiences, contexts, and historical periods. These texts and performances were *rhetorical* insofar as they persuaded certain audiences to identify with them, and others to feel excluded by them, thereby shaping social affinities and identities.[25] Adams's claim that late nineteenth-century immigration trends were "a menace to the preservation of our long-established English civilization" is a good example of this: by using the word "our," Adams called forth an audience of fellow Anglo-identified Americans. Across many such cases, *Here in This Island We Arrived* reveals Shakespearean sites to have been rhetorical sites, where groups defined, defended, circumvented, crossed, and even changed social boundaries at the turn of the twentieth century.

Shakespearean sites were also performative sites, and here I mean to invoke both the colloquial and academic meanings of *performative*. Of course, these sites were performative insofar as they were theatrical. But they were also performative in the theoretical sense of making-real-by-doing. We can understand performative acts or utterances as distinct from expressive or descriptive ones: a descriptive utterance refers to something that is already there ("That boat is hers"), whereas a performative utterance manifests a new reality ("I hereby declare that the boat is hers"). Early modernist Ayanna Thompson makes the case that Shakespeare, as both cultural symbol and body of dramatic work, is not a "stable, fixed, [nor] perfect" text but rather "is always defined through the recreation of his identity, image, texts, and performances."[26] In other words, Shakespeare accrues meaning and matter (indeed, comes *to matter*) solely through action. After all, the playwright's dramas first took shape as performances on the Elizabethan stage and were not published in any definitive editions during his lifetime.

Academic theories of performativity likewise hold that social categories like race, gender, nationality, and class are not inherent features of identity that we simply express in our everyday lives but rather are behaviors that we learn to recognize and represent when we calibrate our own performances against others', be they the same or different. That is, these categories only come to exist (and only come to matter) through human interaction. As such, a performative perspective is essential to exploring how ideas about cultural belonging form within human communities, and therefore essential to making meaning of the stories in this book. This perspective prompts me to see, for instance, how Adams's "Shakespeare and American Culture" assumed *and reinforced* public associations among race, U.S. belonging, and Shakespeare, wherein acting Shakespeare equated with acting Anglo-American. The same lens brings into view how performances like Mencher's Yiddish *Macbeth* or Maiori and Rapone's *Amleto* enacted dominant social codes (i.e., Shakespeare), but enacted them with a difference so as to simultaneously resist and reshape them.

Just as theories of performativity seek out the *doing* at work behind seemingly empirical social categories, performative historians endeavor to see the *doing* at work behind seemingly empirical records of the past. Despite the permanence of texts, the solidity of artifacts, and the stillness of archives, history does not "stay put," to use performance scholar Shannon Jackson's apt idiom.[27] Take the schoolchildren who, by Adams's account, obediently recited Shakespeare's "most eloquent lines": these were living, active bodies whose array of experiences far exceeded what any individual could capture in narrative, let alone an individual so ideologically transparent as Adams. One can imagine spontaneous juvenile responses to Shakespeare's odd-sounding language—girls in the back of a classroom snickering over a raunchy rhyme, for instance, and therein forging friendships. Or a student's mistaking archaic Elizabethan expressions for common U.S. parlance as he made the shift from his native Italian to American English, and the embarrassment he felt when his peers teasingly parroted the mix-up back at him for weeks to come. In her landmark study of cultural memory in the Americas, Diana Taylor precisely captures the value of performativity to history in describing how a "*repertoire* of embodied practice/knowledge (i.e., spoken language, dance, sports, ritual)" can live within and push against an "*archive* of supposedly enduring materials (i.e., texts, documents, buildings, bones)"—namely, that reading between the lines of extant materials for unwritten traces of lived experience can surface historical nuances and complexities, often casting light on marginalized groups' previously obscured pasts.[28]

Performative and rhetorical approaches to history thus share an orientation toward *doing*, where performative perspectives tend to focus on performance *as* knowledge production (be it knowledge of ourselves, of others, or of the past), and rhetorical perspectives emphasize *how* performances influence our ways of knowing (be the performer a body, text, object, or place). As I see it, performative heuristics encourage an especially keen awareness of the embodied experiences that pulse beneath the printed figures or physical contours of historical artifacts, and rhetorical methods bring heightened attention to the cultural activities that embed social expectations and perceptions in public culture.

These two analytical lenses, rhetorical and performative, are my 3D glasses as I examine stories of stage communities and Shakespearean activities more than a century past. Set against the radically shifting social and economic landscapes that characterized urban areas in the United States around 1900, these stories highlight occasions when Anglo-identified groups and non-Anglo-identified groups intersected by way of Shakespeare. Chapter 1 sets the stage for the study, detailing the demographic, industrial, and economic changes that incited Progressivism in the United States in the late 1800s and showing how Shakespeare became a tool for social reform. Like Adams at the Folger Library's opening, Progressive Era activists promoted Shakespeare as a body of knowledge and an embodied knowledge that could serve to "Americanize" recent immigrants. Records of Shakespearean reform efforts—dramatic readings, community performances, ticket voucher initiatives—mostly frame these activities as one-way cultural transactions. But they just as often proved instances of two-way cultural exchange that challenged Progressive representations of Shakespeare as a fixed property that could solve the problem of proliferating racial and class difference in lower Manhattan. More broadly, chapter 1 sets into motion the argument that Shakespeare was not merely an instrument for social mobility at the turn of the twentieth century, but also an arena for social interaction, struggle, and change.

Chapter 2 turns to the immigrant-run theatres that thrived just blocks from Lower East Side reform organizations. Here, Shakespearean translations and adaptations staged by and for immigrant groups intermingled traditionally Anglo texts with non-Anglo languages, music, manners, meanings, themes, settings, and audiences. Whereas the period's social reformers conflated performances of Shakespeare with performances of national belonging, the immigrant entertainers working nearby adapted Shakespeare to the *local* needs and circumstances of the surrounding populations. Contrary to widely held theories that Shakespeare appealed mainly to highbrow sensibilities by the late nineteenth century, immigrant-produced Shakespeare drew mixed publics with varied artistic tastes. In these diverse and interactive settings, Shakespeare was more apt to serve specific instances of community building than ideological agendas for nation making and, in doing so, aided immigrants' adjustments to everyday life as Americans in more immediate and meaningful ways than did activists' Shakespearean reform efforts.

Pivoting from local conditions on the Lower East Side to the perspective of nonlocals, the next chapter introduces a set of well-educated, Anglo-identified drama critics who wrote about immigrant Shakespeare theatre for mainstream magazines and newspapers. Significantly, these writers' commentary reached middle- and upper-class readerships, staging immigrant Shakespeare on the page for bourgeois audiences who may not have viewed it in theatres. Their reviews also circulated complex social beliefs, often betraying the ambiguous racial perceptions that conditioned non-Anglo immigrants' tenuous inclusion in white American culture in the late 1800s and early 1900s. On the one hand, these writers found a point of connection, even identification, with immigrant groups in the familiar terrain of Shakespeare. On the other hand, Anglo-identified critics viewed non-Anglo performers as racially incongruous with Shakespeare, and their reviews and commentary in the English-language press brought otherness into stark focus as they struggled to ideologically reaffirm social and cultural hierarchies in the face of emergent realities.

The final chapter looks uptown to New York's English-language stages, where non-Anglo immigrant actors appeared in Shakespearean roles throughout the late nineteenth and early twentieth centuries. Some delivered their lines in English, while others spoke their native language in polyglot productions. Among the latter cohort was Yiddish-theatre star

Jacob P. Adler, who in 1903 and 1905 played Shylock in *The Merchant of Venice*, speaking Yiddish amid otherwise English-speaking casts. Adler's case richly illustrates how immigrant Shakespeareans' precarious racial status as not-quite-white enabled these actors to simultaneously adopt and *disrupt* conventions of Shakespeare and white American belonging, ultimately proving the fluidity of terms like "Shakespearean" and "American." *Here in This Island We Arrived* may begin with Adams's Folger Library lecture, in which Shakespeare was seen to have safeguarded a racially and culturally homogeneous ideal of U.S. identity. But it gives the final word to Adler, whose performances insisted that the Shakespearean stage and American social categories alike could accommodate diverse performances, encompassing rather than eschewing difference.

Today, too many books about U.S. Shakespeare theatre cement a legacy in which the playwright's value lies in his texts and their power to shape culture—that is, in Shakespeare as *archive*, to revisit Taylor's term. Bill Clinton's foreword to James Shapiro's recent volume, *Shakespeare in America*, expresses this pattern to a T in its closing remark: "I hope that all Americans enjoy their own encounter with the playwright whose work has done so much to illuminate the human condition, and to help us to understand ourselves, throughout our history."[29] But *Here in This Island We Arrived* tells a different story, shifting focus from the culture-shaping force of Shakespeare's words to the culture-making force of Shakespearean activity. The coming chapters do not simply tell of how Americans' encounters with Shakespeare's plays taught them about themselves at the turn of the twentieth century. Instead, they show how Shakespeare occasioned Americans' encounters with *one other* in this period of unprecedented demographic and economic change. And it was through these human encounters that attitudes about Shakespeare clashed, perceptions of what (and who) counted as "Shakespearean" narrowed or broadened, and associations between Shakespeare and certain social categories strengthened or severed.

As I worked on this book throughout 2016, the quadricentennial anniversary of Shakespeare's death brought celebrations, commemorations, and representations of the Bard that reflected the playwright's continued cultural status around the world. Despite the wealth of poststructuralist scholarship that has pointed up the socially constructed nature of Shakespeare's cultural value (and the socially violent nature of some of the ways in which the Shakespearean canon has been put to use over time), four-hundredth anniversary events reaffirmed that value and revealed that Shakespeare's universality remains unquestioned and unchallenged by many all over the globe, viewed with a reverence akin to that which Adams promoted over eighty years ago. And as the quadricentenary drew to a close, intensifying expressions of populist nationalism in the West (the rise of Donald Trump and England's Brexit vote, among them) underscored with particular urgency the continued struggle over who can lay claim to that hallowed symbol of culture.

But, were we to study the year's quadricentenary activities closely, we would likely see how Shakespeare culture also formed an arena for social interaction and exchange in the context of the early twenty-first century's own historically and geographically specific exigencies. Take, for instance, the September 2016 musical adaptation of *Twelfth Night* by Public Works, a New York City–based initiative that "invites members of diverse communities to participate in workshops, take classes, attend performances at The Public, and, most importantly, to join in the creation of ambitious works of participatory theater."[30] At a time when contemporary disputes over U.S. immigration policy and post-Ferguson racial tensions shine a searchlight on social difference in the nation's most diverse and economically divided cities, we would do well to ask how such a production might compare to Progressive Era classrooms or settlement stages, where Shakespeare supposedly schooled the nation's newest inhabitants on the terms of American belonging. But quadricentenary events like this *Twelfth Night* production just as certainly occasioned opportunities for exchange and change, as historical actors from diverse communities came together to perform—off book, and with varying interpretations—the ever-fluid meanings of American identity and belonging.

CHAPTER ONE

Shakespeare and the Myth of the Melting Pot

A May 1904 Shakespeare series presented at the Cooper Union People's Institute in lower Manhattan caught the interest of *Theatre*, a New York–based magazine aimed at "winning favor among the great general public . . . interested in the doings at the theatre and its people."[1] A full-length article in *Theatre*'s July issue focused not so much on the well-respected English company, the Ben Greet Players, who staged the Cooper Union productions but more so on the particular venue and its attendant audience. Founded in 1897, the People's Institute was an educational institution bent on uniting the city's "world of culture" and its "world of labor," as the Institute's founder Charles Sprague Smith put it. However, wedged between the Lower East Side's German-dominated Seventeenth Ward and the largely Italian Fifteenth Ward, and barely five blocks north of the mostly Italian Fourteenth Ward and the predominantly Jewish Tenth Ward known as New Israel, the People's Institute primarily served Manhattan's working-class new immigrant populations—this, despite Smith's hope that his organization would prompt a mingling of groups from across the city. The *Theatre* piece, preoccupied by a perceived incongruence between this downtown audience and Shakespearean drama, declared with a combined tone of curiosity, condescension, and approval: "As a theatrical, nay, as a sociological event, this was one of great importance. Here was the finest of dramatic literature put before the common people at prices which they could afford to pay. . . . In two days 4,000 of New York's proletariat received the most positive mental improvement that the drama is capable of affording."[2] By

Theatre's account, the People's Institute had succeeded in a Shakespearean sociological study that, like one of Prospero's spells, awakened "positive mental improvement" in the industrial metropolis's unruly urban masses.

Titled "Twenty-five Cent Shakespeare for the People," this *Theatre* article aptly expressed the spirit of the Progressive Era, albeit with a heavier dose of paternalism than some of the period's more left-leaning activists would have favored. Class, culture, geography, race, ethnicity, and social uplift in the name of democracy collided in a mere two pages of print. Shakespeare, too, was bound up in this Progressive spirit as a choice instrument for social reformers who sought to educate the so-called masses. The following month's issue of *Theatre* included an article titled "Brewing of the 'Tempest' in New York's Ghetto." Much like "Twenty-five Cent Shakespeare for the People," this piece detailed a recent community production of *The Tempest* at the Educational Alliance, an organization strategically located on the border between the overwhelmingly Eastern European Jewish Seventh and Tenth Wards so as to undertake, in the organization's own words, "work of an Americanizing, educational, social and humanizing character" with the neighborhood's residents.[3] The August *Theatre* article described at length a rehearsal process through which "young people would come into intimate mental contact with classic text, their imagination be stirred to noble ideals, their nature would expand to wider human interests, their bodies be trained to facility of expression, grace and flexibility, their voices cultivated and vocabulary increased and ennobled, their qualities of self-control, industry, and personality strengthened." Having thus relayed the virtues of this preparation as well as of the final production, the author concluded that "[t]he educational value of this work has been demonstrated."[4] Once again, *Theatre* stamped its seal of approval on the Shakespearean social reform efforts taking place on the Lower East Side. Yet, even in these seemingly one-sided cultural transactions, Shakespeare's meaning—and the terms of American belonging—was always in flux, assimilating to a rapidly shifting national demographic as opposed to the other way around.

SETTING THE PROGRESSIVE ERA STAGE (AND THEN, ENTER SHAKESPEARE)

In 1890, journalist Jacob Riis published his hugely successful and highly influential work, *How the Other Half Lives: Studies Among the Tenements of*

New York. This book might be mined as an archive of various pasts—U.S. immigration, social geography, urban housing reform, industrialization, muckraking journalism, photojournalism, orientalism, and other topics. But one need not look past Riis's title to understand how his widely circulated text proves relevant here: as nineteenth-century Americans looked toward a new millennium, Riis marked a clear line between two halves of New York's rapidly swelling human population, halves that were not simply separated by geography or by class, but by ethnicity, by race, and by national belonging as well. Riis's work therein illuminates a history of how urban Americans divided themselves into social categories during this period. *Here in This Island We Arrived* traces Shakespeare's role in this history.

Riis's work gained such wide circulation in large part due to the collection of photographs he took of tenement scenes. In fact, *How the Other Half Lives* began as a stereopticon slide show that led to an illustrated essay in *Scribner's Magazine*, ultimately expanding to a 304-page book with forty-two images, sixteen of which were reproduced in print by new halftone photoengraving technologies.[5] These photographs and line drawings depicted filthy alleyways, overcrowded sweatshops, bodies slumped in opium dens and outdoor stairwells, dust and gravel and trash and dimly lit spaces—and always the viewer observes these bleak scenes as an outsider.[6] "Drawing on the realism of photography," explains cultural studies scholar Reginald Twigg, Riis "[made] the surveyed Other available for dominant-class inspection."[7] The book itself thus staged an encounter between Riis's two halves (or "haves" and "have nots," as he construed them), inviting a socially privileged readership into Riis's wanderings through the city's tenement districts. *How the Other Half Lives* has endured as an exemplar of the ethnographic projects and Progressive reform efforts that proliferated across the three decades following its publication.

Riis's work sets the stage for this book: it places us on the Lower East Side, at the dawn of the Progressive Era, one decade into an unprecedented wave of U.S. immigration, within months of the U.S. Census Bureau's deeming the Western frontier closed, and at the boundary line of socially constructed difference. Further, as a New York newspaper reporter and a *Scribner's* author, Riis combined the discourses of social reform and journalistic reporting that informed privileged readers' perceptions of working-class Lower East Siders, and his pathbreaking use of photographs turns our attention to the

ways in which visual as well as verbal rhetorics likewise shaped these perceptions. In short, Riis's work offers a window into how many individuals of
this period, particularly those who held the social power and communicative
resources to influence public culture, understood themselves and others. As
we will see, this window frames a structure of national and racial feeling that
moved some Progressive Era reformers to bring Shakespeare to "the people"
and further inclined them, as well as the journalists who reported on their
efforts, to imbue this activity with a particular social meaning for the city's
middle- and upper-class publics.[8]

Indeed, Riis was a prime contributor to what historian Mark Pittenger
identifies as "a larger intellectual phenomenon, a theoretical conflation of
the categories of class, race, and culture which can be identified in popular
and academic discourse both during and since the Progressive era." And
while "culture" is arguably a capacious enough term to suggest numerous
other overlapping ideological categories during this period, Riis's work, particularly as it frames this book, demands that we append national belonging
to Pittenger's list. Early in *How the Other Half Lives*, following a brief introduction and condensed history of tenement housing, Riis characterized
the "mixed crowd" that inhabited lower Manhattan in the late nineteenth
century. Emphasizing the "cosmopolitan character" of this neighborhood
and listing the various immigrant "colonies" one might find in the area's
"alleys and courts," he remarked: "The one thing you shall vainly ask for in
the chief city of America is a distinctively American community. There is
none; certainly not among the tenements."[9]

Why did Riis begin with the absence of "a distinctively American
community"? And who (or what) did Riis consider to be "distinctively
American"? The ambiguous yet potent terms of this signifier, as well as the
ways in which historical actors set and challenged these terms, stimulate
the core questions of this book. As for Riis, key clues about his meaning
of "distinctively American" lie in who was apparently *not* distinctively
American: "They are not here," he reasserted. "In their place has come this
queer conglomerate mass of heterogeneous elements, ever striving and
working like whiskey and water in one glass, and with the like result: final
union and a prevailing taint of whiskey." Whatever "distinctively American" signified for Riis must, then, have been clean, pure, and free of the
boozy "taint" and brown tint of whiskey. Perhaps it was something akin
to Nell Irvin Painter's concept of American whiteness, a fundamentally

Anglo-Saxon idea and ideal of Americanness that, Painter argues, has expanded in dominant public consciousness throughout U.S. history to include certain non-Anglo groups. But while the demographic boundaries of American whiteness are fluid, its meaning—no matter what group lays claim to it—remains essentially Anglocentric. The Danish-born Riis might well be viewed as a beneficiary of this adaptable American whiteness, for having spent just over two decades in the United States by 1890, he already felt justified to play arbiter of a distinctive national identity.[10] In light of this biographical information, Riis's sure sense of who was not distinctively American also gives clues as to what reaffirmed his own feeling of American belonging and, further, suggests that Americanness could be defined in relative terms. Working downtown among the poverty-stricken, frequently foreign-speaking, largely non-Protestant tenement dwellers for whom he hoped to instigate a better life, this Danish immigrant shored up his own middle-class, distinctively American habitus.[11]

Riis often explored the tenement neighborhoods in the company of Theodore Roosevelt, one of the most visible and influential Progressive Era reformers who, before becoming U.S. president in 1901, served as New York City Police Commissioner and New York State governor during the 1890s.[12] Although Riis met Roosevelt after publishing How the Other Half Lives, the two men's deep connection formed around the civic concerns of that book. As Riis himself wrote in 1901, "It could not have been long after I wrote 'How the Other Half Lives' that [Roosevelt] came to the Evening Sun office one day looking for me. I was out, and he left his card, merely writing on the back of it that he had read my book and had 'come to help.' That was all and it tells the whole story of the man. I loved him from the day I first saw him."[13] A brief detour to consider Roosevelt's perspective, then, may further illuminate the late nineteenth-century meaning of "distinctively American" for someone in Riis's social position.

Historian Gary Gerstle points to the process by which a new ideal of American nationhood, shaped largely by Roosevelt's early writings, emerged just before 1900, wherein Roosevelt imagined that a fortified "American race" would result from melding Anglo-Saxons together with members of other races, all oriented toward a shared civic patriotism. This Anglocentric vision of an American melting pot bore racial presumptions that profoundly compromised citizenship and national belonging for the country's African American, Native American, Asian, and Latino populations.[14] These fraught histories, however, are mostly beyond the scope of this book, which is primarily concerned with the ways in which Roosevelt's civic and racial nationalism defined the non-Anglo European immigrant populations residing in lower Manhattan, whose whiteness Matthew Frye Jacobson describes as variegated, contingent, and contested, particularly between 1840 and 1924. (I will, however, briefly discuss New York's African American Shakespeare scenes later on.) After all, Roosevelt's liberal attitude toward various shades of whiteness was linked to his belief in a single American race rather than a pluralistic society. "[T]he diverse streams of European humanity flowing into New York had to Americanize," explains Gerstle, who goes on to quote Roosevelt: "'We must American-ize them in every way, in speech, in political ideas and principles.' . . . The immigrant 'must not bring his Old-World religious[,] race[,] and national antipathies, but must merge them into love for our common country. . . . Above all, the immigrant must learn to talk and think and be United States.'"[15]

This paradigm of American belonging depended on, but also aggra-vated, the ambiguous associations between race and ethnicity that marked the late nineteenth and early twentieth centuries in the United States. Histo-rian Mae M. Ngai claims that Eastern and Southern European immigrants, leveraging their whiteness as a legal path to American citizenship under the 1790 Naturalization Act, "constructed their identities in ways that were not racial but ethnic, expressing national and religious ties." In this sense, race and ethnicity moved in separate directions for European immigrants within an American context. But within the Rooseveltian framework, any hint of ethnic or racial identity that deviated from a monolithic U.S. worldview was in conflict with the one race that mattered most of all in spite of its mythic origins: the American race, or Painter's American whiteness. Jacobson maintains that American nativists perceived differences among European immigrants as distinctly racial, even as immigrants developed ethnic rather than racial identities. The latter half of the nineteenth century was thus "marked by a profound ideological tension between established codes of whiteness as inclusive of all Europeans, and new, racialist revisions" that conditioned immigrants' white and American identities as "probationary."[16]

Riis's language bore out these racialist revisions. For him, the Lower East Side's "queer conglomerate mass of heterogeneous elements" was still far from realizing the melting-pot ideal. Hardly a blended solution, this polyglot and polyracial population only just managed to achieve "final union and a prevailing taint of whiskey" among its own ranks. Riis's introductory language thus reflected (and likely encouraged) broadly felt anxieties about the instability and vulnerability of American identity— what English literature scholar Coppélia Kahn has called the "ideological ambivalence at the core of the concept of Americanness," which "intensified" in the 1890s as "the longstanding question of what transformed an immigrant into an American became more urgent than ever before."[17]

These deep ideological tensions and ambivalences surrounding race and national belonging mounted alongside other major shifts in American society—demographic, economic, industrial, and technological—that New York's residents experienced more acutely than most. "It is significant that *How the Other Half Lives* was published in 1890," notes historian Roy Lubove, "the first year of a decade of turbulence such as the nation had not experienced since the Civil War."[18] Immigration numbers rose steadily, peaking in 1907.[19] The 1890 census revealed that the Western frontier could extend no further, and as linguist Thomas Paul Bonfiglio writes, "[T]he closing of the frontier denoted a western wall in the popular imagination, which meant that the eastern foreign tide would rise nationwide."[20] The closing of the frontier thus worsened anxiety over immigration's threat to the Anglo-Saxon essence of American identity. Corporate capitalism gained power and presence in the 1890s, reconfiguring industrial employee relations and spurring labor unrest. A middle class of professionals—experts in medicine, law, science, social science, social work, and education—also emerged. Electric grids shot across cityscapes.[21] "Needless to say," writes Sabine Haenni, "these larger economic, social, and cultural changes attending industrialization, urbanization, and immigration were felt particularly strongly in New York City." Urban historian Esther Romeyn characterizes the city as "the visual embodiment of the contradictions of modernity" at the turn of the twentieth century. "Rapid industrialization and capitalism injected its [*sic*] social effects into the very nervous system of the city," she explains, "producing contradictions that no amount of planning or design could control. . . . The city's public spaces, which, guided by principles of rational design, mapping, and order, allowed for the imagining of the almost theatrical unity of diverse urban populations, coexisted with a vision of a dangerous urban heterogeneity."[22] Work like Riis's had sound intentions of exposing and explaining this "dangerous urban heterogeneity"—this "queer conglomerate mass"—in order to improve conditions. Indeed, *How the Other Half Lives* bravely confronted a significant municipal housing crisis threatening New York's poor. However, such reform efforts often simultaneously reinforced divisions and made social anxieties and hierarchies more publicly visible.[23]

The Progressive Era emerged as a response to this tangle of demographic shifts, industrial expansions, technological advances, and social tensions in late nineteenth-century U.S. urban centers. As historian Steven J. Diner chronicles it, "Anxieties culminated in broad-based reform movements, which became known as progressivism, that began to transform local government in the 1890s and state and national government at the turn of the century." Certain key local initiatives that precipitated national policy change arguably began in New York, where new approaches in social science at the university level found practical application at the civic level in the founding of settlement houses and similar institutions, like the People's Institute. The first U.S. settlement houses—the Neighborhood Guild (later renamed the University Settlement) and the College Settlement—appeared in New York in 1886 and 1889, and the Educational Alliance, although technically founded in 1889 as a mediator between several Lower East Side associations, reorganized in 1893, outlining formal objectives and electing a board of directors. Although the Alliance board held that the organization was not technically a settlement—and was therefore distinct from other reform efforts in the neighborhood—the 1908 *New Encyclopedia of Social Reform* nevertheless listed the Alliance among the United States' 170 settlements, defined as "homes in the poorer quarters of a city where educated men and women may live in daily personal contact with the working people."[24] Four years later, Smith founded the People's Institute, not as a settlement house but as an educational forum that would disseminate knowledge and spur dialogue between the city's "cultured" and "laboring" classes.

Settlement houses and other like organizations thus proliferated in poor neighborhoods densely populated by new immigrant groups, undertaking what influential reformer Mary Simkovich saw as three broad, overlapping functions: community improvement, "social effort," and education. Community improvement included policy and municipal reform campaigns, while social efforts created opportunities for individuals of different origins and socioeconomic backgrounds to gather through clubs, meals, exhibits, and other events. Education spanned a wide range of offerings—vocational classes, courses in English and U.S. government, lectures on the liberal arts and sciences, instruction in practical skills like cooking or sewing, programming in art, music, and drama, reading groups—and charted a fine line between affording non-native residents personal and cultural autonomy and imposing prescribed paths to American assimilation. As such, settlements and similar reform agencies not only precipitated policy change but also lay groundwork for a wider Americanization movement that, by World War I, had shifted focus "from cultural uplift to a more conservative nationalism."[25] By the 1910s, this movement manifested across many societal sectors: certain U.S. states made public evening school compulsory for illiterate minors; factories and industrial plants offered free classes in subjects as wide-ranging as the English language, arithmetic, civil government, "good citizenship," and hygiene; fraternal orders like the Masons and Elks issued nationalist propaganda; patriotic organizations like the American Defense Society disseminated literature and hosted public gatherings for immigrants; and a National Committee on Americanization, founded in May 1915, helped organize and standardize Americanization methods for governmental, educational, religious, and business entities across the country.[26]

Toeing the fine line between social activism and paternalistic patriotism, Progressive organizations' reading clubs and dramatic associations promoted cultural works that reformers felt would improve conditions for the city's working-class communities, and "improve" the community members themselves. At Jane Addams's Hull-House settlement, established in Chicago in 1889 on the heels of New York's earliest settlement houses, an early reading group discussed George Eliot, Dante, and Browning, and a Sunday afternoon Plato Club fostered philosophical discussion. Hull House also staged the plays of the ancient Greeks, and eventually took to producing works by realist playwrights like Henrik Ibsen and George Bernard Shaw. Other settlements likewise programmed classical texts and plays with strong moral messages and/or beautiful settings that might transport performers out of their unseemly surroundings. Historian Mina Carson explains that "as college graduates, most [reformers] had likely seen or participated in the forms of theater familiar on nineteenth-century campuses: classical plays, declamation, pageants, and pantomime. . . . Younger children naturally enjoyed fantasy and mimesis, and there could be no objection to older children's dramatic readings of Shakespeare and Victorian poetry."[27]

Indeed, it seemed Shakespeare never met with objection in these Progressive reform settings, as the playwright proved a steady staple for settlement reading clubs, declamation exercises, and dramatic undertakings. "Appreciation of and participation in productions of Shakespeare's plays were posited as keys to overcoming the taint of foreignness as well as to developing character," observes theatre historian Dorothy Chansky. "This prejudice circulated among hereditary Americans and was also often eagerly adopted by immigrants wanting to better their situation in the United States." Thus, a company called The Players was said to have staged Shakespeare plays at different settlements in the early 1900s, and Shakespearean actors from the American Academy of Dramatic Arts performed many times at the Educational Alliance before the Alliance established its own children and young adults' theatre in 1903. In May 1904—the same month as Ben Greet's appearance at the People's Institute and not long after the Alliance's Children's Educational Theatre produced *The Tempest*—the *New York Tribune* reported that "Jews, Irish, and Bohemians combined to give a performance of Shakespeare's comedy 'The Taming of the Shrew'" at an East Side settlement house, a performance that so successfully stirred the melting-pot spirit that "[a]ll race feeling was lost for the time . . . in the pleasure of seeing son and daughter or brother and sister tread the boards." Ben Greet himself discussed his style of performing Shakespeare in the unedited and scenically bare "manner of Shakespeare's time" in a 1905 *Harper's Weekly* piece, stressing "the educational aspect of such representations of Shakespeare . . . the benefit of which should accrue not only to young people, but to their elders as well." He went on to detail his upcoming season, which included performances "at Mendelssohn Hall, . . . before the Brooklyn Institute of Arts and Sciences, at near-by colleges, and, best of all, at some of the East Side Settlements." Hull-House dramatic groups frequently included Shakespeare in their repertoire (an 1897 production of *As You Like It* was an early success that propelled its director to a permanent post at Hull House), and a Hull-House Shakespeare Club thrived for sixteen years.[28] So it was that the spirit of Progressive reform found a voice in Shakespeare.

Different records of Shakespeare programming at the People's Institute and the Educational Alliance suggest how, and to what ends, Shakespeare figured into the period's reform rhetoric. For Charles Sprague Smith at the People's Institute, Shakespearean drama was a catalyst that spurred social scientific reaction while undergoing no permanent change to its own makeup. For the Educational Alliance's entertainment director Alice Minnie Herts, Shakespeare offered a universal ideal that might be implanted in the minds, morals, and bodies of Lower East Siders so as to incorporate them into American democracy. For journalists who covered this programming in the mainstream press, the Lower East Side of the 1890s and early 1900s seemed an unlikely stage for Shakespeare, but these writers nevertheless appeared open to the possibility that, if properly administered and absorbed, the Bard's plays might prove an antidote to the proliferating forms of social difference afflicting New York's increasingly polyglot, racially diverse, and class-divided population. Thus, a survey of the language and images used to communicate Progressive aims and encourage Shakespeare's role in achieving them reveals a double standard of sorts. Responding to a host of urban problems spurred by rapid demographic and economic shift in the United States, Progressives became deeply committed to social reform; yet for all this talk of change, Shakespeare moved through Progressive Era discourse as a stable entity. A closer look at alternative historical perspectives, however, will challenge this stability.

SHAKESPEARE AT THE PEOPLE'S INSTITUTE

In 1904, Smith, a professor of modern languages and foreign literature and organizer of Columbia University's Modern Language Department, published a short handbook, *Working with the People*, to record the People's Institute's early years of activity.[29] As part of a series called "Handbooks for Practical Workers" edited by Samuel Macauley Jackson, a professor of church history at New York University, Smith's book presumably addressed an audience of scholar-activist peers. *Working with the People* included six photographs distributed across roughly 150 pages. Of these six images, the middle two depict Shakespeare performances, and the remaining four show a Sunday evening lecture, a classroom of students, a club social, and a ladies' club-room. Despite the many activities of the Institute, and despite the fact that the Institute devoted two-thirds of its seasonal program to social science course content, Shakespeare emerged—so far as Smith's choice of photographs suggested—as the centerfold of this chronicle of the Institute's young history.[30]

To understand Shakespeare's part in this history, it is necessary to understand Smith's vision for the Institute. Chapter 1 of *Working with the*

People detailed an initial meeting in the spring of 1897 to "consider the advisability of establishing a new educational institution," during which "[a]ll recognized that, in a democracy, it is neither wise nor safe to neglect provision for instruction in those departments of knowledge that especially qualify the voter for the intelligent use of the ballot." Accordingly, the group resolved that "[f]ree instruction in the laws and facts of social science and a platform . . . where the questions of the day . . . and social theories can be freely discussed, were . . . imperatively needed in order to promote good government, cooperation between all sections of our citizenship, and peaceful social evolution."[31] While Smith's language was never so nativist as to suggest that all individuals should "talk and think and be United States," his statement nonetheless indicated a belief that stimulating, even molding, potential voters' minds would be good for the country.

By June, Smith and his cohort had formally established the People's Institute and gained support from Abram Hewitt, a cofounder of the Cooper Union, who invited them to use the Cooper Union's large hall as a lecture venue. The Institute primarily served as a free evening school that offered, first and foremost, education in social science, as well as courses in literature, art, ethics, philosophy, and natural science. In addition to attending these lectures and classes, individuals could participate in discussion forums, access nonsectarian spiritual services at the People's Church intended for "Jew, Christian, and Nonbeliever," convene recreationally through social clubs, and enjoy concerts through the People's Hall of Music. Smith's ultimate aim was to cultivate "the principles of unity and fraternity . . . as fundamental social truths."[32]

Bringing Smith's mission to bear through literary and dramatic programming, the People's Institute issued Shakespeare to the people through four primary channels. Beginning in late April 1900, Professor Edward Howard Griggs delivered a series of lectures respectively titled "The Humanity of Shakespeare," "From Love's Labor Lost to the Merchant of Venice," "The Roman Plays: Julius Caesar and Antony and Cleopatra," "Facing the Mystery: Hamlet," "The Tragedies of Passion: Othello, Lear, and Macbeth," and "The Serene Acceptance: The Tempest and the Winter's Tale." Such lectures continued in subsequent seasons as part of the Institute's literature curriculum. In the 1900–1901 season, the People's Institute launched a set of Shakespeare recitals performed by actor Marshall Darrach, an annual offering that would continue, with Darrach as reciter, for more than a decade.

Throughout this period, Shakespeare remained the only dramatic material on the seasonal program.[33] In 1904, Smith arranged for the Ben Greet Players to perform several Shakespeare plays at the Cooper Union. Unlike the Darrach readings, these were full-cast productions, led by one of the period's most noted actors. Greet's People's Institute performances garnered large audiences and citywide attention, although, according to Smith, the "audience [was] composed largely of residents of the East Side."[34] By 1905, legal questions surfaced concerning the use of the Cooper Union's large hall for theatrical events, and Smith was forced to discontinue plays, as well as symphony concerts, given in the space.[35] In lieu of bringing Shakespeare to the Lower East Side, Smith coordinated with uptown theatres to offer reduced-price tickets to holders of People's Institute vouchers. In a letter to one associate regarding a production of *Romeo and Juliet* at the Carnegie Lyceum, Smith explained that the initiative was meant "to give under the auspices of the People's Institute, Shakespearean plays for the public schools and the masses of the people. . . . It is hoped," he continued, "that persons desiring boxes, or reserved seats, and who can afford to pay more than the price named, will do so in order to assist in this experiment."[36]

Indeed, Smith placed the utmost value on these dramatic experiments. In an interview for a 1906 *New York Times* profile piece on the Institute, he remarked to the reporter,

> You ask what the People's Institute means? . . . Let me tell you. A few nights ago I was present at one of the leading theatres of the city. The most charming actress we have was giving a representation of a play that delights children. The first and second balconies were filled with boys and girls from the public schools, and during several nights every week they will be filled with a similar audience until the close of the season. . . . In this way some 23,000 such theatrical opportunities will have been provided to those of limited means before the close of the present season.[37]

With this summary of the Institute's meaning, Smith linked the organization's dramatic programming—the vast majority of which constituted works by Shakespeare—with its core mission. Yet Smith's focus in this *New York Times* piece did not so much center on the dramatic program as it centered on the dramatic audience. By foregrounding an auditorium packed, over multiple performances, with "some 23,000" playgoers "of limited means," he emphasized spectatorship over production value. This emphasis seems a logical extension of Smith's view that the voucher initiative was "an experiment," with attention rightly paid to his malleable subjects sitting in the house rather than his control variable, the dramatic performance, on stage.

Smith's *Working with the People*, a social activist manifesto informed by social scientism, likewise traded in the language of "experiment," figuring theatregoers as subjects of Smith's research.[38] The handbook's two Shakespearean images, respectively titled "Shakespeare Recital" and "Merchant of Venice," visually downplayed the performers onstage and amplified the spectators throughout the auditorium. "Shakespeare Recital" orients the viewer toward a sea of seated people, most of whom turn to look directly at the camera rather than facing the stage, where a dimly lit man in a tuxedo holds forth (fig. 2). "Merchant of Venice" likewise reduces Ben Greet's players to obscure figures on a poorly lit thrust stage, whom the viewer, positioned toward the back of the audience section facing the stage's right edge, sees in profile. Beyond these shadowy Shakespeareans, a swath of sunlight bathes the stage-left audience section, and as the viewer's eye scans the photograph clockwise from this haloed group, rows of bodies fan out across the hall, consuming more than half of the image (fig. 3). In both photographs, the effect is overt visual emphasis on the audience as the primary point of interest.

Working with the People's textual content reinforced this visual emphasis on Shakespearean audiences over Shakespearean productions. Describing attendance at the first three years of Shakespeare recitals, Smith wrote, "The course, given at first in the lecture-room, was in the second year transferred on account of overcrowding to the large hall, and has drawn on every occasion an audience of 2,000 or above." He later added in a footnote to a reprint edition, "Since writing the above, the third year's course has begun. The audience is thronging the house, and hundreds are being turned away, unable to find even standing-room." Having read this footnote, one turns the page to find the "Shakespeare Recital" photograph and to see for oneself that very throng, jammed into the large hall, peering out of the image.[39] The significant spectacle was not, it seems, the Shakespeare plays themselves but rather the people who came to see them.

The press took an interest in this audience as well. *Theatre*'s memorable title, "Twenty-five Cent Shakespeare for the People," resonated with similar

FIGURE 2 "Shakespeare Recital," in Smith, *Working with the People*. Courtesy of Northwestern University Libraries.

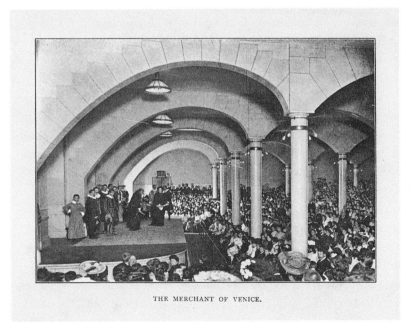

FIGURE 3 "Merchant of Venice," in Smith, *Working with the People*. Courtesy of Northwestern University Libraries.

headlines in the *New York Times* and the *New York Tribune*, like "Shakespeare for the People's Institute," "People's Institute Plays: Sixteen Hundred Girls Enjoy 'Merchant of Venice,'" "Mr. Greet to Play Shakespeare on the East Side," "The People's Institute to See Mantell at Reduced Rates," and "Give 'Romeo and Juliet': The Players Act under the Auspices of the People's Institute."[40] Such headlines relied on their readership to associate terms like "the people," "East Side," and the "People's Institute" with the city's working-class immigrant audiences—an enthymeme that *Theatre* secured with a close-up image of a mostly fair-skinned and dark-featured audience, captioned "types among the spectators," as well as with the mocking comment, "So there seems to be a taste for real art lurking about somewhere, after all—somewhere in the benighted regions of the East Side, among the Russian old clothesmen, the Hungarian grocers and the Italian barbers."[41] It would seem that the mainstream press's consistent and pointed juxtaposition of Shakespeare with East Side audiences catered to a specific ideology presumed to be held by the readership, one that primed readers to do a double take when these "benighted" East Siders were paired with Shakespeare. Whereas Smith's visual and verbal emphasis on the Institute's playgoers showcased the results (and the beneficiaries) of his well-meaning if unfortunately labeled social reform "experiments," New York's newspapers and magazines leveraged a perceived incongruity between "Shakespeare" and "the people" as a rhetorical strategy to get their readers' attention.

However, this perceived incongruity did not necessarily go hand in hand with a felt resistance to Smith's bringing Shakespeare to the masses; rather, the press approved of, even celebrated the People's Institute's efforts to bridge the ideological gap between Shakespeare and "the people." Although the author of *Theatre*'s "Twenty-five cent Shakespeare for the People" called Smith's "proposition to establish genuine democracy . . . amusing," the writer nevertheless recognized that "it is better to be Utopian and attempt the impossible than to do nothing at all" and accordingly deemed the People's Institute "a place for dignified instruction and recreation." Following Greet's appearance on the Cooper Union stage, the *New York Tribune* noted that "[t]hose interested in the development of popular drama perceived from the success of such performances that the people, the masses, if once given the opportunity would show that they also had discriminative taste. They felt assured that Shakespeare would pay on the East Side—pay not only in dollars and cents, but in the more substantial achievement of popular education in the higher drama." Later, in 1907, the *Tribune* covered the People's Institute's collaboration with uptown theatres in a lengthy piece praising Smith's sustained efforts to foster "[s]ocial evolution in the shape of dramatic entertainment at popular prices, or, in other words, the education and elevation of the masses by means of the theatre." "Actually," the article reported, "the movement has revealed a popular passion for Shakespeare."[42] As we will see later on, this popular passion for Shakespeare was welcome among Manhattan's taste-making journalists, but often with the implicit caveat that it be expressed in proper terms. Performances in languages other than English, for example, drew a good deal of comment, as well as occasional critique.

Press reports generally aligned with Smith's own writings, both in giving particular notice to working-class audiences and in praising the work of improving these spectators through Shakespeare. However, newspaper and magazine coverage seemed to overlook the crucial preposition in Smith's handbook title: while Smith understood himself to be working *with* the people, the press put a paternalistic spin on his efforts, promoting them as Shakespeare *for* the people. Literary scholar Christopher P. Wilson's study of Progressive Era print culture helps to explain the similar-yet-different tones of Smith's rhetoric of reform and that of the press. "In certain respects, mass-market authorship bears comparison to fields like social work or academic professionalism," he writes. "As in the social sciences, the essence of the literary professionals' credo would be their claim to explain the root causes of American problems, causes otherwise invisible to the public." Albeit "to a limited degree," Wilson thus groups journalists, social workers, and academic professionals in an "evolving 'knowledge class' so distinctive of late-industrial societies." Riis's standing as a journalist and a social worker, as well as Smith's role as a social worker and an academic professional, further evidences Wilson's generalization. However, Wilson also cautions that "we must keep in mind certain differences between the new literary professionalism and that of more familiar occupations. . . . We must not, for instance, overlook the fact that the more journalistic literary endeavors exhibit a split personality between intellectual culture and entertainment media." In other words, the press's aims were far more commercial than charitable, catering to the tastes of a readership that would not pay for banal news stories, no matter how altruistic or intellectual their scope. "If an incident was commonplace," explains Wilson, "well, by definition, it was not news."[43]

Thus, while Smith and the press reported on identical events and spoke from places of comparable educational privilege (turn-of-the-twentieth-century reporters increasingly held college degrees[44]), they maintained distinct personas, claimed unique relationships to their subjects of discussion, and addressed different, if overlapping, audiences. Smith was an academic-turned-social-worker, physically if not entirely ideologically integrated into the working-class community that he wrote about for a readership of civically concerned scholar-activists—Smith's "fellow-workers," according to his book's dedication. By contrast, journalists were most often informed outsiders, observing rather than participating in the various Lower East Side reform efforts that provided material for their reportage—material that their audiences wanted to read. Major newspapers like the *New York Times* or the *New York Tribune* addressed a broad public of middle- and upper-class readers across the city.[45] *Theatre*, a monthly magazine, and *Harper's Weekly*, a weekly journal, printed long-form and literary content that, although published in New York, circulated nationally, helping to shape an impression of U.S. cosmopolitan culture for middle- and upper-class audiences all over the country.[46]

The press, then, not merely informing but also responding to its market, simultaneously reflected and influenced the period's mainstream public tastes and sentiments, particularly those of New York's socially dominant classes for whom stories of "Shakespeare for the people" were apparently newsworthy. As Smith's own subtle cultural imperialism suggests, he too was implicated in this privileged public sphere, however often his actions and words bucked his peers' paternalistic worldview. Reform workers' enthusiasm "could not in itself change the habits inscribed into their bodies and minds," writes Shannon Jackson. Like the Hull-House settlement workers whom Jackson studies, Smith was among a group "of bourgeois women and men working to share their privileges and, with varying degrees of commitment, working to undo the very system that guaranteed them those privileges." Jackson thoughtfully discourages "contemporary analytic perspectives" that hold reformers' work to be "overdetermined by their class status"; indeed, painting Progressive undertakings as plainly paternalistic flattens history as conspicuously as do the mainstream press narratives cited earlier. But Shakespeare's rhetorical role in reform discourse did bear paternalistic force, as bourgeois attitudes toward the relationship between Shakespeare and working-class immigrant culture took for granted—and reinforced—certain social differences, hierarchies, and boundaries.[47] Despite key differences between Smith and the various newspaper and magazine voices that covered his reform activities, a similar narrative, marked by a shared "uptown" mentality if not by an uptown address, threaded its way across these historical records of Shakespeare at the People's Institute: that is, at the turn of the century, in what was by all accounts a noteworthy experiment, Smith brought Shakespeare before an unlikely audience to catalyze social change on the Lower East Side.

SHAKESPEARE AT THE EDUCATIONAL ALLIANCE

Not fifteen blocks south and a short walk east of the People's Institute stood the Educational Alliance, where Alice Minnie Herts, a social worker by training, became managing director of the Entertainment Department in 1903. The department had been active at the Alliance for years. An 1895 promotional booklet listed "[e]ntertainments in the Auditorium, of a musical and literary character, aiming to educate and refine as well as to afford diversion and amusement, every Saturday evening." *Theatre* indicated that, prior to 1903, students from Franklin Sargent's American Academy of Dramatic Arts "were imported from uptown to reproduce successes from their Empire matinees." And Herts recalled that she "inherited a budget which outlined a number of concerts by professional musicians, entertainments by amateurs, and prestidigitator acts for children."[48]

But unlike Smith, Herts was unsatisfied with merely exposing the neighborhood to what many considered to be good music and plays. Nor was she satisfied with the state of performances undertaken by members of the Alliance. In her 1911 book, *The Children's Educational Theatre*—a record of her work at the Alliance and thus a fitting analogue to Smith's *Working with the People*—Herts somewhat condescendingly reminisced about early productions staged by Alliance dramatic clubs, "the elders" giving their plays "in the Yiddish or the Italian language, according to their nationality, the young folks in what in their vigor and enthusiasm they believed to be the English language." Discontented with conditions under which these people "were as perfectly willing to play 'Hamlet' in a Harlem flat interior as they were to gown Ophelia in a twentieth-century hired wedding-dress," Herts recruited acclaimed actress Emma Sheridan Fry to serve as artistic director of a new amateur young persons' troupe, therein launching the Children's Educational Theatre. "I saw the great opportunity not to impose upon people an ideal from without," Herts reflected, perhaps with performances like Greet's in mind, "but to help people to create an ideal from within."[49] Herts's aim to "help people to create an ideal from within" was akin to Smith's insistence on working *with* rather than *for* "the people," and indeed, her community-based performances saw through this collaborative impulse much more literally than Smith's Shakespeare series. Yet, while her vision of cooperative exchange held the promise of reciprocal improvement for her and her actors, Herts's ideal—at bottom, an ideal of American belonging, as her published work lets on—was as one-sided as Smith's Shakespearean catalyst.

What, then, did Herts really mean by "help people to create an ideal from within"? And how did she draw on Shakespeare to make manifest such an ideal? To address the second question first: Among Herts's earliest productions at the Children's Educational Theatre were Shakespeare's *The Tempest* and *As You Like It*, and a good deal of commentary about Herts's work referenced Shakespeare as a stand-in for "educational drama." In fact, her 1911 history of the Children's Educational Theatre included a lecture by Harvard professor George P. Baker entitled "The Educative Value for Children Acting in Shakespeare's Plays," one of a series of six lectures that Herts organized and hosted in New York's Lyceum Theatre in 1909.[50]

But before turning to discourse about Shakespeare at the Children's Educational Theatre, and to how this discourse illuminates Herts's mantra "create an ideal from within," we need more background on Herts and the setting in which she was working and writing. Like Smith, Herts was a formally educated, bourgeois reformer who believed that disadvantaged communities should actively participate in their own uplift; yet, also like Smith, she often exhibited the morally and culturally paternalistic worldview of those in her social position at that historic moment. What is more, prior to 1908, when she incorporated an independent Educational Theatre for Children and Young People, Herts was working under the auspices, and therefore within the ideological ethos, of the Educational Alliance. A brief introduction to the Educational Alliance is therefore necessary if we are to understand fully Herts's own work.

The work of the Educational Alliance largely centered on a philosophy of controlled mental, physical, and moral development for immigrants new to the Lower East Side. The aforementioned 1895 promotional booklet, quoting an 1893 agreement that codified the Alliance's objectives, described the "scope of the work of the Educational Alliance" as being "of an Americanizing, educational, social and humanizing character" and further specified that the proposed work of the Alliance "was grouped under the following heads: Social Work, Educational Work, Physical Work and Moral Work." In the spring of 1905, just over a year after the Children's Educational Theatre's first performance, the general objectives of the Alliance were revised slightly but remained "of an Americanizing . . . character," namely, "[t]o help newly arrived immigrants to an understanding of the English language and of the Constitution and institutions of the United States and offer them opportunities for self-betterment and encourage them to avail themselves of the facilities therefore open to the people generally, to the end that they may in due course correctly comprehend and appreciate the rights and obligations of American citizenship and intelligently adapt themselves to the new conditions here confronting them." In April of the same year, the Alliance board brought Herts's work as director of the Entertainment Department into alignment with the organization's Americanizing aims, resolving that all dramatic performances at the Alliance "should be so adjusted as to comprise performances for children, while for adults only such entertainments or performances should be given as may aid in Americanizing immigrants."[51]

Any introduction to the Educational Alliance demands a description of its primary leadership and membership. Although leaders and members were mostly Jewish American, their common ground arguably ended with their shared claim to this ambiguous identity category. The majority of Alliance leaders and benefactors hailed from New York's class of wealthy, well-educated Jews of Western and Central European descent, a group that saw significant midcentury immigration to the United States but had by and large assimilated by the 1880s, when hundreds of thousands of Eastern European Jews began to settle on the Lower East Side. The Alliance's members drew mostly from this second group—new immigrant Jews from Russia, Poland, Hungary, and Romania who occupied the "other half" of Riis's social split. Assimilated Jews in the United States, who couched their Jewish American identity in an Anglo-American habitus, feared that this new group of foreign-born Jews in downtown Manhattan would call attention to an alien element of Jewishness— one that might overwhelm the "American" (and therein the American whiteness) in the hyphenate identity that old-immigrant Jews had constructed over several decades. Thus, Manhattan's assimilated Jewish elite set out to Americanize new immigrants through social reform efforts. Americanist Laura R. Fisher has called settlement houses "[a]n enduring symbol for the fraught process of assimilation and for the patron-client relations between 'uptown' and 'downtown' Jewish constituencies" as well as "a site through which key period debates over Americanization [and] identity . . . were waged." Tellingly, then, the proposed spring 1905 revision of the Educational Alliance's general objectives initially began, "to help the newly arrived Jewish immigrants to an understanding of the English language and of the Constitution and institutions of the United States," but, "[u]pon Motion, seconded and carried, the word 'Jewish' in the first sentence was crossed out."[52]

Herts's work with the Children's Educational Theatre brought a refreshingly collaborative approach to social reform while simultaneously upholding the ethos of mental, physical, and moral control at the core of the Alliance's Americanization efforts. At her most broad-minded as a social worker and educator, Herts expressed a sincere intent to inspire youthful imagination and foster character development through engaging, confidence-inspiring dramatic work. She railed against "ignorant 'elocution teachers' who had not helped [children] to any understanding of the characters they wished to portray, but who had merely taught them to mechanically learn lines and make gestures," explaining that "[n]o growth whatever had taken place in these young people, because no attempt had been made to develop their imaginations." She approached dramatic character development—which, for her, doubled as social character development—as "guiding, not coercing; stimulating, not exciting; establishing relations, not specializing in personality." Reflecting on the rehearsal process for a 1904 production of Shakespeare's *As You Like It*, she wrote, "Where dull, cramped habit interfered, the player's *will* was kindled to stimulate action and the master's play received worthy interpretation in genuine sincerity of expression and in unself-conscious portrayal."[53] Such statements capture the brightest potential of Herts's reform vision, where collaboration might take place not only between her and her players but also between her players and "the master's play"—a process of interpretation and self-expression that molded Shakespeare to the player rather than the player to Shakespeare.

Ultimately, however, Shakespeare did not prove so mutable for Herts as these excerpts might suggest. For one, across Herts's writings is the implied presumption that the dramatic characters in the plays she chose were mentally, physically, and morally superior to the plays' participants. In fact, Herts placed the entire world of each play on a rhetorical pedestal, explaining that she selected only repertoire that would "represent a suitable ideal to the neighborhood." Recalling preparations for *As You Like It*, for instance, Herts wrote, "[I]n the majority of cases the people's English was so unintelligible, their voices were so poor, their bearing so slovenly, that it was impossible to meet the obligation to our audiences with this material. Yet these were the very ones who deserved all the comfort and strength which come from spiritual fellowship with a higher type of human being." Here, "spiritual fellowship" referred to the kinship forged between actor and dramatic character, the latter (fictional) party serving as the "higher type of human being" which the (living, breathing) former should strive to embody. Settings as well as characters incorporated Herts's players into an idealized world. She chose *The Tempest*, for example, "because its scenes are laid in Nature's own abode, significant contrast to the tall and forbidding tenements of the neighborhood."[54] Of course, plotlines represented Herts's ideal as well: *The Tempest* upheld the civilizing powers of Duke Prospero over the lowly island native, Caliban, and Herts's other repertoire choices—*As You Like It*, *Ingomar the Barbarian*, *Little Lord Fauntleroy*, and *The Prince and the Pauper* among them—likewise told of transformations or reentries from humble or uncultured status into courtly gentility that led to happy endings. Although Herts herself never explicitly articulated this particular theme, it is nonetheless relevant to an understanding of Herts's "ideal from within." Like Smith, Herts seems to have taken Shakespeare for granted as a stable catalyst, a "suitable ideal" that might engender a better life for her players.

Herts made the value of players' and playgoers' imaginative growth her mantra, but even this space of invention took on conformist rather than collaborative connotations. Imagination, she wrote in a chapter on "purposeful play used as a preventive of crime," was not only "the warp and woof of which is woven of dramatic instinct" but was also "the force which makes the soldier on the battle-field grasp his country's flag. . . . It sustains the monk in his vigils, the statesman in his patriotism, the preacher in his pulpit. Through proper cultivation it may be made a force in education so far-reaching that under its organized impulse the entire character may be developed, mind quickened, sympathies broadened, ambitions ennobled, and bodies lifted and remade." In other words, for Herts, imagination some-how bound individuals to social institutions like church and state rather than freeing them to pursue independent character and thought. Phrases like "proper cultivation" and "organized impulse" stressed the normative dimensions of Herts's work, and references to flag and patriotism evinced the nativist streak running through her project. At what was roughly the midpoint of *The Children's Educational Theatre*, this "warp and woof" pas-sage tenuously linked imagination, Shakespeare, and national allegiance as part and parcel of the same idealized American character, mind, and body. Indeed, as she concluded her final chapter, Herts made plain that "the Educational Theatre, properly developed, [will] be a great educational asset throughout our country—a citizen-making institution, implanting ideals of true democracy."[55] The imaginative "ideal from within" laid out in Herts's chapter 1 thus shaded into her fourth chapter's "suitable ideal" for the neighborhood and, by book's end, became conflated with an implanted ideal of American belonging.

While Herts's 1911 book demonstrated the ideological tensions at the core of her work—showing how her liberal attitude often collided with a troubling nativism typical of the period's most conservative reformers—pithier publicity materials tended to flatten her educational project into a more strictly paternalistic enterprise. For instance, in a July 1904 interview with the *New York Tribune* that addressed the Children's Educational The-atre's upcoming rehearsals for *The Tempest*, *As You Like It*, and *Ingomar*, Educational Alliance Superintendent David Blaustein explained, "From these plays the actors gain a wealth of knowledge of manners and customs. The observance of social forms that is necessary in the portrayal of the characters they represent often remains with them and is carried into the homes." The *Tribune* writer took care to underscore how these productions might incorporate the young people *and* their families into American social norms, adding, "Dr. Blaustein believes that the good social effects resulting from the performances of the dramatic club are felt by the families and friends of the students as well as by themselves."[56]

A 1908 fundraising booklet, issued when Herts and a small board of directors established an independent offshoot of the Children's Educa-tional Theatre, did not mention imagination or "creating an ideal from within" when outlining the scope and results of Herts's program at the Educational Alliance. Instead, its opening paragraph touted the Alliance Entertainment Department's "work in character building" wherein "[d]ramatic instinct . . . is here trained and directed to operate upon both player and audience."[57] The booklet also included roughly a dozen letters of praise for the Children's Educational Theatre, sent to Herts through the years from respected public figures who collectively reasserted the one-dimensional view that Shakespeare "operated upon" Lower East Siders rather than "creating an ideal from within" them. Among this correspondence was a letter from renowned Shakespearean actor Richard Mansfield, who proclaimed, "Nothing could be better of worthy support than so excellent a method of brightening the existence and enlivening the mind of the hewer of wood and drawer of water. What it must mean to the girl who had hitherto spent her long and dreary and hopeless days at the treadmill. . . . [O]ne can only surmise, but it must be like the sight of a hospitable shore to a shipwrecked mariner." Through figurative language, Mansfield painted a dramatic divide between the unforgiving working-class ocean and the magnanimous shoreline of genteel culture. George C. Chase, president of Bates College, likewise perceived and, further, had trouble reconciling the edges of this divide, confessing, "I could not have believed that a children's theatre in such an unpropitious and depressing environment, could, even under the most careful training, have developed the literary appreciation and the power of interpretation and expression that were in such evidence at that Sunday afternoon performance." Jacob Riis himself contacted Herts in 1908 to remark, "It has been on my mind since I saw your children act the other night at the Educational Alliance, to tell you that you have your hand upon one of the most powerful springs for shaping character where the growth of it has been terribly handicapped by the tenement environment. . . . [I]n giving the real child a better chance you have not only opened the safety-valve wide that keeps him out of mischief, but you are helping him grow, grow whole and grow right." Here Riis implied that educational drama might aid passage from the handicapping, mischievous world of "the other half" into the (not-other) half of society that Riis (ironically) viewed as "whole"—a world that was "right," and perhaps even distinctively American. Brander Matthews, a highly respected dramatic critic and Columbia University professor, certainly seemed to think that a distinctively national identity was operative in Herts's efforts: "It seems to me," he told Herts in a 1906 note that she then published in the 1908 booklet, "that your project ought to be very helpful in making good Americans."[58]

By way of giving more formal testimony, the fundraising booklet reprinted an address in praise of Herts's work delivered by Charles W. Eliot at Boston's Simmons College in 1908. Eliot's text summarized the themes expressed by Mansfield, Chase, Riis, and Matthews, serving as an exclamation point to the series of letters preceding it. As president of Harvard University, Eliot embodied the "world of culture" at its most authoritative, and he therein cemented for readers—via Shakespeare—what Progressives held to be the Children's Educational Theatre's ultimate contribution. Characterizing Herts's actors as "a population which would not seem at first sight to be very well adapted to Miss Herts's plan—Russian Jews, Polish Jews, large elements of the Jewish stock throughout the neighborhood; poor people, very poor people," Eliot finally concluded, "Imagine what the environment of those children on the East Side of New York is—how squalid, how depressing, how compelling of the lowest side of life; and then imagine the lifting up into the emotions of 'The Merchant of Venice,' for example, or of 'Julius Caesar.'" It is a presentation of a great picture of a great world, an intellectual world, a moral world, a world of physical beauty also. . . . What better influence can you put as a permanent force into the minds and hearts of the Children of the East Side of New York?"[59] Here, Eliot underscored what Herts merely implied in *The Children's Educational Theatre*: Shakespeare was a permanent force (one that could be transferred "into the minds and hearts" of "the other half"), a world intellectually, morally, and physically distinct from, indeed superior to, the East Side of New York that might nonetheless improve this "lowest side of life."

Likewise viewing the Bard as both a mismatch and a messiah for Lower East Siders, mainstream reporters covered Shakespeare at the Educational Alliance in much the same way that they did Shakespeare at the People's Institute—with an attitude that coupled approving nods with raised eyebrows. A *New York Tribune* preview of the Alliance's 1904 production of *The Tempest* displayed this mixed sentiment on a number of levels, the first of which was visual. A photograph, three times as wide as the single-column article, bifurcated the text midsentence in the middle of the page. The image shows three figures dressed as goofy male characters huddled in the center of the frame, the middle figure, presumably Caliban, crouching while the two flanking fellows, Stephano and Trinculo, lean in. The figure on the right, dressed

"THE TEMPEST." (*Produced 1903.*)
STEPHANO: "*Here's my comfort.*"

FIGURE 4   "The Tempest," featured in "To Give the Tempest," *New York Times*, 22 May 1904, A4. This version of the image is from Herts, *Children's Educational Theatre*. Courtesy of Yale University Libraries.

somewhat like a court jester, looks at the camera bug-eyed, cheeks puffed out a bit, and holds his left hand high in the air, raising what appears to be a bottle. The backdrop is a simple set that suggests a forest, and the caption reads, "A scene from 'The Tempest,' to be given tonight at the Educational Alliance" (fig. 4). On the one hand, this image called attention to the young thespians' transformation from tenement dwellers into Shakespearean players, which in turn emphasized the assimilative value of Herts's dramatic programming. On the other hand, knowledge of this scene within *The Tempest*'s plot, which many of the *Tribune*'s readers doubtless had, poses a more cynical meaning. Having taken a swig of Stephano's "comfort," Caliban swears himself to be Stephano's subject, which prompts Trinculo's remark, "A most ridiculous monster, to make a wonder of a poor drunkard!"[60] It is conceivable, then, that some readers perceived Herts as analogously ridiculous in her efforts to make wonders of poor Lower East Siders. Moreover, it is also conceivable that this image invited the *Tribune*'s middle- and upper-class readers to imagine themselves as Prospero and therein to shore up their own superior social positions as they gazed at the lowly Caliban and company.

While one risks making too much of this photograph's possible meanings, the textual content and physical layout of the *Tribune* article further support a multilayered reading. As if to make the image speak, the article opened in the voice of one of the young players rather than the journalist: "'Everybody around here knows the 'Tempest'—that is, all the educated ones—and them that don't, I tells them.'" The piece then went on to explain, "In these words the little ten-year-old boy who will take the part of Ariel in the play to be presented at the Educational Alliance this evening summed up the Shakespearian knowledge of his neighborhood; and his statement, if not strictly grammatical, was absolutely accurate. As Mrs. A. Minnie Herts, director of entertainments at the Alliance, puts it, the play has soaked into the neighborhood."[61] The *Tribune* thus celebrated the production's educational value—its "soaking into the neighborhood"—while simultaneously snickering at the affair through a subtle rhetorical wink at its implied genteel readership: "if not strictly grammatical." The charm in this snarky parenthetical comment seems to have ridden on the expectation that few among the *Tribune*'s readers would expect grammatical finesse from an immigrant child living on the Lower East Side.

What is more, the other articles and images that surrounded the *New York Tribune*'s *Tempest* preview collectively affirmed the social value of the performance while slighting its dramatic significance. The photograph of the three young actors loomed large in the center of a spread that comprised the "Woman's Realm" section of the paper. While a handful of smaller drawings appeared around the *Tempest* image, the only other photograph of comparable size displayed "the new 'Girdle' Corset" in the top left corner—a device that was, much like the Alliance Shakespeare production, intended to mold bodies into culturally acceptable forms through highly controlled means. An adjacent "Lenten poem for the good of the many" along with an article about a new cookbook for the sick and convalescent framed *The Tempest* as a social service rather than a significant theatrical event.

While Smith programmed lectures and forums in ordered areas of knowledge to breed fraternity and healthy democratic participation at "the ballot," Herts expressed a more overt agenda of Americanizing immigrants through embodied practice. Corset-like, she aimed to discipline bodies as well as minds. But both reformers leveraged Shakespeare to transform a community perceived by many as a threat to the nation into a neighborhood of individuals who could contribute and succeed as Americans. Across the extant records of their efforts, reformers and reporters alike implied an unquestioning faith in the stable, symbolic power of Shakespeare to effect positive change in material circumstances of social disadvantage.

In a study of present-day "Shakespeare reform programs" for groups like prisoners and urban youth, Ayanna Thompson explores the ways in which, even today, Shakespeare is employed "as the ultimate tool to reform and unify a population into a cohesive identity (nationally, culturally, socially, *and* racially)." By illuminating how "Shakespeare symbolically [stood] in for the body politic that," in Thompson's words, "[sought] both to accept and to digest/melt away the racial, ethnic, cultural, and social differences" of those who were not initially seen as "part of the whole," the public records of Smith's and Herts's programs—like Riis's *How the Other Half Lives*—offer a history of how social hierarchies circulated and cemented in public culture. Thompson holds that today's Shakespeare reform initiatives "walk the tightrope of espousing the value of Shakespeare through the rhetoric of liberal humanism and espousing the value of Shakespeare through the rhetoric of neocolonialism."[62] For their part, Smith and Herts helped to string up and secure this discursive tightrope, clumsily toppling toward colonialist rhetorics as they made a case for Progressive drama.

SHAKESPEARE AND THE MELTING POT

Shakespeare's privileged place in Progressive Era reform rhetoric is consistent with a broader history of how culturally empowered groups in the United States understood and used Shakespeare at the turn of the twentieth century. For Progressives, Shakespeare represented "a great world, an intellectual world, a moral world, a world of physical beauty also," to recall Eliot's view. What is more, for the likes of Matthews, this was a world that somehow instilled in groups of working-class immigrants some knowledge of how they might become American, or, in the words of Roosevelt, "talk and think and be United States."

Scholars have amply demonstrated Americans' appropriation of Shakespeare as a national author throughout the nineteenth century.[63] By Lawrence L. Levine's account, Shakespeare was ubiquitous across the United States in the antebellum era, often mixed with other forms of entertainment and frequently parodied. Further, Levine writes, the early to mid-nineteenth century was "a period when melodrama became one of the mainstays of the American stage," and "Shakespearean plays easily lent themselves to the melodramatic style." In addition to parodies and melodramas, performances advertised Shakespearean works intermingled with gymnastics, farces, songs, and stories. Among Levine's central and most convincing claims is his sense that although "[t]hese afterpieces and divertissements most often are seen as having diluted or denigrated Shakespeare . . . they may be understood more meaningfully as having *integrated* him into American culture." In their study of "Shakespearean educations," Coppélia Kahn and Heather Nathans suggest that "Americans' growing affinity for Shakespeare during the nineteenth century can also be explained by a kinship between the long established role of oratory, in both schools and public life, and Shakespeare's fine declamatory speeches." They cite the elocutionary manuals "that circulated both inside and beyond schools" as another mode by which tampering with Shakespeare—that is, excerpting his speeches for study and recitation—influenced U.S. identity formation, as Americans young and old wove the Bard's passages into an emergent national discourse. Whatever the explanation for the nineteenth-century uptake of Shakespeare in the United States, the country undoubtedly developed a claim to Shakespeare as American. James Fenimore Cooper called Shakespeare "the great author of America" as early as 1828, and American poet William Cullen Bryant remarked at the 1872 dedication of Central Park's Shakespeare statue that "the fame of our great dramatist fills the civilized world," wagering a confident "our" before some six thousand persons and therein inviting them to count Shakespeare as one of their own at that commemorative moment.[64]

Bryant's use of the word "civilized" reflects an ideological shift in the late nineteenth century, not necessarily of Shakespeare's place as American, but of Shakespeare's primary place in American public culture. Shakespeare metamorphosed, Levine asserts, "from popular culture to polite culture, from entertainment to erudition, from the property of 'Everyman' to the possession of a more elite circle." Shakespeare scholar Virginia Mason Vaughan observes the playwright's gradually becoming "a source of American cultural capital, and knowledge of his plays a mark of gentility," citing actor-manager Augustin Daly, actor Edwin Booth, and scholarly editor and collector Horace Howard Furness as major American contributors to an emergent intellectual and purist approach to reading and performing Shakespeare that was divergent from the popular, colloquial approach of the previous decades. Kahn points to an American "genteel elite that tended to identify its Anglo-Protestant heritage with the nation's," linking these "Anglo-Saxonists' sense of English culture and language as a signifier of racial superiority" at the turn of the century to their use of Shakespeare. And although Katherine West Scheil contends that the spread of U.S. women's Shakespeare clubs after 1880 counters claims that Shakespeare's presence in the lives of ordinary people waned in the late nineteenth century, her guiding notion that "reading Shakespeare was connected with public and personal improvement" and her sense that "the exclusive nature of many clubs accorded Shakespeare privileged status as worthy reading material" are commensurate with the theory that Americans by and large moved away from viewing Shakespeare as everyday culture toward extoling him as cultural capital.[65]

Reviews of famous turn-of-the-twentieth-century American Shakespeareans E. H. Sothern and Ada Rehan display this new taste. The New York Times suggested in 1902 that Sothern's "vigorous and dignified" performance of Hamlet was in accord with his recent "ambition to act in plays of the highest literary and dramatic value," and the New York Tribune reported that Rehan's delivery of Katherine's closing speech in a 1904 production of The Taming of the Shrew would "long be remembered for gentle dignity of demeanor and lovely refinement of utterance." Even Greet's performance at Cooper Union earned praise from the New York Times for its textual purity: "Most welcome of all, the text was spoken entire. . . . The net result of it all was that the dramatic harmony of the play was preserved." Describing the Shakespearean shift in question, Levine writes, "Gone were the entr'acte diversions: the singers, jugglers, dancers, acrobats, orators. . . . Those who wanted their Shakespeare had to take him alone, lured to his plays by stark playbills promising no frills or enhancements."[66] Shakespeare, having spent decades in the U.S. melting pot, emerged in the late nineteenth century as a highbrow cultural icon of American whiteness—and a clear means by which to incorporate new immigrants into a white American ideology.

PLAYERS AND PLAYGOERS AS POACHERS

Of course, Shakespeare's cultural authority in the United States rested on socially constructed values rather than universal standards. Sociologist Pierre Bourdieu's work on social distinction demonstrates how manners of using and/or consuming culture—Shakespeare in this case—become ideologically and habitually linked to certain class positions, and literary theorist Barbara Herrnstein Smith has put "value" under a microscope to expose how universal truths, classifications, and evaluations of art and literature can be traced to deeply and complexly entangled social and historical forces, not least of all the press and other public texts. As Shakespeare scholar Gary Taylor writes, "In the appropriate cultural conditions certain ideas are more likely to be thought, and having been thought are more likely to be communicated to others, and having been promulgated are more likely to win and sustain adherence." Thus, Smith's *Working with the People*, Herts's *Children's Educational Theatre*, and all of the surrounding publicity and press materials about Shakespeare at the People's Institute and Educational Alliance were not merely historical records of dramatic activity on the Lower East Side but were also historical actors, "creat[ing] and destroy[ing] boundaries" among social groups and "shaping what would be validated as common beliefs and values," to draw on rhetoric scholar Angela G. Ray's apt characterization of rhetorical action.[67] Moreover, as material texts of public address, these discourses circulated—widely, in the case of mainstream newspapers and middle-class periodicals—and etched notions of taste and social difference onto the imaginations of their readers, not only deploying but also reproducing Shakespeare as a stable icon of cultural capital and American whiteness.

Such textual records are privileged historical actors because, unlike the past's human performers, they endure physically through time. Further, as a result of this material longevity, they also privilege a certain history—in this case, a history in which Shakespeare was a "permanent force," as Eliot put it, incongruous with, even superior to, "the people" but also ultimately "good for" them and therein good for the country. But what of the everyday embodied performances and human interactions associated with these Shakespeare-centered reform efforts that tell a more complex, if less definitive, version of the past? That is, what of the unrecorded or overlooked behaviors and experiences of People's Institute and Educational Alliance audiences and actors that bore rhetorical force without necessarily claiming rhetorical intent? The whispered commentary among Greet's audience members when they turned away from the camera and resumed spectatorship, or the intimacies and in-jokes that formed between Herts's adolescent actors backstage. Such historical performances are often "transformative

... overflow[ing] [their] borders, marking and filling other performances, running off unpredictably, growing exponentially," in performance scholar Della Pollock's words. Indeed, they may run clear off the pages of history, or at least off the pages of more formalized records of the past produced by socially dominant individuals and institutions, but the historical meaning of these performances is no less potent for their archival elusiveness. "[T]he printed word," Jackson reminds us, "was not the only medium that did the work of historical mediation."[68] It is therefore crucial to look beyond and beneath the surface of traditional archives, mining records for subtle contextual factors and details that work against the grain of dominant narratives. Doing so reveals that Progressive Era efforts to bring "Shakespeare to the people" did not simply transmit controlled knowledge about democratic practice and American identity to Manhattan's immigrant communities but also produced new knowledge—new expressions of Shakespeare, of whiteness, and of national belonging.

The immigrant press, for instance, offers an alternative (albeit textual) historical site in which to explore Shakespearean social reform efforts. Just as surrounding content in the *New York Tribune*'s February 1904 preview of *The Tempest* at the Educational Alliance framed the production as a social welfare effort consistent with the Alliance's efforts to Americanize new immigrants, so too did advertisements for the same performance in the Yiddish press frame the production's social meaning—but in a very different light. On 28 February, a small advertisement appeared in the *Forverts* (*Forward*), an influential Yiddish newspaper, publicizing a "second performance of Shakespeare's *Tempest*" under the auspices of the Educational Alliance. "The piece is performed by members of the clubs and classes of the Educational Alliance," it read. "New scenery, new costumes and music." To the right of this understated preview—which made no fuss over the uptake of Shakespeare by working-class members of the Alliance—was a social-democratic column called "The Worker's World," the first headline of which announced a new weekly newspaper distributed by the Jewish trade union. To the left and above the *Tempest* announcement appeared ads for a Yiddish-language opera and a concert. Here, *The Tempest* at the Educational Alliance was situated alongside radical politics and popular entertainment, not corsets and cooking for convalescents. A March 26 *Forverts* announcement for the Alliance's final performance of *The Tempest*, positioned between an ad that read "Concert and Ball" and a notice that renowned Yiddish actor Bores

Thomashefsky would not be performing in New Haven, Connecticut, also marketed the production as show business rather than social betterment.[69]

More than merely framing *The Tempest* as entertainment, the *Forverts* dislocated Shakespeare from a scene of Anglo-American social propriety, seamlessly and unquestioningly incorporating the playwright into an American immigrant milieu. In fact, Shakespeare had already mingled considerably with this milieu despite self-aggrandizing suggestions to the contrary from voices like Smith, Herts, Eliot, and the *New York Tribune*. According to ads in the *Forverts*, February 1904 not only saw the opening of *The Tempest* as an English-language production at the Educational Alliance but also saw multiple Yiddish-language performances of *Shaylok, oder der koyfman fon venedig* (*Shylock; or, The Merchant of Venice*) and *Der yidisher kenig Lier* (*The Jewish King Lear*) at the Lower East Side's Grand Theatre. Similarly, Greet's performance of *The Merchant of Venice* at the People's Institute on May 13, 1904, coincided with a Yiddish production of *Hamlet* at the Yiddish-run (formerly German-run) Thalia Theatre.[70] These contextual factors expand the implications of "Shakespeare for the People" and render headlines such as *Theatre*'s "Twenty-five Cent Shakespeare for the People" not just tonally paternalistic but factually naïve as well.

Mainstream records also yield alternative histories for readers alert to absent or unelaborated experiences rather than intentional narratives—a reading practice somewhat like examining the photographic negative of an archival document. In this sense, whereas Herts told the *New York Tribune* that *The Tempest* had "soaked into the neighborhood," a photo-negative approach to extant records suggests that a more accurate, or at least equally plausible, remark may have been that the neighborhood had soaked into Shakespeare. Of course, privileged accounts never framed the scene as such. Instead, the mainstream media marshaled immigrant voices, experiences, and images to corroborate its misguided conclusion that the neighborhood had simply and wholly absorbed Shakespeare. For instance, *Theatre* characteristically described Greet's audience at the People's Institute using a series of passive verbs: "Here were a number of the common people and their children being improved. In many of them latent tendencies towards good thinking were awakened, others were directly stimulated to the study of the best that is to be found in books, others yet felt encouraged to continue and enlarge the already existing habit of communing with the choice spirits of the past." Such a passage illustrates cultural theorist Michel de

Certeau's claim that, although the image of a passive public "is not usually made explicit" in the mainstream media, "[i]t is nonetheless implicit in the 'producers'' claim to *inform* the population." Yet De Certeau also provides an alternative perspective through which to read American immigrant histories, pointing to a "misunderstanding [that] assumes that 'assimilating' necessarily means 'becoming similar to' what one absorbs, and not 'making something similar' to what one is, making it one's own, appropriating or reappropriating it."[71]

Understanding assimilation in this latter sense animates images of "the people" against the grain of dominant narratives and illuminates a scene of cultural complexity, instability, and hybridity that mainstream media underplayed if not resisted completely. One finds, for example, that Jewish immigrant culture asserted itself in the literal fabric of the Alliance *Tempest* performance. The *New York Tribune*, along with other sources, reported that "[n]ot only the players, but the costumes, scenery, and music, are all local. . . . the materials were bought in the neighborhood, some of them even from pushcarts." The *Tribune* also quoted a local dressmaker, who revealed that she knew "all the leading parts" and remarked that "Prospero must have a wide sleeve. . . . A narrow sleeve would not look well when he raises his wand and says, 'One midnight fated to the purpose.'" Thus, despite the fact that artistic director Emma Sheridan Fry herself called for the costumes to be "modelled after historic pictures," and despite the probability that the *Tribune* highlighted the dressmaker's ability to quote Shakespeare as an unexpected novelty for its readers, such details point to a multidimensional community of assimilators, in De Certeau's sense of the term: local craftspeople laboring over costumes and offering their own interpretations of characters; the neighborhood trade economy, called upon for materials, outfitting the final stage product; and nearby musicians providing incidental music for the production.[72]

De Certeau calls readers "poachers," neither of a privileged cultural text nor outside it but "simultaneously inside and outside, dissolving both by mixing them together."[73] So too were Alliance audiences and actors simultaneously inside and outside, and therein making something new, of Shakespeare. *Charities and the Commons*, a weekly philanthropy journal, reported that "[a]lmost a thousand copies of ['The Tempest'] were sold during the performance, and The Tempest really created a tempest in the neighborhood, for it was talked about and discussed in every aspect."

Further, *As You Like It* "was read and studied throughout the whole section of the city in settlements, schools and in classes."[74] Although this writer's intent was to show how far Shakespeare's reform powers stretched across the Lower East Side, his effect—for those attentive to De Certeau's perspective on assimilation—is an understanding of how Lower East Siders made Shakespeare their own. Perhaps an enterprising pushcart operator pocketed a copy of *The Tempest* on his way home from work and discussed it in rough English with his more fluent children over dinner. Or two sweatshop employees debated the pound of flesh in Yiddish over the whirr of their sewing machines. Whatever the scenario, individual or group interactions with Shakespeare took on social meaning relative to the circumstances and feelings of a specific moment—a father's increasingly rare chance to connect with children raised in a different country than he was; an energizing intellectual outlet for women confined to wretched working conditions—and not necessarily with respect to Shakespeare's symbolic status.

Even the Greet performances at the People's Institute, which focused on exposure to rather than engagement with Shakespeare, prompted such audience proactivity.[75] Describing the playgoers at the 1904 People's Institute production of *The Merchant of Venice*, the *New York Times* reported that "[m]any followed lines in pocket editions of the play, and when the single cut was made, that of the fifth scene of the third act, the fact was noted and commented on." Smith likewise observed in an article for *Charities* (formerly titled *Charities and the Commons*) that "[c]opies of Shakespeare, with the page open at *The Merchant of Venice*, were in evidence everywhere." Far from passive sponges soaked through with Shakespeare, Lower East Side audiences took a critical and creative role in these productions. While the press rarely quoted audience members themselves, a letter from a young girl who had seen Greet's *Merchant of Venice* appeared in both the *New York Tribune* and *Charities* as proof of the play's good influence. "Saturday morning I was so happy over the prospect of seeing 'The Merchant of Venice,'" she wrote. "While helping mama, I was continually saying, 'In sooth I know not why I am so sad,' until she said her ears buzzed. The whole morning I was dreaming of Portia, Antonio, Shylock, Bassanio." Assuming that this girl was indeed a real child and not a public relations fabrication, we can extrapolate an image of someone dreaming, making characters her own—their words, their images, their relationships. Describing the performance, she confessed, "Even though I knew the pound of flesh was not to be forfeited

I forgot it for the time being, and imagined that I saw it being confiscated, but that is because of the way in which Shylock sharpened that knife." Despite reformers like Greet, then, who "lay all possible emphasis upon the importance of a faithful and effective rendering of the text," and Herts, who demanded that her young actors' interpretations of character and plot be "founded on text, not on opinion," this particular girl strayed from the text to imagine and improvise new possibilities.[76] Conceivably, so did the tens of thousands of other spectators and performers who participated in the People's Institute and Educational Alliance Shakespeare activities. Thus, while it is crucial to expose the neocolonial currents in Progressive Era reform rhetoric, it would be unfortunate to stop with such a critique. To do so would be to discount the active and contributory individual and community experiences that were obscured by neocolonial accounts—to misunderstand the agency of assimilation so often discounted by the rhetoric of Progressive Era assimilation agencies.

But my suggestion that the community "soaked in" to Shakespeare perhaps still misses the point. It is a metaphor far too permanent and unidirectional for what was really taking place in New York City at this time. In their efforts to nurture social change, Smith and Herts staged sites of social and cultural *ex*change. For example, according to *Theatre's* report of the Educational Alliance's *Tempest*, Broadway theatre producer "Daniel Frohman lent bits of the Daly production of 'The Tempest'" to Herts and Fry—an indication that Broadway materials, carrying the cultural weight of the late actor-manager Augustin Daly's professional authority over Shakespeare as highbrow drama, combined with pushcart fabrics and locally stitched seams. *The Tempest's* audience manifested this hybridity as well. *Theatre* reported that "[u]ptown folk got wind of what was in progress, and stormed for entrance." The same was true of the People's Institute Shakespeare productions, particularly those that provided vouchers for Lower East Siders to attend uptown performances. Mainstream press coverage, Smith's correspondence with various associates, and the extant vouchers themselves—all carefully preserved in the People's Institute Records at the New York Public Library—emphasized the Institute's "power to enable those classes to which it ministers to see good plays," as the *New York Tribune* put it. However, the Institute's efforts also filled uptown theatres with thousands of people who would have been otherwise unlikely to attend these performances, producing a new and diverse public as a result of Smith's initiative. Haenni's study of New York's immigrant scene between 1880 and 1924 argues that, "especially in the light of the heavy restrictions on people's actual mobility" during this period, "spaces of leisure provided forms of virtual mobility" for groups all over the city by staging and screening cross-class and cross-ethnic experiences.[77] In fact, the People's Institute vouchers provided a new form of actual mobility, filling spaces of leisure with highly mixed audiences—a scenario that was new not only to those utilizing the vouchers, but also to those well-off patrons who would continue to pay full price at the theatres.

Across these scenes of exchange, we see how cultural assimilation entails not so much "a clean erasure of one identity substituting another" but rather "combination and transaction . . . negotiated in a moving ratio that always retains traces of the previous identity," to borrow American studies scholar W. T. Lhamon Jr.'s excellent metaphor. Indeed, as "moving ratios," processes of assimilation are always reciprocal and never complete, even if this ineffable historical reality often eludes the public texts that produce social truths.[78]

———

The 1890s not only marked the dawn of the Progressive Era but also launched an especially vibrant period for New York's immigrant stages. In 1887, Gustav Amberg moved his German company, formerly housed in the Thalia Theatre along the Bowery south of Houston Street, to the new Amberg Theatre—soon to be renamed the Irving Place Theatre—in Union Square, giving over the Thalia to a Yiddish company. Jacob P. Adler came to the city in 1889, joining Bores Thomashefsky, David Kessler, and Sigmund Mogulesco, all of whom had emigrated in the 1880s, to establish a golden era of Yiddish theatre in Manhattan. Antonio Maiori, the Lower East Side's chief Italian tragedian and company manager, came to the United States around 1892. Acclaimed Yiddish actress Bertha Kalich, who eventually had a major career on the English-language stage, arrived in 1894.[79] These talents and others gained loyal followings among Lower East Side audiences, developing large and diverse publics for whom they often performed Shakespeare. Fusing Anglo-Shakespearean traditions with non-Anglo immigrant performance milieus and thus drawing spectators from around the city, such performances offer up another site where different social groups converged around Shakespeare.

CHAPTER TWO

Shakespearean Translations, Immigrant Adaptations, and Community Formations

In the decade or so following 1890, programs and playbills advertising productions of *Hamlet* on New York's East Side might have read like this:

Thalia Theater
Bowery, nahe Canal Str.
. . .
Freitag, den 5. Februar 1892:
Gastspiel von
Josef Kainz
und
Gustav Kober.
„Hamlet"
Prinz von Dänemark.
Trauerspiel in fünf Aufzügen von William Shakespeare.

*****

Talia teyater, 46–48 Boyry.
. . .
Madam Bertha Kalish
Mitvokh abends 30 Yanuer
Tsur afirung komt
Shekspirs berimte drame
Hamlet

*****

201 Bowery. Pipel's teyater, 201 Boyry.

. . .

wMontag abend, den 18sten November, 1901
Durkh groyse miye und fiyele kosten vider afgefirt
Shekspirs unshterblibe tragediye, H. Thomashefsky's unvber-
trafener sukses
Hamlet
der prints fon Denemark

*****

Teatro Italiano
Villa Giulia 196 Grand Street.
Compagnia Comico-Drammatica Italiana
A. Maiori e P. Rapone
Questa Sera
Venerdi' 30 Agosto, ore 8 Pom. precise
Si Dara
Amleto
Principe di Danimarca
Tragedia in 6 atti dell'immortale G. Sakespeare.[1]

That is to say, at the turn of the twentieth century, the city's German, Yiddish, and Italian American playhouses translated, and often altered, Shakespeare's work for immigrant audiences, therein mingling Anglo Ur texts with non-Anglo languages and performance traditions.

These immigrant-run Shakespeare productions not only overlapped in time with the Shakespearean reform efforts coordinated by Progressives like Charles Sprague Smith and Alice Minnie Herts, but they also overlapped in space. The performance venues advertised in the above excerpts, for example, map onto the physical urban terrain precisely between the street addresses of the People's Institute and Educational Alliance, as the following narrated walking tour illustrates: Begin at the Cooper Union People's Institute at the northernmost end of the Bowery and walk downtown for a half mile to reach the People's Theatre at 201 Bowery, where Yiddish and Italian troupes performed at the turn of the twentieth century. Next, walk three blocks south on the Bowery and, at the third cross street, take a right to find 196 Grand Street, the temporary location of the Teatro Italiano, where Antonio Maiori and Pasquale Rapone's *Amleto* (*Hamlet*) took place on 30 August 1901. Return to the Bowery and continue south for just over two blocks, past Hester and Canal Streets, to 46–48 Bowery, where the Thalia Theatre stood for decades as the home of German, Yiddish, Italian, and Chinese theatre companies. Finally, from the Thalia, walk down the Bowery past Bayard and Pell Streets to the intersection where Doyers Street (the home of Manhattan's turn-of-the-twentieth-century Chinese theatre) turns into Division Street; take a sharp left on Division, walk less than half a mile, and bear slightly right on Canal Street; follow Canal to where it ends at East Broadway and turn left; another block will lead you to the corner of East Broadway and Jefferson Street—the site of the Educational Alliance (fig. 5).

But while immigrant productions of Shakespeare overlapped in time and space with reform efforts, they did not overlap in ideological motivation or effect. Just blocks from where Smith partnered with powerful performers and theatre managers to ready working-class immigrants for "intelligent use of the ballot" and where Herts tirelessly rehearsed immigrant youth so that they might become "good Americans," Manhattan's largest immigrant populations put Shakespeare to work for themselves in their own languages, on their own stages, and on their own terms.[2] As such, two adaptive processes were entwined in the same historic moment. The largely linguistic and stylistic process of adapting Shakespeare to an American immigrant milieu became mutually constitutive with immigrant groups' cultural and social adjustments to their lives as Americans in lower Manhattan. Put another way, the act of going to an East Side venue to see Shakespeare performed in German, Yiddish, or Italian was the type of everyday, "old-culture-meets-new-culture" experience that organically influenced immigrants' transitions into New York life; at the same time, the diverse artistic tastes and demands of this consumer-community-in-transition shaped how theatre managers, directors, and performers adapted Shakespeare for immigrant audiences.

Shakespeare thus entered the East Side's theatrical economy not as a fixed ideological category to which immigrant bodies might conform, but as a broadly recognized and malleable cultural space that accommodated and encouraged what Sabine Haenni identifies as "a heterogeneous collective ethnic identity in which people of diverse affiliations could participate."

FIGURE 5 "Hagstrom's Map of Lower New York City, House Number and Subway Guide." From the New York Public Library, https://digitalcollections.nypl.org/items/a8338fc0-f79f-0130-5e5e -58d385a7b928, with annotations by the author.

Historian Mario Maffi's study of the Lower East Side reminds readers that "immigrant communities are living organisms. They are class structured. . . . They contain the past, and they entertain a continuous, osmotic relationship to the present. They give birth to new traits, and they remould old ones."[3] In other words, south of the dividing line between Jacob Riis's two halves—a line that was at once geographic, socioeconomic, and ideological—the New York neighborhoods most densely populated by immigrant

groups at the turn of the twentieth century bristled with their own ideological, economic, artistic, religious, and linguistic differences. As Lower
East Side residents moved about their daily routes and routines, inter-
and intragroup negotiations precipitated a "moving ratio" of assimilation
as forcefully as (and more frequently than) immigrants' exchanges with
bourgeois reformers, necessitating "combination and transaction" of social
behaviors, tastes, beliefs, dialects, languages, and identities.[4]

Theatres were important sites for such exchanges. "In its heterogeneity,"
explains Maffi, "the theatrical scene of the Lower East Side clearly mirrored
the complex, ethnic and cultural stratification brought on by decades of
immigration." In her study of the Lower East Side, Haenni makes a related
case for how immigrant-run theatres staged diverse, often opposed, styles
and tastes that in most cases attached to social and cultural hierarchies,
therein congregating multifaceted publics. She contrasts theatres' function
as "modern urban subculture[s]" with their oft-attributed function as "communal (and community building)" institutions. But whereas Haenni pits
the theatre's communal qualities against its heterogeneity, I view these two
functions as commensurate. That is, at the turn of the twentieth century,
New York's immigrant-run theatres—and their Shakespeare productions
in particular—enabled community in the face of difference.[5]

Thus, while social activists on the Lower East Side used Shakespeare as
a reform strategy to incorporate immigrant groups into a normative white
American habitus in the 1890s and early 1900s, the neighborhood's immigrant groups concurrently adapted Shakespeare to a diverse set of local
needs and circumstances. Indeed, if the Bard's work was a means to any
social end in New York's East Side immigrant-run venues (other than the
obvious aims of artistic expression and public entertainment), it was as a
force of community building rather than nation making. By "force of nation
making," I mean the dominant worldviews that corral different groups
within a given nation-state into a common set of beliefs, values, attitudes,
mannerisms, and behaviors—a shared knowledge of *how to be* a member
of what Benedict Anderson terms an "imagined community"—whereas
a "force of community building" signals the interpersonal networks and
experiences that encourage different social groups to *be* together in shared
physical localities.[6] Accordingly, new modes of American being and belonging took shape from *within* this heterogeneous community, rather than
being imposed *on* it or imagined *for* it.

HIGHBROW AND LOWBROW

Scholarly literature has decisively marked the end of the nineteenth century as the juncture when "rigid, class-bound definitions of culture [were]
forged" in the United States.[7] Managers and producers increasingly distinguished "high" from "low" entertainment forms, Americans began to
correlate cultural taste with social status, and audiences self-segregated
accordingly. Shakespeare became the stuff of highbrow theatre, or so many
historical narratives would have it.[8] But the period's immigrant venues
staged a range of entertainments that spanned the high-low continuum and
catered to socially diverse audiences. In one sense, then, immigrant-run
theatres flouted the highbrow/lowbrow binary that scholars trace to the
late nineteenth century. But in another sense, these venues *depended* on this
binary, combining aspects of both cultural orientations in order to develop
a uniquely heterogeneous space between the two. And Shakespeare played
a vital role in venues' striking a balance between highbrow and lowbrow
to convene diverse immigrant groups in artistically and socially hybrid
gatherings. Lower Manhattan's German, Yiddish, and Italian playhouses
translated, staged, and advertised Shakespeare's plays with precisely this
mixed community of playgoers in mind—a community with varying
artistic tastes rather than the privileged group of elite consumers whose
aesthetic disposition is customarily classified as "highbrow."

Indeed, a history of Lower East Side immigrant venues demands an
ampersand where Lawrence W. Levine famously inserts a slash between
highbrow and lowbrow in his landmark work, *Highbrow/Lowbrow: The
Emergence of Cultural Hierarchy in America*. Perhaps the best-known
account of U.S. performance culture's late nineteenth-century social stratification, especially where Shakespeare was concerned, Levine's study
links Shakespeare's changing place in U.S. culture to the concurrent shift
in the makeup and mannerisms of American audiences during the latter
half of the nineteenth century. Before 1850, Shakespeare was ubiquitous
in the nation's theatres, which "housed both the entire spectrum of the
population and the complete range of entertainment from tragedy to farce,
juggling to ballet, opera to minstrelsy. The theater drew all ranks of people
to one place," he continues, "where they constituted what Erving Goffman
has called a 'focused gathering'—a set of people who relate to one another
through the medium of a common activity. The term is useful," Levine

notes, because it reminds us "that in the theater people not only sat under one roof, they interacted." Theatres across the early nineteenth-century United States, then, were "microcosm[s] of the relations between the various socioeconomic groups in America." Early American theatres not only stimulated audiences' interpersonal engagements with one another but also encouraged playgoers' "engagement in what was happening on stage—an engagement that on occasion could blur the line between audience and actors."[9] The decades following 1850, however, saw the gradual emergence of separate theatres meant for "highbrow" and "lowbrow" entertainments (artistic qualifiers that functioned as class markers for the audiences in attendance), with Shakespearean repertoire generally confined to the former and participatory spectatorship relegated to the latter.

Shifting American ideas about Shakespeare performance were thus intertwined with a period of "audience construction" in the United States, to borrow Dorothy Chansky's term for "the creation of attitudes and behaviors concerning theatergoing in the minds and bodies of actual or potential spectators as well as other Americans. The purpose of audience construction," writes Chansky, was "to create and maintain a permanent audience class and a public belief in the importance of theatre in civic and personal life." While Chansky's work attributes this process to the Little Theatre movement that developed in the United States in the 1910s and '20s, her description of audience construction, its purposes, and its effects resonates strongly with Levine's central thesis about the emergence of American cultural hierarchy in the late nineteenth century. "Audience construction may be imposed from the outside in the form of actual instruction by an usher, a columnist, a teacher who is about to take a group of students to their first play, or program notes requesting or forbidding certain behavior," Chansky explains. "Or it may be generated by playgoers who create their own theatre in order to inhabit it as spectators and to fill it with others who are like-minded." Citing drama scholar W. B. Worthen, she summarizes the salient dynamic between onstage performance and audience construction, wherein "producing a certain kind of experience for the audience" leads to "producing the audience itself," and vice versa.[10]

Levine's account tracks this reciprocal influence via print advertisements from the first half of the nineteenth century. More so than records of where and when a production took place, what costumes the actors wore, or how much tickets cost, such materials offer clues about the artistic appetites, attitudes, and ambitions of the groups who created and consumed them. For example, early nineteenth-century promotional pieces that presented Shakespearean repertoire "amid a full range of contemporary entertainment" evidence for Levine Shakespeare's popularity among mixed audiences. He also links the period's melodramatic acting style to the enthusiastic, even bombastic spirit of publicity materials, which often appended an exclamation point to Shakespearean titles. Further, the playbills on which Shakespeare's dramas appeared alongside various divertissements and afterpieces convince Levine of the ways that theatres and theatregoing "*integrated* [Shakespeare] into American culture. Shakespeare was presented as part of the same milieu inhabited by magicians, dancers, singers, acrobats, minstrels, and comics. He appeared on the same playbills and was advertised in the same spirit."[11]

Whereas publicity materials in the early 1800s excitedly advertised Shakespeare alongside a variety of other entertainment forms, late-century posters and playbills *distinguished* Shakespeare from what Levine calls "the broader world of everyday culture." Variety acts—singers, jugglers, dancers—disappeared from programs, as did "the purple prose trumpeting the sensational events and pageantry that were part of the Shakespearean plays themselves. Those who wanted their Shakespeare had to take him alone, lured to his plays by stark playbills promising no frills or enhancements." While theatre history icon Marvin Carlson's study of the development of the American theatre program stresses that evolving conditions of production also played a role in the changing aesthetics of publicity materials, Levine's argument nonetheless holds up under rhetorical scrutiny.[12] Early nineteenth-century posters and playbills addressed a broad American public who welcomed their Shakespeare in all contexts, be they parody, farce, circus antics, or musical spectacle, while late-century posters addressed a narrower, more intellectually discriminating demographic, one inclined to hold Shakespeare as privileged, pure, and even sacred.

Two Shakespeare posters, one advertising actors E. H. Sothern and Virginia Harned's Broadway run with acclaimed New York manager Daniel Frohman in 1900 (fig. 6), and the other announcing Robert Mantell's 1904 New York appearances with Marie Russell (fig. 7), illustrate Levine's case.[13] Both posters are rich in color and imagery but sparing in text—certainly no "purple prose trumpeting . . . sensational events" and no exclamation points, no enthusiastic details about jugglers, dancers, or divertissements.

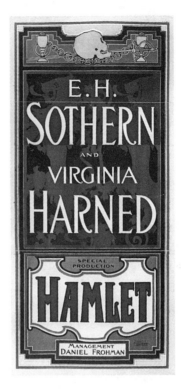

FIGURE 6 "E. H. Sothern and Virginia Harned, special production of Hamlet." Theatrical poster collection, Prints and Photographs Division, Library of Congress, LC-USZ62-19687.

Even the colors and imagery are austere; the posters appear more like tapestries than entertainment bills. In fact, neither poster so much as displays Shakespeare's name—instead, the Sothern/Harned poster offers *Hamlet* as a sort of proxy that audiences were expected to recognize, and the Mantell/Russell poster details a series of "classic and romantic productions" by way of four character portraits that surround a profile of Mantell. On the Sothern/Harned poster, the name "Hamlet" looms across the poster's base, combining with an image of what we can presume to be poor Yorick's skull in the top banner to signal what the performance will entail. In the Mantell/Russell poster, Hamlet appears only in pictorial form, a figure posed with Yorick's skull in the top right corner of the portrait set. Whereas a melodramatic spirit characterized early nineteenth-century Shakespeare performance, a more "cerebral" acting style accompanied Shakespeare's exit from popular culture, according to Levine. He supports this claim by contrasting images of two famed American tragedians, picturing Edwin Forrest's early nineteenth-century Macbeth opposite Edwin Booth's

FIGURE 7 "Rob't B.
Mantell assisted by Miss
Marie Booth Russell and
a company of players
in classic and romantic
productions." Theatrical
poster collection, Prints
and Photographs Division,
Library of Congress, POS -
TH - POR .M35, no. 1.

late-century Hamlet to underscore Forrest's forceful energy and bellicose
stance as compared to Booth's "cerebral" mood and "restrained" posture.[14]
It is fitting, then, that both *Hamlet* advertisements described above feature skulls, as this prop belongs to the graveyard scene that stages Hamlet's
introspection in the extreme and may have drawn turn-of-the-century audiences whose tastes preferred a staid, intellectual approach to Shakespeare
theatre over the more vigorous, spectacular performance styles of the early
1800s.

But New York's immigrant-run playhouses were not artistically or
socioeconomically stratified like other American theatres at the turn of
the twentieth century, and their publicity materials tell a different story.
In fact, these venues instigated "focused gatherings" much like the theatres
that Levine claims faded from the American cultural landscape by the late
1800s. Immigrant audiences represented a range of artistic, intellectual,
and socioeconomic positions, and the commercial demands of sustaining
a theatre compelled managers of immigrant venues to stage a wide range of
repertoire. For instance, Haenni links Heinrich Conried's success as manager and director of the German Irving Place Theatre with his use of diverse
programming, aptly calling this mixed repertoire of "serious" plays and
"popular" entertainments "a pragmatic tool that allowed [Conried] to cater
to a diverse, heterogeneous constituency." Antonio Maiori and Pasquale

Rapone's Teatro Italiano likewise played to varied theatrical sensibilities. "Maiori would ply his audiences with classic productions of Shakespeare and other known European writers," historian Emelise Aleandri explains, "but the working class patrons could always be assured that Rapone would follow up with a Neapolitan farce." Yiddish venues also struggled to satisfy mixed dramatic dispositions. It is nearly impossible to trace the history of Yiddish theatre on the Lower East Side without addressing the artistic— and inevitably social—tensions that emerged at the turn of the century between "low" and "high" tastes, as stage luminaries like Abraham Gold-faden and Morris Horowitz, who produced mainly historical operas and comic operettas, clashed with pioneers of realist theatre like playwright Jacob Gordin and actor Jacob P. Adler, who advocated for simple, serious onstage content, free of music or bombast.[15]

An Irving Place Theatre program for an 1896 performance of *Romeo und Julia* (*Romeo and Juliet*) compels Haenni's commentary on the German theatre's dual appeal to high and low tastes, as the booklet featured Shake-spearean production and casting details on the left-hand page opposite the full week's repertoire—"current light comedy," a "merry! funny!" Sunday concert, and other "serious" fare, all jammed together on the facing page. In fact, the Thalia Theatre program for the 1892 Kainz/Kober *Hamlet* quoted at the beginning of this chapter looked very similar, as do most of the German Thalia and Irving Place theatre programs from that period. These programs also featured busy collages of advertisements—so busy that at times it proves difficult to spot the dramatic details in the midst of commercial products—that, as Haenni also discusses, evidence the varied consumer tastes that came with audiences' diverse aesthetic tastes. For example, on the front cover of an 1899 Irving Place Theatre program, the cast list for *Othello* is wedged between ads for pianos atop and below it, and flanked by a column of ads to its right for "fine furs," "exquisite per-fumes," "highest grade champagne," and still more pianos. The booklet's inner pages, by contrast, err more toward hodge-podge than high-end: ads for Burnham's Clam Chowder ("A Whole Dinner in a Can"), Capsicum Vaseline, Her Majesty's Corset, Adams' Pepsin Tutti-Frutti ("How to feel good for a nickel"), Newman's "photographic palace, one of the sights of New York," and over a dozen other brands hail a motley audience of con-sumers. By and large, the German theatre's programs employed a mix of English and German, another indication of its assorted clientele.[16]

The playbill for Maiori and Rapone's 1901 production of *Amleto*, cited at the outset of this chapter and pictured in figure 8, likewise shows how the Teatro Italiano simultaneously promoted highbrow *and* lowbrow culture. The playbill seems plain enough; it does not include the exclamation points or "purple prose" (aside from a reverent nod toward "dell' immortale G. Sakespeare") that Levine associates with early-century playbills' tendency to "announc[e] Shakespearean plays as spectacles in their own right." But beneath the cast listing for *Hamlet* is a notice for a large vocal concert, the talent for which is given rather prominent billing relative to the *Hamlet* cast. The names of the three vocal performers, printed bolder and larger than the surrounding text, are seemingly intended to catch a viewer's eye. Of the three, Eduardo Migliaccio in particular signals the genre of this concert, as he was among the Italian American theatre's most celebrated variety stars. "Accompanied by a small orchestra," Haenni explains, "Migliaccio, under the name of 'Farfariello,' usually performed six . . . character impersonations that included a prose part as well as a song . . . during a half-hour vaudeville segment." Sure enough, the name "Farfariello" appears in parentheses following Migliaccio's concert credit. A closer look at the cast list reveals that Migliaccio also played Marcello in this production of *Amleto*, but "Farfariello" does not accompany his given name in that context.[17] Thus the playbill, historically located firmly on the "no-frills Shakespeare" side of Levine's trajectory, lured its audience not merely with Shakespeare, as the Sothern/Harned and Mantell/Russell posters did, but also with a musical spectacle featuring a local variety performer.

The posters for the aforementioned Yiddish productions of *Hamlet*— Kalich's January 1901 performance and Bores Thomashefsky's appearance the following November—reveal a hybridity similar to the German programs and Maiori playbill, albeit in different respects (figs. 9, 10). Like the Sothern/Harned and Mantell/Russell posters, neither Yiddish poster advertises auxiliary entertainments (although Yiddish directors, particularly Thomashefsky, frequently incorporated music into their productions). Both posters hold Shakespeare in high esteem, implying the Bard's highbrow, literary appeal. The Kalich poster emphasizes the actress's preparation for the role, noting that "it's been six months that she's been studying . . . with one of the greatest professors in the area . . . the same professor also taught the greatest artists such as Sothern, Maude Adams, and others." Here, it is noteworthy that the poster brings Kalich into parity with the period's

FIGURE 8 "Teatro Italiano ... Amleto Principi Danimarca [playbill]." By permission of the Folger Shakespeare Library.

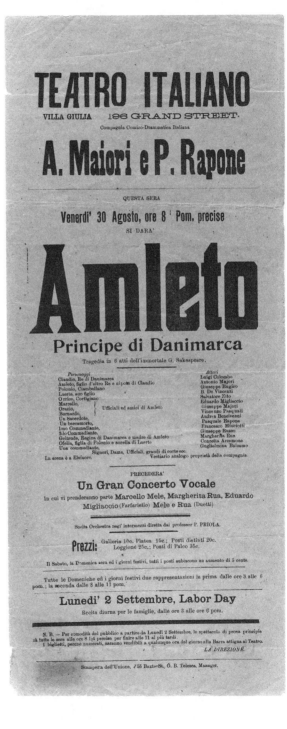

FIGURE 9 "Madam Bertha Kalish als Hamlet." From the New York Public Library, https://digitalcollections.nypl.org/items/510d47db-1488-a3d9-e040-e00a18064a99.

most respected Anglo-American Shakespeareans, even as it draws the obvious connection between Kalich and Sarah Bernhardt, the internationally recognized French tragedienne who was the period's best-known female interpreter of Hamlet. This was a curious move, as the comparisons would have certainly bolstered Kalich's credibility among English-speaking spectators but were less likely to register with the Yiddish-speaking community to whom the poster was addressed. On the second poster, Thomashefsky appears sullenly and pensively draped across the floor, arguably emulating the late-century cerebral style of Edwin Booth, whom he had seen and called "the most famous Hamlet of America and England"—the interpretation of the role "chiefly engraved in [his] memory." A description below this image further likens the Thomashefsky poster to the Shakespearean

FIGURE 10 "Hamlet, der prints fon Denemark." From the New York Public Library, https://digitalcollections.nypl.org/items/510d47da-dc52-a3d9-e040-e00a18064a99.

publicity materials that Levine identifies with the period's "highbrow" tastes: inviting audiences to luxuriate in the play's "beautiful scenes and elevated dialogue," the poster puts Shakespeare's work on a literary pedestal and therein classifies it as high culture.[18]

But certain characteristics of these two Yiddish posters suggest a Shakespeare scene more akin to Levine's early "popular" phase than his later "polite" period. For example, below its long-winded assurance that Kalich's Hamlet was as thoroughly studied as that of the period's best Anglo-American performers, the poster includes a note: "Pay particular attention to Hamlet's duel with Laertes." While a small detail, this note reveals a good deal about the Yiddish theatre's diverse audiences, as the promise of a duel, reinforced by the long sword that Kalich stands poised to draw in the poster's central image, was likely aimed at spectators less interested in, or totally unaware of, the likes of Bernhardt, Sothern, and Adams—perhaps even indifferent to or unfamiliar with Shakespeare altogether.[19] Sword fighting was typical of the melodramatic style that found favor among Yiddish audiences. Although certain Yiddish actors and directors, along with the Yiddish intellectual elite, pushed for a more naturalistic repertoire that wrestled with the period's serious social issues, many Yiddish playgoers expressed an opposing desire for onstage spectacle, song, sentiment, and sensation. The histrionic tone of Thomashefsky's *Hamlet* poster suggests that the larger-than-life actor was also happy to deliver on this front (and, indeed, he generally was). The two lines of text above the title "Hamlet" read, "Through great effort and great expense, is presented Shakespeare's undying tragedy, Mr. Thomashefsky's unparalleled success, *Hamlet*," recalling the "purple prose" that had supposedly vanished from U.S. Shakespeare advertisements in the late nineteenth century. Further, a note under the play's title specifies that the play had been "updated and made into scenes by Mr. Thomashefsky"—again, a move reminiscent of the early 1800s, when altering, parodying, and supplementing Shakespeare were common on U.S. stages. Finally, both the Kalich and the Thomashefsky posters indicate an interactive dynamic between actors and audience more characteristic of the American Shakespeare culture that Levine consigns to the early 1800s than the exclusively highbrow Shakespeare scene he ascribes to the latter half of the century. Energetically hailing their viewers with cries of "extra! extra!" the Kalich and Thomashefsky posters convey a turn-of-the-twentieth-century theatre space that welcomed Shakespeare *and* audience engagement. The prose sections at the base of each poster even read like correspondence between performers and playgoers, beginning with the salutation "worthy public!" and signing off, "the Thalia Theatre Company" or "with respect, the Committee," respectively.

Various anecdotes about the Lower East Side's Yiddish and Italian theatres likewise paint this interactive audience dynamic, evidencing spectators' involvement in the Shakespearean action on stage. For instance, multiple sources recount an evening at the Thalia Theatre in 1895 when, during the closing scene of Thomashefsky's *Hamlet*, the audience's enthusiasm swelled to great heights. "The general slaughter, the lively dueling, the flashing of swords and the sobbing of death cries simply set the [playgoers] crazy," a *New York Sun* writer reported, and the star performers grew weary from curtain calls. After a time, the appreciative audience began to cheer "Author! Author!" so relentlessly demanding the playwright's onstage appearance that, rather than sending out a manager to explain that Shakespeare had been dead for hundreds of years, the backstage team costumed a young stagehand in a fake beard and linen collar so that he might address the crowd as Shakespeare. In the Italian theatre, following the fourth act of a 1900 production of *Othello* at the Germania Assembly Rooms—a performance that Italian actor Guglielmo Ricciardi deemed "a night to remember"—the audience sent the lead actor "what seemed a bunch of flowers done up in tissue paper," according to an usher's account (retold by journalist Hutchins Hapgood in his investigative work, *The Spirit of the Ghetto: Studies of the Jewish Quarter in New York*). "But when Othello took it in his hands," the usher recalled, "the paper dropped off and revealed a cabbage. He was applauded so wildly that the last act was not played, and Desdemona did not die."[20] In the Italian theatre's case, the audience not only interrupted the production but also changed the course of the Shakespearean action, adapting the plot of *Othello* to the circumstances of that particular moment. For their part, the Yiddish spectators recharted the course of Shakespeare's biography, so powerfully voicing their demands that management had no choice but to improvise an appearance by the deceased playwright himself.

Levine's version of "William Shakespeare in America," as he titles his groundbreaking chapter, is not so much incorrect as it is incomplete. His chosen archive of mostly mainstream theatre ephemera steers his analysis toward dominant groups' histories, and he therefore constructs a national narrative that neglects the nation's full social spectrum. To be sure, Levine's observations of the ways in which early nineteenth-century modes of Shakespeare performance "integrated [the playwright] into American culture" point to a rich instance of assimilation as a moving ratio. In the century following the Revolutionary War, Americans developed a new group identity that at once retained and reimagined the Anglo culture whose dominance they eschewed in founding their new nation. In this sense, early Americans were "poachers" of Shakespeare, "simultaneously inside and outside" the text, "dissolving both by mixing them together."[21] But so too did New York's immigrant theatre scene, decades later, perform analogous acts of Shakespearean poaching—and of group identity building—by simultaneously adopting and adapting the dominant culture's canonical works so as to forge community in a new home. Coppélia Kahn and Heather Nathans's

assessment of how early nineteenth-century Americans "denatured" Shakespeare's work by using Shakespearean speeches as material for elocutionary
practice could just as readily apply to immigrant groups' denaturing of
Shakespeare around 1900: Thomashefsky's "updating" *Hamlet* and making
it into scenes, Kalich's featured sword fight, Maiori's pairing *Hamlet* with a
Farfariello act. "While this denaturing of Shakespeare's work might initially
seem to diminish his power and authority," Kahn and Nathans write, "it
allowed his texts to become a kind of palimpsest upon which Americans
continually reinscribed new notions of identity and belonging."[22]

THE OLD WORLD IN NEW YORK

One of the Yiddish community's primary modes of denaturing Shakespeare
was to "Judaize" the Anglo Ur texts, as theatre historian Joel Berkowitz
terms it—to make "the characters and settings Jewish." Take for example
a poster for an 1898 production of *The Jewish King Lear*, performed in Yiddish at the Windsor Theatre: An image of an old man occupies the center
of the page. He stands next to a small table that is draped with an ornate,
tasseled covering. Leaning on the table with his left hand, he raises his
other in a fist and looks off to his right, past his fist and past the image's
frame, with a hardened gaze. The man has a fair complexion and a long,
full white beard. He wears a long dark coat and a substantial prayer cap
atop his white hair. He appears righteous—rabbinical, even. The image is
captioned, "Herr Adler als kenig Lier" (Mr. Adler as King Lear). Beneath
this caption, about three-quarters of the way down the page, the words
"kenig Lier" (King Lear) are displayed in huge Hebrew characters, prefaced by the phrase "Der yudisher" (The Jewish), printed to the right in
much smaller font such that the full title reads, "Der yudisher kenig Lier."
The play's title sits atop an acknowledgment, "fun Herr Jacob Gordin" (by
Mr. Jacob Gordin), indicating an author other than Shakespeare (fig. 11).[23]
Shakespeare's legacy thus leaps off the center of the page in the form of his
tragedy's original title, but the pious protagonist pictured above, the petite
qualifier printed beside, and the authorial imprint stamped below the aged
king's famous name signal to readers that this production is something distinctly different—and distinctly Jewish.

    In fact, the Jewishness of this *Lear*—the way it summoned the local
East Side community—made Gordin's play one of the most beloved in

FIGURE 11 "Der yudisher
kenig Lier." From the New
York Public Library, http://
digitalcollections.nypl.org
/items/510d47db-1487-a3d9
-e040-e00a18064a99.

the Yiddish repertoire and made its title character, a Jewish businessman
named Dovid Moysheles whose actions toward his three daughters recall
Lear's, one of Yiddish-stage giant Jacob P. Adler's most celebrated roles.
The play opens in the Moysheles home in Vilna, at that time in Western
Russia, where the family is celebrating the Jewish festival of Purim with
food and song while simultaneously negotiating tensions between "the
more traditional members of the family" and the youngest, more progressive daughter, Taybele. Taybele has invited her tutor to the Purim meal, but
her tutor is a German Jew who, to this group of pious, Old World Jews, represents modern and secular thought, "the source of ideas that challenge[d]
traditional Jewish life."[24]

The fallout that occurs between Dovid and Taybele staged a strain of
social difference all too familiar to Jews living on the Lower East Side in
1898, where the rift between Old World religious sensibilities and modern

secular attitudes grew ever wider in an urban American context. But Shake-spearean adaptations like *The Jewish King Lear*—in which Dovid and Taybele inevitably reconcile by play's end—helped mitigate this rift by creating a space of shared identification for New York's diverse turn-of-the-twentieth-century Jewish audiences.[25]

In the predominantly Yiddish-speaking Seventh and Tenth Wards of the Lower East Side, Old World, ultrareligious traditions and observances min-gled with the increasingly secular lifestyles of Eastern European immigrants to New York. This shift can be seen as an extension of the Jewish Enlighten-ment that began in Germany in the eighteenth century and led a number of Eastern European Jews to exchange their religious practice for a more secular, intellectually progressive way of life in the mid- to late nineteenth century. As Jews settled in the United States, customary dress, arranged mar-riages, and *mikvah* ritual baths disappeared from daily life; Jewish women and men danced together, and some Jews had factory jobs that required them to work on the Sabbath. Jewish studies scholar Ruth Gay writes, "If Jews could go to work on the Sabbath, they could certainly go to the the-ater as well! And the Yiddish theaters in New York had no hesitation about giving five performances on the weekend, one on Friday night and two each on Saturday and Sunday." Yiddish theatres thus responded to and bore out the neighborhood's hybrid immigrant scene, staging Jewish-themed plays, integrating religious considerations into popular commercial conscious-ness, and encouraging the secularized culture of Jewishness that began to characterize New York's turn-of-the-twentieth-century Yiddish immigrant community more so than religious observance.[26]

Given Shakespeare's significance in wider American culture, as well as the playwright's worldwide status as a genius of the early modern West (a status that developed in the wake of the Enlightenment), Yiddish play-wrights' Shakespearean adaptations, which often staged traditionally Jewish settings, characters, holidays, festivals, prayers, and music, were particularly apt to signal both New World secular modernity and Old World religious observance. In this sense, *The Jewish King Lear*, along with likeminded productions like Thomashefsky's *Jewish Hamlet*, also called *Der yeshive bokher* (*The Yeshiva Boy*), in which a Jewish seminary student returns home to find that his father has died and his mother has married his uncle, or *The Oath on the Torah; or, The Jewish Romeo and Juliet*, which transposed the balcony scene to a synagogue, were what Diana Taylor calls *multicoded* performances, transmitting multiple "layers of meaning" to multiple viewers at once.[27] Such multicoded performances, Taylor explains, operate as "form[s] of multiplication and simultaneity rather than surrogation and absenting," cultural transfers that "preserv[e] rather than eras[e] . . . antecedents."[28] In other words, rather than advocating nation-ness at the expense of difference, Judaized Shakespeare adaptations preserved traditional antecedents in a secular space and therein enabled community despite the cultural conflicts that frequently divided Lower East Side Jews.

Music was a key mechanism for intertwining the secular, modern connotations of Shakespearean source texts with the Old World sacred sentiments of Jewish song. When Yiddish Shakespeare adaptations incorporated such music, mixed audiences experienced communal reverence, be it toward the famous playwright or the religious melodies—or both. Avigdor, the protagonist of *Der yeshive bokher*, sang the Kaddish, the Jewish prayer for the dead, when he learned of his father's death. In its opening Purim meal scene, *The Jewish King Lear* featured a Kiddush, a prayer sung before holiday meals. *The Jewish Romeo and Juliet* began on Simchat Torah with a ritual procession around the synagogue altar that, according to a *New York Times* review, "resolve[d] into a choral dance."[29] On the one hand, these musical interludes fulfilled Thomashefsky's "opinion [that] the Yiddish theater must be Jewish. . . . The music must be authentically Jewish; the melodies must penetrate the hearts of the Jewish audience." On the other hand, as historian Irene Heskes notes, "the music and particularly the popular songs of American Yiddish theater properly belong[ed] to the dual continuities of Judaic inspiration and American expression." As such, music operated as a "pendulum" that accrued energy and movement in the space between old and new cultures, fulfilling cultural critic Rustom Bharucha's model for ideal intercultural theatre. Jewish studies scholar Seth L. Wolitz elegantly captures how Yiddish repertoire combined the secular and sacred, turning the theatre into a new kind of house of worship. He writes, "[T]he stage itself becomes the place where a rite is performed, and where a traditional culture can find fresh expression of its core beliefs. In the context of Judaism, Yiddish theater resacralized Jewish history, its traditions, and its people."[30] In my own view, the *music* of the Yiddish theatre precipitated this "resacralization," fusing sacred with secular and, in many cases, incorporating and modifying Shakespeare's sacredness on the American stage as well.

Some of the music produced for New York's turn-of-the-twentieth-century Yiddish Shakespeare theatre was mass published—songs from *The Jewish King Lear*, for example—and this music's community-building effects therefore circulated outside of the theatre, reaching Jewish homes where traditionalist and modern-minded groups (often split along generational lines) not only experienced shared identification with the musical content but physically joined in song to re-create the stage melodies. "Almost from the start," writes Heskes, "sheet music had a strong and consistent market, even among the many who could neither read music nor play any musical instrument. Everyone could sing the widely known melodies, especially if all the lyrics were printed in broadside fashion." Along with the Hebrew Publishing Company bookstore, Heskes cites "at least a dozen music publishers with little outlet stores located on East Broadway, Canal Street, and the side streets" between 1890 and 1910. She also emphasizes that piano-vocal versions of songs were "deliberately simple, playable by modestly capable pianists," explaining that "an upright piano in the parlor had social advantages for a Jewish home; young women might enhance their qualities by singing and playing the latest favorite songs of the Yiddish stage."[31]

A close look at a *Jewish King Lear* piano-vocal score reveals another social advantage particular to Shakespearean Yiddish stage music: it addressed and appealed to multiple audiences who otherwise might not have gravitated toward the same forms of cultural expression. The cover for an 1899 edition, issued by the Hebrew Publishing Company, features bold blue letters printed against an ecru background. At the top of the page, Hebrew characters spell out "Der yudisher kenig Lier," the words "kenig Lier" appearing in larger font than "Der yudisher," as in the aforementioned poster (albeit with a smaller size differential). Immediately below this Yiddish text, however, are the same words in English: "The Jewish King Lear." Again, "The Jewish" appears substantially smaller than "King Lear" and is printed in a much simpler font, the first two words of the title sitting atop the latter two, nestled discreetly between the "N" of "King" and the "E" of "Lear." The original Shakespearean title flaunts its ornate, three-dimensional font from center-page, calling all Shakespeare worshipers. The remainder of the cover text is also in English (or English transliteration), crediting the piece's arranger ("H. A. Russotto"), listing the four pieces inside ("No. 1. Kiddush Al Tiro Avdi Jacob . . 2. Aude Lo-Eil No. 3. Couplet Shamai . . 4. The Chsidim Dance"), indicating the instrumentation and price ("Piano and Vocal 75 Cents"), and detailing the publisher and copyright information. While the titles of the songs, particularly the Kiddush and Hasidic dance, evoke Jewish rituals, the affordable price would have enticed turn-of-the-twentieth-century U.S. consumers, who, in purchasing sheet music and assembling their families around the piano, could participate in a popular American parlor practice of the time. On the inner leaves of the eight-page booklet, the Anglo, secular connotations of "King Lear" all but melt away, as musical language dictates traditional Jewish sonorities, and transliterations of Yiddish text prescribe the lyrics (save for the Chsidim Dance, which is for piano only). The sheet music's back page, which features a "Catalogue and Price List of Popular Hebrew Melodies for Piano and Violin," also positions *The Jewish King Lear* squarely in a Jewish context, associating it with Yiddish theatre standards like *Shulamith* and *Bar Kochba*, biblical operettas like *König Ahasverus* (*King Achashverosh*), sacred chants like "Kol Nidre," and other "Traditional Religious Melodies."[32] As a whole, this sheet music represents a multicoded artifact (in Taylor's sense of "multicoded") that gathered together disparate traditions and diverse audiences in shared song.

While many sounds of Yiddish Shakespeare theatre are lost to history, and most others are reduced to lines in extant play scripts, descriptive fragments in newspaper clippings, or song snippets in scores and sheet music, Avidgor's Kaddish from *The Jewish Hamlet*, performed by Thomashefsky, remains available as a sound recording.[33] Unlike the traditional script, in which Hamlet enters having already learned of the King's death and Gertrude's subsequent marriage to Claudius, Avigdor's Yiddish Hamlet hears of both his father's death and his mother's remarriage while on stage and is thus moved to sing the prayer for the dead. Berkowitz attributes this adaptive choice to the Yiddish community's taste for theatrical melodrama, but the change also created an occasion to infuse Hamlet's grief with the sounds of Jewish mourning. Thomashefsky's voice feelingly and resonantly intones the chromatic lines, the mood of his sound shading from anguished moaning to defiant bellowing as an accompanying chorus of klezmer strings ebbs and flows between phrases. Such use of Yiddish music as a way of signaling and staging Jewishness was important regardless of a play's text, but characteristically Ashkenazic sonorities became especially significant when combined with Western canonical texts, as the sound and meaning of the music reassigned a symbolically Anglo figure like Hamlet to a specifically

Yiddish setting. Jewish playgoers honoring recently deceased family may well have risen that morning in *shul* (synagogue) to recite Kaddish themselves, the visceral (and spiritual) memory of choking back tears through the prayer as they stood among a seated congregation still raw while taking in Thomashefsky's spin on Shakespeare. Moreover, the sounds of the Yiddish theatre also exposed non-Jewish spectators—of whom there were plenty, as we will soon learn—to a Yiddish soundscape, informing their perspective on what Shakespeare could mean to this American-immigrant audience.

Such examples suggest a Shakespeare scene that navigated cultural gaps on a local versus national level. Whereas Smith and Herts imagined immigrant groups absorbing and adapting *to* Shakespeare performed in English, Jewish immigrants' more meaningful cultural adjustments occurred when Yiddish theatres adapted Shakespeare for the community—when Adler's conservative-minded Lear reconnected with his progressive daughter (who earns her medical degree over the course of the play), when Thomashefsky's Jewish Romeo chanted the balcony scene in a synagogue, or when Yiddish audiences experienced musical numbers from *The Jewish Hamlet* or *The Jewish King Lear*, which traveled beyond Yiddish theatres into countless homes in the form of mass-published sheet music. To recall Maffi's observation, immigrant communities bear their pasts even as they reflect and respond to the present, "giv[ing] birth to new traits" and "remould[ing] old ones."[34] Striving for commercial success with an audience that ideologically straddled the Old World and New York, Yiddish playwrights and directors responded to neighborhood exigencies by remolding Shakespeare.

A CULTURE OF EXCHANGE

On the Lower East Side, differences existed between immigrant groups as well as within them, and Shakespeare facilitated intergroup contact and collaboration across such social borders. On January 31, 1901, for example, the *New York German Journal* reproduced a photograph of Bertha Kalich—costumed in princely garb, poised with ruffle-covered shoulders back, studiously considering a book held in both hands at chest level—over the caption "Frau Bertha Kalich als 'Hamlet'" (Madame Bertha Kalich as 'Hamlet'). Above the image, the announcement "'Hamlet' im jüdischen Theater aufgeführt" ("Hamlet listed in the Jewish theatre") attuned

German-speaking readers to recent goings-on in the Yiddish theatre. A small note beneath the caption relayed the previous night's performance by Kalich and detailed the various Eastern European locations in which she had trained and performed before becoming a star in the Bowery's Jewish theatre. *New York Journal* critic Alan Dale, reviewing the same performance, reported that Kalich in fact spoke her lines in German while the surrounding cast spoke Yiddish, and the *New York Daily Mirror* also noted that Kalich used a "German version of the play." Although Berkowitz cites a Yiddish translation for Kalich's 1901 production of *Hamlet,* and a preview article in the *Forverts* likewise suggested that Kalich employed a Yiddish text, it would seem that Kalich did engage a German translation at some point, as the Bertha Kalich Papers at the New York Public Library house an undated German-language copy of *Hamlet* with Kalich's name penciled onto the back page beneath a scrawled set of closing stage directions (written in German) appended to the printed text in red ink. What is more, Dale emphasized the multilingual audience in attendance at Kalich's performance, remarking, "The Yiddish theatre teemed. Every language under the sun seemed to be fluently spoken." Therein posing an exception to Carlson's observation that "the theatre has often, consciously or less consciously, been seen and employed as an instrument of cultural and linguistic solidification," downtown Manhattan's Shakespearean activities also encouraged cultural and linguistic exchange.[35] And because the Lower East Side's German-, Yiddish-, and Italian-language venues all programmed Shakespearean repertoire, the Bard's work was particularly apt to join these groups in focused gatherings.

Crossovers and collaborations between German and Yiddish Shakespeare scenes were relatively frequent. For one, Berkowitz notes that Yiddish translators and adapters often looked to German translations of Shakespeare rather than working from the English texts, and the German translation of *Hamlet* preserved in the Bertha Kalich Papers certainly supports this claim.[36] The flow of acting talent between German and Yiddish theatres offers another example of overlap between these groups. For instance, Morris Morrison, a German actor of Jewish descent, appeared on the Yiddish stage alongside multiple companies. Berkowitz cites a lengthy 1892 advertisement printed in *Di arbeyter tsaytung (The Workman's Newspaper)* that detailed Morrison's upcoming performance of *Othello* at the Thalia Theatre, "with an exceptional first-class German company of artists."[37] At this point in history, the

Thalia was transitioning from a primarily German to a primarily Yiddish playhouse, as Gustav Amberg's German company had moved north to the Irving Place Theatre at Union Square not five years prior. German star Josef Kainz appeared as a German-speaking Hamlet at the Thalia in January 1892, and Thomashefsky debuted his Yiddish-speaking Hamlet on the same stage in November 1893.[38] But Morrison's appearance at the Thalia does not necessarily correlate to the theatre's transition from German to Yiddish, as the actor performed in other Yiddish venues as well. An undated poster announces Morrison's double bill of *Othello* and *Hamlet* at the Yiddish Windsor theatre, and although the poster does not indicate the year, it does specify that the performances were scheduled for Monday, June 11, which points to either 1894 or 1900. Indeed, Morrison could still be found on the Yiddish stage into the 1900s: in 1904, the New York correspondent for the *Jewish Exponent*, an English-language paper published weekly for Philadelphia's old-immigrant Jewish population, reported Morrison's "successful performances of classic plays" at the Lower East Side People's Theatre "with an [*sic*] Yiddish-speaking company," and in 1910, New York's Jewish weekly, the *American Hebrew and Jewish Messenger*, reviewed Morrison's appearance as King Lear alongside a Yiddish-speaking company at the Thalia Theatre.[39] Although he performed with both German and Yiddish companies, Morrison himself performed "exclusively in German," and it is therefore easily conceivable that he drew German-speaking audiences to the Yiddish venues where he performed, congregating immigrant groups in a polyglot Shakespearean space.[40]

Yiddish artists' drawing on German translations or talent prompted much of the collaboration between Yiddish and German Shakespeareans. After all, the German stage had a longer history in New York than the Yiddish theatre, and Germany had a rich record of Shakespearean scholarship and performance.[41] Thomashefsky's memoirs, published in 1937, explain how he relied on local German influences to prepare his own *Hamlet*, which he rehearsed hastily in 1893 so as to compete with Adler's more or less concurrent staging of *Othello* in a venue across the street. "[Moyshe] Zeifert did the translation of *Hamlet* for me. In 24 hours' time, he put together the Yiddish text," Thomashefsky remembers. "I took a producer from the Irving Theatre (the famous German theatre of that time), and this producer immediately began to stage the play. He also practiced the role of Hamlet with me. He was a good actor, and a great producer. His name was Walter. He actually put every word into my mouth." Thomashefsky continues, "[Walter] showed me the meaning of the most important parts, explained to me the thoughts that Shakespeare wanted to express in his work. I studied my role for whole days and nights. Seven o'clock in the morning ... I was already in the theatre on the stage, with Mr. Walter studying. He planned every step that I was supposed to take, showed me each tone of the words, and every transition. . . . Walter also helped me order the necessary scenery, clothing, wigs, and other proper things." Thomashefsky's recollection of his partnership with Walter reveals the hybrid influences on Yiddish Shakespeare theatre. According to Thomashefsky's imagery, the German producer artistically shaped the Yiddish performer's interpretation of the famous Shakespearean role and physically engineered the performance in terms of blocking, costumes, and scenery, the latter two of which may well have been on loan from the Irving Place Theatre. But while Walter figuratively put every word into Thomashefsky's mouth, the actual translation was Moyshe Zeifert's, the same Yiddish playwright who translated *Othello* for Adler's competing performance. Thus, despite Thomashefsky's deference to "the thoughts that Shakespeare wanted to express," the final stage product, performed for mainly Yiddish-speaking audiences, expressed a cultural collage reflecting multiple stage traditions. And while the flow of resources and talent frequently ran from the German to the Yiddish stage, musicologist John Koegel points to a reverse flow such that "Jewish attendance at the German theaters in New York City was essential to their survival for much of their history."[42]

Shakespeare also convened the Lower East Side's Yiddish and Italian immigrant groups. It was "not uncommon during this period for the Yiddish and Italian theatre companies to share the use of theatres on alternating schedules," explains Aleandri, "and quite possibly the reciprocal use of costumes and/or sets." A publicity booklet for a series of plays performed by Maiori in June 1902 subtly points to these cultural (and material) exchanges. The series, bookended by Italian translations of *Othello* and *Hamlet*, took place in the People's Theatre, which at that time was jointly leased by Adler and Thomashefsky. The booklet was printed in English, but the performances were given in Italian, and Italian-speaking audiences were seemingly encouraged to attend, as Aleandri cites an ad for the same set of performances in *L'Araldo Italiano* (*The Italian Herald*), an Italian-language daily issued in New York. In addition to announcing the June 9 through 15 production dates, the *L'Araldo* ad also noted that costumes "were supplied by J. P. Adler and Company"—an indication that Adler's Yiddish troupe had shared both its stage and its garment collection with Maiori's actors.[43] Indeed, Shakespeare proved a prime area of repertoire overlap for theatre companies that claimed distinct performance traditions, catered to disparate audiences, and performed in different languages—markedly different, in the case of Yiddish and Italian. It is therefore not difficult to imagine that sharing costumes or scenery was especially likely in the case of plays like *Othello* or *Hamlet*, each of which were Yiddish and Italian stage staples on the Lower East Side at the turn of the twentieth century.

This shared Shakespearean repertoire also enabled a community of critique among different immigrant groups, as is evidenced by a 1905 editorial that Maiori published, in English, in the *New York Times*, in which he publically disagreed with Adler's interpretation of Shylock. In May of that year, Adler and Maiori both appeared as Shylock in different productions of *The Merchant of Venice*, Adler with an English-speaking company on Broadway on May 15 and Maiori at the People's Theatre on May 29. In the days following Adler's performance, the Yiddish-speaking star garnered enthusiastic praise from audiences and critics alike. (Incidentally, the *New York Times*'s review of Adler was among the more measured, reporting "a sincerely enthusiastic multitude" of spectators and calling Adler "a striking figure of this famous Jew of Venice," but hedging this praise with the proviso that "Adler [was] never a poetical Shylock.") On May 26, Maiori wrote to the editor of the *New York Times* to weigh in with his own review of Adler.[44] Reflecting on his peer's performance (and likely priming critics for his own), the Italian celebrity declared, "Mr. Adler's interpretation of Shylock is undoubtedly all wrong." Offsetting his criticism with collegiality, however, Maiori quickly added, "With these remarks I do not intend to diminish the art of the bravo actor whom I have admired in many other plays (not of Shakespeare,) and for whom I profess the greatest admiration."[45] With that, Maiori detailed his own interpretation of Shylock and confidently concluded his editorial, "This is Shylock, and it will be in this way I will impersonate Shylock." Albeit a short missive (the editorial occupied only about a third of a newspaper column), this artifact offers considerable insight into the Lower East Side's Shakespeare scene. Maiori's admiration for Adler implies that the former had attended the latter's performances—yet another indication of the polyglot immigrant audiences who patronized the theatres along the Bowery. Further, Maiori's parenthetical comment, "not of Shakespeare," suggests that he was content to credit Adler's talent in "other plays" but, where familiar Shakespearean territory was concerned, did not admire Adler's artistic choices—that, or he simply had not seen Adler in any other Shakespearean roles. In any case, Shakespeare offered Maiori grounds for direct comparison between himself and Adler, and although such comparison yielded rivalry and criticism in this particular case, it nonetheless nurtured an interactive professional community of immigrant actor-directors on the Lower East Side.

While Shakespeare certainly facilitated a community of exchange among German, Yiddish, and Italian American stage scenes, the above examples also reflect the implicit hierarchies that affected these immigrant-run playhouses, as the dynamic between German and Yiddish Shakespeareans suggests. Berkowitz emphasizes the "Yiddish theatre's inferiority complex" relative to the German stage, and Haenni points out that "Italian theatre was less successful than either German or Yiddish theatre," stressing the lack of a permanent venue for Italian-speaking performers.[46] Later on, we will learn more about how New York's Anglo-identified tastemakers perceived and promoted these unofficial hierarchies, but for now the key point is that immigrant groups frequently looked to one another—not necessarily to a privileged genteel class or to an Anglocentric tradition—for the artistic talent, direction, and materials that would shape their Shakespeare productions. In this sense, whereas Progressive Era reformers framed the aspirational goals of immigrant Shakespeare performance in terms of social standards—that is, normative American behaviors and beliefs—immigrant groups articulated their aspirational goals for Shakespeare performance in terms of artistic standards—quality of acting, interpretation, costumes, and scenery.

This difference between Progressive reform organizations and immigrant-run theatres goes along with a wider nineteenth-century trend that developed in tandem with the United States' uptake of Shakespeare as a sort of national author and icon of bourgeois American whiteness. Even as culturally empowered U.S. groups claimed Shakespeare for their own nation-making purposes, other "countries of the world appropriated Shakespeare and in many cases adopted him as a national figure, for quite different dramatic, cultural, social, and political reasons," as Krystyna Kujawinska Courtney and John M. Mercer make clear in their introduction to a collection of essays, *The Globalization of Shakespeare in the Nineteenth*

Century. Implicit in Courtney and Mercer's comments is the argument that, while Shakespeare's global reach may have been sparked by British and American imperialist efforts to export the playwright as an icon of Anglo authority, the Bard's nineteenth-century "mobility," to borrow Peter Holland's term from his foreword to the same volume, more lastingly *untethered* Shakespeare from Anglo culture to precipitate his place as a world author and a form of internationally recognized artistic capital. As the poster for Thomashefsky's 1901 *Hamlet* put it, "We . . . have not spared any effort or money, and have for our brothers, and for our beloved public, found the greatest drama in the world."[47] Immigrant-run theatres' Shakespearean translations and adaptations, then, were not so much strategic plays for cultural acceptance and national belonging in a U.S. context as they were plays for artistic affiliation with, representation in, and recognition by the global stage community.

FOR THE BENEFIT OF COMMUNITY INSTITUTIONS AND ENDEAVORS

This last idea—that immigrant translations and adaptations of Shakespeare were not necessarily efforts at Americanization, at least not on elites' terms—may be seen to conflict with two key features of the publicity booklet for Maiori's June 1902 People's Theatre engagement. First, the booklet was printed entirely in English, save the Italian translations of certain titles (not the Shakespearean ones) included parenthetically in italicized small type beneath each main title. Second, the prices for these performances were unusually high: lower-box seats were listed at $2.00 per seat, upper-box seats at $1.50, orchestra seats at $1.00 and $0.75, balcony seats at $0.50, and gallery seats at $0.25. By way of comparison, ticket prices for Maiori's 1901 *Amleto* at the Teatro Italiano at 196 Grand Street ranged from $0.10 to $0.35. These 1902 performances, or at least this particular publicity booklet, thus appear to have been addressed to a well-off, English-speaking American public.[48]

In fact, Maiori's audience did include well-off, English-speaking Americans at this time. The year 1902 corresponds to the period when a society of wealthy Manhattan socialites known as the Four Hundred took enthusiastic interest in Maiori's talent and career, turning trips to his theatre into a fad of sorts—what Aleandri calls "the Maiori 'phenomenon.'" That March, Philadelphia-born artist William Sartain, son of British-born engraver and magazine proprietor John Sartain, wrote an editorial in the *New York Times* praising the Maiori–Rapone company's production of *Amleto*, which he felt was "given with great art," and deeming Rapone's Gravedigger the only "proper acting" of the role he had ever seen. "I think, if you saw it," he advised the editor of the *Times*, "you could write an interesting note on it. I am going with a party Friday, the 21st. If you should be there I could get some one to interpret for you." The following August, a *Brooklyn Eagle* headline declared, "Brilliant Dramatic Star, Playing in an Unknown Italian Theater, Discovered by the Four Hundred," and the news spread to Boston, where the *Sunday Herald* proclaimed, "Dramatic Lion Discovered: Mrs. H. O. Havemeyer and Her Friends Have Found Him."[49] Such clear evidence that Maiori performed for Manhattan socialites like Sartain and Havemeyer may tempt historical interpreters with the possibility that Maiori's June 1902 appearances were efforts to gain social mobility through Shakespeare performance. But, while his choice of repertoire might be seen as an appeal for acceptance among American elites, it appears upon closer inspection that Maiori was actually leveraging Shakespeare's appeal in service of the Italian American community—as a way to sustain rather than transcend immigrant difference.

To be sure, Maiori courted nonimmigrant theatre audiences, but his commercial efforts were primarily directed toward securing the future of his Italian-immigrant stage. According to *L'Araldo*, the proceeds from a run of performances that the Maiori-Rapone company staged at the People's Theatre the week prior to their June 9 through 15 series "went in part to benefit colonial institutions and endeavors," and Aleandri clarifies that "'colonial' [meant], of course, Little Italy." The following week's appearances, which began with *Othello* and ended with *Hamlet*, may well have also directed profits toward community institutions and endeavors (although the Friday performance of *La Tosca* was billed in the publicity booklet as a "Grand Benefit Night" for Maiori and his wife, Concetta Arcamone). The *Brooklyn Eagle* further supports this possibility, noting that "Majori [sic], having outgrown his cramped quarters in Spring Street, is looking forward to building a suitable theater for his company. . . . a house that will seat perhaps 1,000 or 1,200. It must be located not lower than Broome street, and not higher than Eighth. . . . Frankly," the article continued, "Majori looks to Mr. Sartain or some other of his American friends to interest American capital to some extent in his plan. To help stir up such interest he hopes to give a special performance up on Broadway before long. Othello will be the play given, and Majori himself will play that part."[50] Note that Maiori's desired venue would remain below Fourteenth Street and could ideally seat a large number of presumably Italian-speaking playgoers; in other words, it was to be an Italian American community institution. What is more, the play chosen to "stir up" emotional and financial investment from "American" associates—that is, white Americans by Nell Irvin Painter's definition— was none other than Shakespeare's *Othello*. While this hypothetical production of *Othello* was not the same aforementioned June 9, 1902, production—after all, the *Brooklyn Eagle* published its article the following August—it stands to reason that the June performances were also efforts to "interest American capital" in Maiori's plan for a permanent Italian theatre since the June publicity booklet was printed in English and listed such high ticket prices. In Maiori's case, then, Carlson's observation that theatre is "an instrument of cultural and linguistic solidification" certainly applies: a permanent theatre could preserve space for Italian American community identification in a city of white bourgeois norms.[51]

A May 1901 performance of *The Jewish King Lear*, staged by Adler's company at the very same People's Theatre, similarly underwrote community institutions and endeavors on the Lower East Side. A "souvenir-programme" for the production called it a "grand benefit" for the Seward Park Playground, a relatively small urban park that extended north from East Broadway between Jefferson and Canal Streets, just blocks southeast of the People's Theatre and only steps from the Educational Alliance. Like Maiori's June 1902 booklet, this program was printed entirely in English. It also addressed readers who were unfamiliar with the plot of Gordin's adaptation, with the Yiddish language, with certain Jewish terms, and with the playground itself. A four-page plot synopsis summarized each of the play's four acts with a degree of thoroughness that would have retained even non-Yiddish speakers' attention throughout the performance. And given the play's continued popularity among Yiddish playgoers after its 1892 debut, such a detailed plot summary further suggests an audience of non-Yiddish speakers from neighborhoods other than the Lower East Side. Following the plot summary, the program offered an "Explanation of the Terms, 'Chasid,' 'Mithnagid,' and 'Chalukah' used in the Play," familiarizing non-Jews (along with American Jews who lacked an Old World Jewish vocabulary) with the social and cultural significance of these terms. The program's back page introduced readers to the Seward Park Playground, taking care to stipulate its location, its value for neighborhood children, and its funding infrastructure, which relied "wholly . . . upon private contributions."[52] Taken together, these features suggest that the *Lear* program aimed to "stir up interest" among Anglo-identified Americans who possessed economic capital.

As in Maiori's case, Shakespeare proved a strategic appeal to this target demographic, and the Seward Park program and other surrounding publicity for the event played up the production's Shakespeare connection. The plot synopsis, for example, was prefaced by a note that read: "The chief motive based upon Shakespeare's King Lear; but with original material founded upon Jewish Life." Advertisements for the performance in the *American Hebrew* and the *New York Tribune* likewise called the play a "paraphrase of Shakespeare's tragedy," and the *Jewish Messenger* headlined its announcement, "King Lear in Yiddish," implying a straightforward translation rather than a recently authored adaptation. The *American Hebrew* and *Jewish Messenger* were Jewish weeklies printed in English, primarily addressed to New York's class of well-off, well-educated Jews of Western and Central European descent—the old-immigrant population whose members could be found on the boards and donor rosters of organizations like the Educational Alliance.[53] By contrast, the Yiddish-language poster for Adler's 1898 appearance as Lear at the Windsor Theatre, which was addressed to the theatre's customary, largely working-class Yiddish-speaking audience, did not mention Shakespeare, nor did the daily *Abend blat*'s (*Evening Paper*'s) Yiddish-language listing for a December 1901 performance of the play.[54] In the case of the Seward Park benefit, Shakespeare seems to have been strategically placed so as to attract those among the city's dominant social groups for whom the Bard had become a symbol of prestige. However, the benefit performance was no effort to incorporate immigrant actors into this dominant social scene. Instead, the performance parlayed Shakespeare's cultural capital among certain demographics into economic capital that would support a community gathering place on the Lower East Side.

As it happens, the Seward Park Playground was part of the same Progressive reform impulse that motivated Smith's drama series at the People's Institute and Herts's children's theatre at the Educational Alliance; however, key differences in the nature of these initiatives and Shakespeare's role in them distinguish the Seward Park benefit performance of *The*

Jewish King Lear from Smith's and Herts's Shakespearean reform efforts. The park benefit, although performed by "Jacob P. Adler and his Company," was "Given under the auspices of the Federation of East Side Clubs," an "organization, which represent[ed] nearly all of the young men's clubs on the East Side, . . . established in December 1900 'to further the welfare of the community through active work looking to the social, physical, educational, moral and intellectual welfare of the East Side,'" according to a *New York Tribune* announcement for the Federation's 1902 annual meeting. Among the speakers listed for this meeting was Jacob Riis, who, in addition to advocating for Lower East Side housing reform, became a vocal proponent of the Progressive Era playground movement. In 1894, Riis published a piece in *Century Magazine* called "Playgrounds for City Schools," in which he argued that urban playgrounds could mitigate crime and gang activity. By way of example, he described a "neighborhood as desolate as it was desperate" that "changed as if by magic" when "the wicked old tenements were torn down, and a public playground was opened on the site of them."[55] Clearly, the Seward Park benefit performance of *The Jewish King Lear* was tied up in the spirit of Progressivism that compelled reformers like Riis to imagine that Shakespearean drama and public playgrounds might aid in "making good Americans."[56] Even so, while reform-driven playgrounds and Herts's children's theatre both structured leisure time for immigrant children, the space of a playground invited improvisatory play, whereas Herts's efforts scripted young people's speech and movement, at least insofar as she envisioned them playing out. In this sense, playgrounds encouraged community interactions on the Lower East Side where immigrant youth could connect with one another and develop identities as Americans on spontaneous, unscripted terms. And Shakespeare's role in the Seward Park benefit was not to steer immigrant bodies toward an ideologically entrenched mode of American belonging, but rather to raise money for a space where local families could come together and create new networks of belonging in New York.

It was also crucial that an immigrant-run, Yiddish-speaking company staged the Seward Park benefit performance. Although all of the immigrant translations and adaptations of Shakespeare discussed here can be seen as figurative sites where Anglo Ur texts came into contact with non-Anglo languages and performance styles, the Maiori and Adler fundraising efforts also fostered physical spaces where Anglo- and non-Anglo-identified social groups connected with one another via Shakespearean repertoire. Moreover, the souvenir program for Adler's benefit performance of *The Jewish King Lear*, which endowed its readers with new knowledge about immigrant life through its plot summary and glossary, beautifully enacts a model of assimilation as reciprocal cultural exchange. The *New York Times* review of the benefit performance also captured this process of exchange, however smugly, when it acknowledged, "It is safe to say that a part of the audience had never heard of the Jewish King Lear or of Jacob Adler until their attention was called to both by the announcements of the benefit." To illustrate this demographic's unexpected cultural gain, the *Times* quoted a representative member of said "part of the audience": "'I confess I had my doubts,' said one man, whose judgment in theatrical matters is above the average. 'I had read a great deal about these Yiddish players, but I set down the praise they received to tolerance for things foreign. I was not in a friendly mood when I came in. But my skepticism soon gave way to admiration.'" The *Times* reviewer then added, "There were many similar expressions from persons who had come to scoff and who remained to be convinced."[57] Thus, just as translations and adaptations of Shakespeare facilitated immigrant groups' various adjustments to new ways of life among a diverse, rapidly expanding population of Lower East Side neighbors, so too did these immigrant groups adapt Shakespeare to new purposes, styles, and cultural surroundings. Moreover, performances like Maiori's June 1902 People's Theatre run and Adler's Seward Park benefit also exposed Lower East Side outsiders to these new meanings for Shakespeare and, by extension, to new modes of American cultural expression.

———

The variety of scenarios wherein Shakespearean repertoire appealed to and appeared before immigrant audiences in the decades surrounding 1900 shows how German, Yiddish, and Italian translations and adaptations of Shakespeare stimulated opportunities for community building—as opposed to serving efforts at nation making—on New York's Lower East Side. This is not to suggest that Shakespeare theatre provided a singular outlet for community building in this area of New York during that time. Indeed, street markets, political gatherings, and other Bowery entertainments were among the many settings where downtown Manhattan's increasingly diverse populace engaged in everyday interaction. But the fact that Shakespeare fostered one such setting contrasts markedly with

Progressive reformers' idea that they were introducing Shakespeare to Lower East Siders, as well as with the press's representation of Shakespeare as elevated drama that might mold the masses into "good Americans."

These scenarios also reveal a slice of turn-of-the-twentieth-century U.S. Shakespeare history that is often overlooked, and indeed appears quite different from widely accepted accounts of this period. In *Highbrow/Lowbrow*'s 1988 epilogue, Levine recognizes that "we have in recent decades begun to move gradually but decisively away from the rigid, class-bound definitions of culture forged at the close of the nineteenth century." To underscore this point, he cites conductor Michael Tilson Thomas, then principal conductor of the London Symphony Orchestra and now music director of the San Francisco and New World Symphonies, who "proclaimed in 1976: 'There has been altogether too much separation of different types of music, such as so-called 'classical' and 'rock.' In the future, people will have to open up their ears and their souls to many kinds of sounds."[58] But there is a lovely irony here, as this late twentieth-century soundbite points to that very slice of turn-of-the-twentieth-century Shakespeare history absent from Levine's work: Tilson Thomas is the grandson of Bores Thomashefsky, whose Yiddish *Hamlet, der yeshive bokher,* and *Jewish Romeo and Juliet* exposed American ears to Shakespeare's compatibility with the aesthetically and culturally varied sounds of immigrant life nearly a century earlier, as did numerous other Shakespeare translations and adaptations staged by the likes of Adler, Kainz, Kalich, Maiori, Morrison, and Rapone. Indeed, these productions flourished at the very historic moment that ostensibly ushered in Shakespeare's rigid classification as highbrow. Assimilating Shakespeare to these various American immigrant contexts, German, Yiddish, and Italian troupes produced flexible meanings for the iconic playwright that percolated in the slash between "highbrow" and "lowbrow," in the gap between Old World and New World, in the exchanges among different immigrant groups, and in the minds of affluent uptown patrons who "had come [downtown] to scoff and who remained to be convinced."[59]

In assembling such diverse communities of playgoers, immigrant troupes also produced new audiences for Shakespeare in the United States. Just as mainstream American theatres constructed genteel, highfalutin Shakespearean audiences by way of programming changes, tempered acting styles, and new expectations for audience conduct, so too did Lower East Side theatres develop mixed audiences eager for Shakespeare in German,

Yiddish, and Italian translation. Publicity materials for these translations implicitly instructed playgoers that Shakespeare paired well with "current light comedies" and Capsicum Vaseline in the case of the Irving Place Theatre, raucous sword fights and religious melodies on the Yiddish stage, and variety show performances at the Teatro Italiano. At the Yiddish theatres, in particular, spectators grew to love Shakespeare through adapted plots, settings, and characters. And at least one Italian-speaking audience left a performance of *Othello* in 1900 with the sanguine impression that Desdemona does not die. Thus, while a mainstream theatre archive yields compelling evidence that the decades leading to 1900 solidified American views of Shakespeare as strictly high culture—educative, sacred ground that should not be tampered with or staged alongside inferior entertainments—immigrant stage ephemera show how lower Manhattan's German-, Italian-, and Yiddish-run theatres convened audiences with alternative Shakespearean sensibilities.

Indeed, the social and cultural diversity of immigrant theatre audiences, and the ways in which immigrant-produced Shakespeare translations, adaptations, and print materials addressed and sustained that diversity, illuminate a complex yet critical dynamic between dramatic adaptation and cultural assimilation. In his own study of Shakespeare on the American Yiddish stage, Berkowitz cautions, "without writers and theatre companies to tailor ... [Shakespeare's] original works to the expectations of a Yiddish audience, [his] plays would have meant little more than box-office poison at worst, an evening's diversion at best." So too did the Italian and German theatres imbue Shakespeare with stylistic, aesthetic, and aural qualities that played to local tastes. In light of Michel de Certeau's view of assimilation as "'making something similar' to what one is, making it one's own, appropriating or reappropriating it," these publicity materials for immigrant Shakespeare performance begin to show how assimilation happens when abstract categories of "Culture" (with a capital "C") such as "Shakespearean" or "American" adjust to local instantiations of culture in its everyday sense.[60] In his study of Chinese Shakespeares, Alexander C. Y. Huang aptly frames this dynamic as the "mutually constructive grammar of the global and the local."[61] For no matter how rigidly dominant groups may define certain social and cultural terms of national belonging, the physical reality of everyday community interactions means that assimilation is improvisatory rather than deterministic.

We now turn from the grammar of Lower East Side locals to that of non-locals—specifically, a cohort of socially privileged, English-speaking New York drama critics who, like Havemeyer, Sartain, and their friends from the Four Hundred, brought a set of dominant meanings for Shakespeare and American belonging to bear on immigrant translations and adaptations of the Bard's plays. By routing immigrant Shakespeare performance through the outsider viewpoints of these English-language critics, we can better see how dominant ideologies clashed with immigrant realities.

CHAPTER THREE

Slumming with Shakespeare

Eight years after the initial publication of Jacob Riis's *How the Other Half Lives*, drama critic John Corbin riffed on Riis in a *Harper's New Monthly Magazine* piece called "How the Other Half Laughs," an eighteen-page profile of the Lower East Side's Italian, Yiddish, and German theatres. Responding to Progressive reformers' focus on the squalor of tenement life, Corbin aimed to show a more uplifting and empowered sphere of daily doings in lower Manhattan, as his titular twist so cunningly hinted. Corbin's first paragraph made clear this alternative angle: "We have heard of the terrors of the tenements . . . but the reports of organized charity have neglected to remind us that the people who support the theatres of the Bowery get as much fun of their sort out of life as most of us," he instructed his readers. "You may pity the people of the East Side, if you must, ten hours a day, but when the arc-lights gleam beneath the tracks of the elevated, if you are honest you will envy them." Cautioning that reform rhetoric obscured the "vital and spontaneous" spirit of the Bowery's immigrant theatre scene, Corbin gave his middle- and upper-class readers a virtual tour of the neighborhood from his perspective as a theatre expert. Significantly, the tour began with a vivid account of Antonio Maiori's *Otello* at the Teatro Italiano.[1]

In fact, Shakespeare played a prominent role throughout "How the Other Half Laughs." From Maiori's *Otello*, to Jacob P. Adler's *Jewish King Lear*, to comparisons of immigrant stage business with Elizabethan practices, the Shakespeare tradition wove its way across Corbin's account of New York's Lower East Side venues. And Corbin was not the only English-language journalist to investigate the "other half's" Shakespeare scene. A number of drama critics for the English-language press took interest in immigrant-run playhouses' Shakespearean undertakings, reviewing individual performances or making note of Shakespearean repertoire in longer special interest pieces about the Bowery's so-called foreign stages and stars, as Corbin did in "How the Other Half Laughs." Unlike Charles Sprague Smith and Alice Minnie Herts, who presented Shakespeare to immigrant groups as a gateway into normative white modes of knowing and being, these critics offered Shakespeare to their readers as a gateway into immigrant culture.

As a record of English-language critics' encounters with immigrant adaptations and translations of Shakespeare, this press archive captures another Shakespearean scenario where different social groups came into contact with one another in Manhattan at the turn of the twentieth century. In fact, this dynamic was manifold, as critics' press coverage not only recorded journalists' own reception of immigrant performance but also circulated their reception to wide readerships, restaging immigrant Shakespeare on the page for uptown and out-of-town audiences who may not have viewed it in New York's downtown theatres. And their reception was complex: On the one hand, Shakespeare offered something familiar in a part of the city that felt increasingly foreign to these critics. The well-known plays invited them to better *recognize* immigrant performance, both in the sense of making it more legible, and in the sense of acknowledging its place in New York's theatre scene. But Shakespeare was sacred ground as well as common ground. And as such, Shakespeare also prompted critics to bristle at a perceived incongruity between the Bard's oeuvre and immigrant culture. These mixed sentiments ultimately informed public impressions of German, Yiddish, and Italian performances, shaping Americans' perceived associations between race, class, national belonging, and Shakespeare. Thus, like settlement productions and immigrant-stage adaptations, this press archive sheds light on Shakespeare's role in a history of how urban Americans divided themselves into social categories during the Progressive Era. And it likewise shows how certain Shakespeare-related activities just as surely confounded these presumed social categories.

Of course, much like the journalists who reported on Shakespeare at the People's Institute and Educational Alliance, these critics brought a privileged worldview to bear on their experiences of Lower East Side life. To be sure, this privileged perspective has had ample airtime over the decades, but there is nonetheless value in examining it here. For "it is impossible to understand the lives of ordinary Americans without appreciating the ways those cultures are influenced and delimited by the ideals, plans, and needs of the powerful," as cultural historians Richard Wightman Fox and T. J. Jackson Lears elegantly put it.[2] Furthermore, to grasp the workings of these dominant ideals, plans, and needs—which the mainstream press participates in shaping in any modern society—is to expose the mechanisms by which empowered classes continually readjust and reassert their authority over nondominant groups. By isolating the journalistic viewpoints that addressed (and therein shaped) mainstream U.S. audiences around 1900, we can better understand Shakespeare as a site of both exchange and struggle for privileged and marginalized Americans alike during this period: Anglo-identified groups' Shakespearean encounters with recently settled, non-Anglo European Americans stimulated progressive understandings of immigrant culture (i.e., exchange), but they also stoked divisive impulses to reaffirm certain Anglocentric terms of social and cultural acceptance (i.e., struggle). Looking ahead, this dynamic helped lay the groundwork for non-Anglo groups to act both within and against white American norms so as to develop new performances of national belonging.[3]

THE CRITICS' TAKE: SHAKESPEARE IN NEW YORK'S MAINSTREAM
THEATRES

By now we have a general sense of how culturally empowered Americans understood and used Shakespeare at the turn of the twentieth century. But going forward, we need a more site-specific grasp of Shakespeare production on Manhattan's mainstream stages during this period, or at least a grasp of how leading drama critics saw things. These journalists made it their business to become experts on the contemporary theatre world, after all, and brought this holistic perspective to bear on all of their writing. As such, their coverage of immigrant-produced Shakespeare did not exist in a vacuum but was instead colored by their views of Manhattan's wider Shakespeare scene—which, as it turned out, had seen better days. Despite the city's flagging quality and quantity of Shakespeare theatre, however, critics on the whole maintained a steadfast reverence for the Bard and an unyielding belief in his plays' essential value.

Several press publications and critics appear in the coming pages. Along with Corbin's writings in *Harper's* and the *New York Times*, where he was drama critic from 1897 to 1900 and from 1902 to 1904 respectively, we will encounter articles from other widely circulated New York papers and magazines, including the *New York Sun, New York Journal, New York Tribune, Theatre,* the *New York Dramatic Mirror, Forum,* and *The Bookman: A Review of Books and Life.* Such publications generally reached middle- and upper-class readerships and numbered among the city's most respectable press outlets.[4] Occasionally, we'll see newspapers published outside of New York—the *Baltimore Sun* or the *Washington Post,* for example—in instances where they printed special correspondence articles by New York writers or reprinted articles or excerpts originally issued in New York. Although reviews and commentary did not always include bylines, a handful of named critics gain mention in addition to Corbin, including Franklin Fyles, who became a special correspondent to a number of major cities' newspapers after serving as the *New York Sun's* drama editor and critic for thirty years; *New York Journal* critic Alan Dale; William Winter of the *New York Tribune;* magazine contributor and *New York World* writer Henry Tyrrell; and essayists Norman and Hutchins Hapgood, the latter of whom is also known for his book-length account of New York's Yiddish community, *The Spirit of the Ghetto: Studies of the Jewish Quarter in New York.* With the exception of Dale, who was born and brought up in England, all of these critics were native-born Americans. They were also a highly educated bunch: Corbin, Winter, and both of the Hapgoods held Harvard degrees. Corbin studied Shakespearean drama in graduate school at Harvard and Oxford, and Winter earned a reputation as an authority on Shakespeare theatre following law school, publishing biographies and stage histories along with his dramatic criticism.[5]

With rare exception, writers for the above-named newspapers and periodicals implicitly addressed a well-off, Anglo-Saxon readership. Whether or not their readers empirically fit this description matters less than that this cohort of writers relied on readers to *identify* with such a persona. In fact, as will become more clear, critics' reviews took part in creating the very Anglo-identified, bourgeois readership that they presumed to address.[6] Critics produced this group subjectivity in large part through pronoun use, as well as through shared cultural references. Take the previously quoted passage of Corbin's "How the Other Half Laughs," for instance: "We have heard of the terrors of the tenements . . . but the reports of organized charity have neglected to remind us that the people who support the theatres of the Bowery get as much fun of their sort out of life as most of us. You may pity the people of the East Side, if you must, ten hours a day, but when the arc-lights gleam beneath the tracks of the elevated, if you are honest, you will envy them." Through combined use of "we" and "us" in contrast to "them" and "their," Corbin affirmed that his readers were not tenement dwellers, or even East Side residents. His presumption that his audience had "heard of the terrors of the tenements" suggested that *Harper's* readers might have picked up a copy of Riis's *How the Other Half Lives*, or perhaps an issue of the Progressive reform journal *Charities*. And a later reference to his own "Saxon pride" in the same essay confirmed that Corbin's "we" was meant to hail Anglo-Saxon, or at least Anglo-identified, readers. American studies scholar Michael Epp cleverly calls this implied readership "the *Harper's* half," and while I occasionally borrow Epp's phrase, I more often use the term "Anglo-bourgeoisie" in order to capture the racial and class categories with which drama critics expected their readers to identify.[7]

At the helm of dominant U.S. culture, these critics and their Anglo-bourgeois readers found themselves in the midst of a changing Shakespeare scene at the turn of the twentieth century. While Shakespearean drama ascended into the realm of high culture for many American audiences, Shakespeare production on New York's stages generally struck critics as declining in both quality and quantity. "Shakespeare Spells Ruin" was a refrain among producers who feared box-office failure as popular consciousness increasingly regarded Shakespeare's plays as literary rather than theatrical fare.[8] But Lawrence W. Levine suggests that this mantra may have been a self-fulfilling statement as well as a symptom of the times, given how New York's theatre management operated at the turn of the century. "In 1896, a half dozen important theater owners and booking agents from New York, Philadelphia, and Boston forged these local circuits into a centralized national booking system," he explains. This Theatrical Syndicate "soon controlled bookings in some five hundred to seven hundred theaters throughout the nation. . . . The actor-managers who had dominated the nineteenth-century theater were replaced in the twentieth century by the producer–booking agents centered in New York City. Broadway and the American theater became more and more inseparable, the repertory of the former becoming the standard fare of the latter." Deducing that "the businessmen who managed the new theater chains and huge booking agencies approached their tasks . . . with the belief that Shakespeare was 'highbrow' culture of little interest to the masses and therefore of slight potential profit to producers," Levine ultimately concludes that the Syndicate was "another decisive factor in Shakespeare's transformation from popular to elite culture."[9]

Critical opinion from the period supports this narrative and also reveals a shared frustration among many dramatic writers who rued the lack of quality Shakespeare theatre in New York. Tyrrell's 1904 dramatic year-in-review piece for *Forum*, a New York–based quarterly magazine staffed by a group of established journalists and academics, offered a particularly glum take on the state of the theatre world. "What then, is the actual condition of things in this theatrical world?" he asked his readers. "That something is wrong, the professional people themselves admit and deplore, and even uninterested laymen cannot have failed to observe. It has been surmised for some years past," he continued, "that the real students and lovers of the drama, and the more liberal church-members who read Shakespeare as well as the Bible, in short, the very classes that normally should constitute the best body of theatre-goers, do not go to the theatre at all." Like Levine, Tyrrell blamed the Syndicate: "The commercial managers have almost ceased to bid for their patronage, finding it easier and more immediately profitable to 'cater' to the frivolous, the vulgar, and too often the downright degraded elements of an abundant, lavish, and mixed populace." Linking the "classes that . . . constitute the best body of theatre-goers" with Shakespeare, and Shakespeare with the Bible, Tyrrell lamented the commercial climate that eschewed what he considered to be substantive, morally sound drama. Winter expressed a related theory and sense of disappointment, suggesting in his 1911 book, *Shakespeare on the Stage*, that the "Parrot Cry, 'Shakespeare spells Ruin,' . . . has had the deleterious effect of discouraging even a judicious use of that author."[10]

Still, in spite of the perception that Shakespearean repertoire was not the stage staple it had been throughout the better portion of the nineteenth century, the playwright's works were consistently produced in New York's Broadway theatres and faithfully reviewed by the city's dramatic critics. Although acclaimed actor Edwin Booth's death in 1893 in many ways marked the end of a golden era in American Shakespeare performance (as one *Harper's* writer suggested in 1903 when he wrote that Booth "probably engaged the last company of actors who were bred in the traditions of Shakespeare"), stars like Maude Adams, Henrietta Crosman, John

Drew, Nat Goodwin, Ben Greet, Virginia Harned, Percy Haswell, Henry Irving, Richard Mansfield, Robert Mantell, Julia Marlowe, Edith Matthison, Ada Rehan, Annie Russell, and E. H. Sothern carried the tradition forward on New York's English-language stages, emerging as the Shakespearean protagonists of theatre commentary published at the turn of the century. Actor-manager Augustin Daly—a close colleague of Booth and a known champion of Shakespeare—was perhaps the chief hero of New York's Shakespeare scene during this period, producing sixteen of Shakespeare's plays over the course of his career. Even after his death in 1899, Daly's Theatre continued to stage Shakespeare revivals, replicating the late manager's productions. Critics' headlines for these various Shakespearean goings-on in New York also suggest that the Bard's plays maintained wide recognition—so much so that character names often stood in for a play's title, as in Dale's 1898 *New York Journal* headline, "Miss Ada Rehan as Portia," and the *New York Tribune*'s 1903 title, "The Drama: Miss Crosman as Rosalind. Manhattan Theatre." In a 1905 *New York Times* piece, Corbin confidently, albeit cynically, asserted Shakespeare's continued relevance on the American stage, even under the commercially driven reign of the Syndicate: "[T]he public has been taught for a generation that they are the ablest and most intelligent exponents of our classical comedy," he wrote, with a characteristic "our" that implied his belief in American co-ownership of Shakespeare. "No business principle is sounder than that the American public believes in the best. . . . For the drama as drama it has no love; but it knows that Shakespeare is great, and if it feels assured that it is not being cheated it will spend its money to see Shakespeare."[11]

Despite overtones of disappointment, frustration, and cynicism, then, critics' coverage of Shakespeare theatre in New York conveyed a steady faith in the Bard's absolute literary and moral value. A look at commentary by both Dale and Winter shows how this belief in a Shakespearean ideal spanned the gamut of reviewers, as these two men were at the extremes of what literary scholar Keith Gandal, summarizing the work of historian Warren Susman, calls "'one of the fundamental conflicts of twentieth-century America': a 'profound clash between different moral orders,' . . . 'an older culture, often loosely labeled Puritan-republican, producer-capitalist culture, and a newly emerging culture of abundance' or consumption." For instance, Winter's *New York Tribune* career ended in 1909 in part because his fundamentally Victorian moralist rants ruffled too many feathers, whereas

Dale, who welcomed entertainment for entertainment's sake, resigned in 1914 as William Randolph Hearst's dramatic critic, having faced pressure for his flippant style, which, according to theatre historian Tice L. Miller, frequently "attacked the 'stuffed images and idols' of late Victorian culture."[12] With respect to Shakespeare, the conservative Winter called the Bard's plays "the best that the English-speaking race possesses," insisting that "knowledge and practical use of them are essential to the dignity, influence, and welfare of an intellectual stage." Dale, on the other hand, brashly condemned what he called Broadway's "Shakespearean 'fetich'" on the grounds that managers and audiences were kidding themselves to believe that Shakespeare's plays made for entertaining stage business, particularly for those spectators who lacked a studied appreciation of the texts.[13] In spite of their extreme differences in tone and taste, however, Winter and Dale both put Shakespeare on a pedestal, insisting on the truth of his plays' meaning and merit. "There is only one way in which [Shakespeare's] great characters can be greatly represented," wrote Winter, "and that is the right way—the way in which they were drawn by the poet who drew them." Dale's disdain for Shakespeare on stage in fact traced to a similar belief in the plays' essential value: "I am a Shakespeare lover," he declared, "and that is why I think that many of his great poems should never be staged. They should be studied, ransacked for their gems of thought, rifled for the exquisite jewels they contain."[14]

Thus, in the face of changing material conditions for, critical opinions about, and public attitudes toward Shakespeare performance at the turn of the century, the *idea* of Shakespeare as a fixed property held strong among New York's Anglo-bourgeoisie. One *New York Times* writer, very likely Corbin, expressed this quite plainly in 1903 when he wrote that "'Hamlet,' 'Shylock,' 'Othello,' and 'Lear' are symbols of life—fixed, immutable. They cannot be tampered or juggled with. The actor who attempts their interpretation may make as many changes in the text as he likes, he may introduce any new business he may choose, or follow the lines laid down by tradition without deviation, but if his portrait is to stand out as true these details matter not at all, so he has invested himself with the innate spirit and purpose of the poet." As the melting-pot paradigm's imagined category of American whiteness conditioned immigrants' everyday performances of national belonging, so too did critics' imagined ideal of Shakespeare set certain terms of acceptable onstage performance. Dale began his review of E. H. Sothern's 1900 performance of *Hamlet* with a fitting image for this bounded ideal: "Somebody has described 'Hamlet' not as a play but as a hoop," he wrote, "through which every eminent actor was bound to jump."[15]

THE CRITICS' TAKE: NEW YORK'S IMMIGRANT-RUN THEATRES

As commercial aims and booking agencies secured a stranglehold on Broadway, the German, Yiddish, and Italian venues on New York's Lower East Side thrived apart from the Theatrical Syndicate, and many liberal-minded critics turned their attention downtown in the hopes of finding dramatic fulfillment. The German-language Irving Place Theatre stood for many of them as an exemplar of artistic merit. "What makes the little house on Irving Place so notable is something thoroughly familiar and intimate to the minds of cultivated Americans," Norman Hapgood commented in his contribution to a *Bookman* magazine series called "The Foreign Stage in New York" that ran in the summer of 1900. "It is merely that the drama, as we know it, is on a higher plane than it is in any other theatre in this city." Hapgood went on to credit the diverse repertoire that included "meaningless farces," "some classic" each weekend, and "the very best to be found either on the library shelves or in the serious productions of the day." Further, he continued, the Irving Place Theatre's German-speaking actors "know how to recite verse, and they know the meaning of poetry. This is a prime requisite, if we are ever to have in English anything corresponding in quality to what we have in German. It is even more necessary, because almost the whole of the English drama which holds any place in the general literary heritage of our race is in verse," he added, giving a nod to Shakespeare, to whom he obliquely referred as "the great national dramatist." Corbin likewise lauded the German playhouse, remarking in a 1900 *Harper's* piece, "If the question were to be asked, what is the most interesting dramatic institution in the country, an intelligent theatre-goer would almost certainly answer, Herr [Heinrich] Conried's Irving Place Theatre."[16]

Sabine Haenni has suggested that "what made German American theater different from other immigrant theaters . . . was its ability to claim autonomous culture as a legitimizing horizon, which ultimately guaranteed the theater's alternativity while simultaneously furthering German Americans' assimilability." That is, at the turn of the century, the German American theatre's "Germanness," its autonomous culture, held a certain cachet among New York's Anglo-bourgeoisie that aided and likely resulted from Germans' upward mobility and increasingly secure status as white Americans. Haenni also points out that the geographic location of New York's German theatre paralleled its social position. Having moved just before 1890 from the Thalia Theatre, located squarely in the Lower East Side's Bowery district, to the Irving Place Theatre on Fifteenth Street, technically a block north of what is traditionally recognized as the Lower East Side's northernmost cross street, the German players performed on the border between Jacob Riis's two halves, which split the city geographically (in a literal sense) as well as racially and socioeconomically (on an ideological level).[17]

The Yiddish theatres along the Bowery also captured English-language critics' attention. "A down-trodden people, used through generations to hopeless persecutions, is leaping into individuality and power through the new liberty they have found," observed Corbin in 1898. And in 1900, Hutchins Hapgood, writing for the same *Bookman* series as his brother Norman, remarked on the Yiddish theatre's varied repertoire, writing, "In the midst of the frivolous Bowery . . . the theatres of the chosen people alone present the serious as well as the trivial interests of an entire community." The Yiddish stage's reputation extended beyond New York, too. In anticipation of a touring performance by Bertha Kalich, a *Washington Times* reporter declared, "Contrary to the notion that these Jewish or Yiddish theaters are small affairs with little to offer in the way of dramatic art, they are, as a matter of fact, of very large seating capacity, are extremely prosperous in a financial way, and the plays produced compare very favorably indeed, in point of dignity and importance, with those offered at the Broadway playhouses."[18]

Turn-of-the-twentieth-century Yiddish and German companies in Manhattan shared more than their East Side locations, their favor in the eyes of Anglo-bourgeois critics, and their diverse programming. As we have already learned, they overlapped in the Thalia Theatre venue for a short time, with Yiddish troupes leasing from German management before the German players fully transitioned to the Irving Place Theatre. And because the modern Yiddish and German languages both etymologically trace to medieval German, Yiddish and German troupes occasionally exchanged acting talent (like Morris Morrison), and Yiddish playwrights often drew on a heavily Germanic dialect called *daytshmerish* when scripting more heroic, "cultivated" characters (a choice that likely capitalized on Germans' widely esteemed literary traditions and upward social mobility relative to newer immigrant groups).[19] Given such connections, New York critics perceived the Yiddish and German theatres on something of a continuum: the Yiddish playhouses were proximate to but geographically just south of the German theatre. Yiddish performances were linguistically related to but far more foreign-sounding than those on the German stage. Yiddish playwrights occasionally drew on German repertoire, and both Yiddish and German troupes were among the pioneers of theatrical realism in New York, but the city's tastemakers did not regard Yiddish productions to be as artistically sophisticated as those staged at the Irving Place Theatre. And Yiddish performers and audiences were further seen to be socially beneath those in German venues. (This imagined social hierarchy was surely linked to actual economic disparities, as the city's Yiddish-speaking community was proportionately more working class at the turn of the century than the socioeconomically diverse German community.) No English-language critic, for example, would have offered praise for the Yiddish theatre comparable to Norman Hapgood's comment: "What makes the little house on Irving Place so notable is something thoroughly familiar and intimate to the minds of cultivated Americans." Mainstream critics from this period simply did not perceive Yiddish culture as "familiar," "intimate," or fully "cultivated." In Corbin's blunt words, "The Yiddish troup[e] that took the Thalia from the Germans are working along the same general lines," but "[t]heir performances are not yet up to those of the Germans."[20]

Antonio Maiori's Italian-language theatre was less established than the nearby German or Yiddish theatres, alternately sharing space with Yiddish companies and occupying a dedicated house. To highlight this disparity for his readers, Corbin compared Italian to Yiddish promotional signs, remarking that the Yiddish "billboards, compared to the modest placards of the Italians, speak of prosperity." Most accounts also suggest that Maiori's dramatic efforts held a lower position on critics' implied cultural continuum than the neighborhood's Yiddish stages, as critics viewed the Italian productions primarily as a source of levity and sentiment rather than intellectual substance. Describing the afterpiece to *Otello*, for example (presumably performed by Pasquale Rapone), Corbin commented, "The drop was scarcely down, however, when . . . the comedian—the sometime Duke of Venice—bounded out in a song-and-dance costume, and bellowed forth a Neapolitan ditty. Then . . . Cassio came out in black street clothes, somewhat threadbare and shiny, if the truth be told, and sang us a sentimental song while we were putting on our coats. Alas for our uptown manners! The simple and kindly Italians did not turn from the delights of the stage until the last mournful cadence was ended." Hutchins Hapgood similarly explained to his *Bookman* readers that the Italian theatre's "farce is allied to their serious play in one important respect: it is pure fun, never approaches the comedy of manners, as it lacks entirely the intellectual and critical element; just as the serious play is pure passion and sentiment, without the reflective or philosophic element, which distinguishes the tragedy of the Anglo-Saxon, the German and the Jew." Hapgood's comment not only shows how critics grouped German and Yiddish performances in a more distinguished category than Italian productions but also alludes to the nuances of whiteness in the United States at the turn of the twentieth century, where Anglo-Saxons, Germans, Jews, and Italians were perceived as different, and differently classed, races—"variegated whiteness," as Matthew Frye Jacobson terms it.[21] Setting such nuances aside for later on, it suffices to emphasize here that immigrant-run theatres' status among English-language critics roughly corresponded to critics' perceptions of class and race as well as to their estimates of artistic merit.

Yet, despite the Italian American theatre's perceived lack of "manners," critics paid notice to Maiori and his company. In a 1902 *Theatre* article titled "Little Italy's Great Actor," Tyrrell commented, "Antonio Majori [*sic*], tragedian, and Pasquale Rapone, comedian, are the two partners who have here fostered and directed the precarious destinies of the Italian drama in exile, maintaining its traditions with a zeal worthy of better encouragement than—until very recently—they have received."[22] Nine months prior to publishing "How the Other Half Laughs," Corbin issued a *Harper's* profile of Maiori that drew direct comparison between the disappointing Broadway Shakespeare scene and the Lower East Side's theatrical offerings. "The dearth of tragedy which has of late fallen on the Broadway theatres has been indifferently laid to the lack of good actors and to the abundance of ballets and vaudeville shows," he began.

> It would perhaps be more just to lay it to the lack of a school of tragic acting. . . . That melodrama is slowly and steadily retreating to the Bowery is well known; and the fact has suggested that on the East Side there is still a spontaneous interest in the deeper and more permanent emotions. The announcement, therefore,

that "Othello" and "Hamlet" were to be brought out in the Italian Theatre in the Bowery raised the question . . . whether the tragic muse had been brought down from the clouds of ballet girls uptown to live among the men of the East Side. It would not be the first time that the best things in dramatic art flourished most among the multitude.[23]

Corbin's racialized associations between immigrant groups and emotional expression notwithstanding, this passage usefully summarizes one motivation for English-language critics' attention to immigrant-run playhouses. No mere response to some supercilious curiosity about what many among the bourgeoisie saw as "exotic" or "primitive" populations south of Fourteenth Street, critics' coverage reflected a sense of journalistic integrity that compelled them to comment on the full range of New York's successful theatre institutions, be they on or off Broadway, as well as a desire to seek fulfilling alternatives to the city's mainstream theatre activity. Of course, given that the "announcement of 'Othello' and 'Hamlet'" piqued Corbin's suspicion that the "tragic muse" might be living "among the men of the East Side," it is safe to say that his interest in the Italian American theatre also hinged on Shakespeare.

SLUMMING WITH SHAKESPEARE

To be sure, dramatic critics for the English-language press traveled to the Lower East Side in pursuit of Shakespeare and the tragic muse, but they also made the trip because "slumming," or touring lower Manhattan's working-class immigrant enclaves for sport, was in vogue among the city's Anglo-bourgeoisie at the turn of the twentieth century. Slummers frequently wrote about their experiences, and slumming narratives— which include journalistic endeavors like Riis's *How the Other Half Lives* and Corbin's "How the Other Half Laughs" as well as fictional works like Stephen Crane's *Maggie: A Girl of the Streets*—comprise a diverse body of writing that yields rich sociological insights. A quick review of some probable motivations for slum writing sheds light on the range of social impulses that, in addition to dramatic and journalistic commitments, moved critics to seek out Shakespeare in the slums. And the consequences of slum writing frame the social stakes of critics' published reflections on what they saw.

Some scholars interpret slum writing as a self-affirming bourgeois response to late nineteenth-century anxieties about the changing urban American landscape. In this sense, narrated accounts of the slums empowered middle-class writers and readers via working-class denigration, spectacularization, or commodification. For example, in her analysis of Corbin's "How the Other Half Laughs," Dorothy Chansky aptly notes how Corbin "expressed empathy while also reinforcing boundaries," ultimately "reasserting the cultural authority of the WASP bourgeoisie." Similarly, Epp positions "How the Other Half Laughs" in a historiography of American humor to show how Corbin wanted his "readers to understand humor practices in relation to a hierarchy of national characteristics." Scholars in this camp generally agree that realism—in this case, slum realism—served as "a conservative force whose very act of exposure reveal[ed] its complicity with structures of power," as American studies scholar Amy Kaplan characterizes this particular critical view.[24]

Other scholars embrace the inevitable complexities of social interaction to offer subtle accounts in which slummers admired aspects of immigrant life, productively foregrounded marginalized voices, or even subverted certain dominant norms (conventions of morality or sexuality, for example), while admittedly still reinforcing hierarchies of class and race.[25] For her part, Haenni links "How the Other Half Laughs" to the middle class's "attempt to gentrify the ghetto without abandoning its cultural specificity, to create an intimacy that keeps it different yet makes it acceptable to the middle classes." While this intimacy did not guarantee exchange—slummers by and large "ma[de] the foreign proximate through spectatorship," getting the thrill of the foreign while preserving spectatorial distance—Haenni nonetheless allows that Corbin's contact with Lower East Siders led him to discover below Fourteenth Street "a truly democratic, national-popular culture that, according to him, America's increasingly commercialized and class-stratified stages seemed to be so sorely lacking." Relatedly, Gandal maintains that slum narratives "were responses not only to middle-class worries about the slums but also to middle-class anxieties about itself" and accordingly attributes the "outpouring of interest in the slums in the 1890s" to "a new and diverse quest for intense experience in response to a perceived 'feminization' and 'overcivilization' of American life."[26] Once again, take Corbin's essay as an example: "[W]hereas our plays in English are apt to be either imported or stupid," he explained to readers, "a candid observer will admit that the artistic spirit is more vital and spontaneous in [these foreign plays] than in the plays of the most prosperous uptown theatres." Insisting on his own class's cultural shortcomings, Corbin turned to the "vital and spontaneous" slums. Such a turn was noteworthy because "[p]reviously, the urban poor were absolutely inferior, both morally and aesthetically, and held at a distance," explains Gandal, "but now the middle class is carrying on a more intimate contact with them, even borrowing from them, and so implicitly acknowledging that they are superior at least when it comes to the issues of excitement and toughness."[27]

Critics' dissatisfaction with Broadway Shakespeare theatre, then, as well as their quest for dramatic fulfillment on the Lower East Side, may in fact have stemmed from this broader structure of feeling that turned the American bourgeoisie against its own seemingly "feminized" and "over-civilized" surroundings in pursuit of the exotic alternatives, the "intense experience[s]," and the "excitement and toughness" that the Lower East Side ostensibly offered. So too did critics' theatre-focused newsprint effect a broader social imprint. To Haenni's point, the Anglo-bourgeoisie's presence in immigrant venues, not to mention the appreciation for Shakespeare shared by critics, playgoers, and performers alike, enabled intimacy, albeit with an observer's privileged distance, between otherwise segregated social groups. Yet critics viewed Shakespeare as a fixed property—an abstract category of culture, like "Americanness," to which immigrant bodies could assimilate by performing it on acceptable terms. Accordingly, their accounts of Shakespeare in the slums "reveal[ed] [their] complicity with structures of power" and with dominant ideologies.[28] Refereeing what sights and sounds transgressed the boundaries of Shakespeare, critics betrayed an implicitly Anglocentric claim to the Bard that in turn shored up their readers' position at the top of an emergent U.S. cultural hierarchy and, moreover, helped to nurture this hierarchy into being.

"EXIT THE OLD BOWERY": SHARED SHAKESPEAREAN SPACE

Above all, the turn-of-the-twentieth-century slumming mentality that drove bourgeois, uptown New Yorkers to working-class Lower East Side settings rested on ideological associations between urban space and social meaning. The word "slum" is itself both a spatial and social referent, simultaneously evoking geography, class, and even race. What is more, for the

English-language critics who patronized Manhattan's immigrant-run theatres, the slum also evoked particular Shakespeare histories, insofar as
Bowery venues recalled earlier American Shakespeare traditions, including
early nineteenth-century performances by English and American (both
white and black American) tragedians, as well as midcentury minstrelsy
spoofs of the Bard. Indeed, "[t]o anyone who cares for the stage and for
the art of the player in America," as Corbin advised his readers at the outset
of "How the Other Half Laughs," "the theatres of the lower Bowery are of
special interest."²⁹ The historical significance of these shared spaces—shared
in critics' nostalgic musings if not in real time by immigrant performers and
ghosts of Anglo, black, and blackface Shakespeareans past—combined with
their significance as slumming hotspots and shaped how Anglo-bourgeois
critics consumed and construed the immigrant Shakespeare productions
staged there at the turn of the twentieth century.

Shannon Jackson's concept of "interspatiality" usefully elaborates on
how single spaces like theatres can contain multilayered significance. A
means of "theoriz[ing] the semiotic hybridity of interpreted spaces, the
term *interspatiality* gestures to a 'space as text' paradigm," she writes. "Like a
complex text that contains allusions, suggestions, parodies, and quotations
from other texts, strains of many spaces may permeate selected spaces."³⁰
As interspatial sites, the theatres of the Lower East Side placed critics at
the crossroads of early nineteenth-century U.S. Shakespeare performance,
a subsequent period of melodrama and minstrelsy at midcentury, and the
immigrant stage scene that ushered in the 1900s. As such, these spaces also
signaled more abstract phenomena: the formation of postrevolutionary
American identity through early nineteenth-century stage performance
and spectatorship; the city's shifting racial makeup, including the sharp-
ening of the color line and the increasing diversity of white-identified
bodies throughout the nineteenth century; emergent associations between
cultural taste, class, and urban geography (for example, the divergent connotations of "uptown" versus "downtown" theatres) in the latter half of the
1800s; and proliferating socioeconomic divisions across the turn of the
century, to name a few.

In the early nineteenth century, Shakespeare thrived in the theatres
along the Bowery, where Anglo and Anglo-American tragedians like
Edmund Kean, Edwin Forrest, Junius Brutus Booth, and Charlotte Cushman played to enormous, enthusiastic, and primarily Anglo-American

audiences. These venues and the New York culture they represented pre-dated the slum, but while the social scene in and around them changed over the course of the 1800s, gradually ceding cultural clout to the Broad-way theatre district that developed further uptown, their social meaning lingered and layered onto later significances. Located at 46–48 Bowery, the Thalia Theatre served late-century drama critics as a synecdoche for the neighborhood's theatrical history. At its founding in 1826, the Thalia, originally called the New York Theatre and then, after a few seasons, the Bowery Theatre, was among the most esteemed English-language venues in the Bowery theatre district. In 1879, it came under the management of a German company and was renamed the Thalia. Before the end of the cen-tury, the Thalia became a thriving hub of Yiddish theatre and later went on to house Italian and Chinese troupes in the 1910s and '20s before burning down in 1929.[31] The historic venue, which many called the Old Bowery even after 1879, thus staged the social and cultural evolution of New York's Lower East Side during the peak years of immigration and became a recurring trope for dramatic critics like Corbin.

Sometimes the theatre was a trope of common ground. For instance, linking the Old Bowery's Shakespearean past to its Shakespearean present for readers of "How the Other Half Laughs," Corbin noted that "[t]he early history of the theatre" was "strangely prophetic." He proceeded to illustrate this early history by quoting an address delivered on the occasion of the theatre's opening: "'At last, as Hope, bright, sandalled Hope, went by," the address intoned, "She calls on Shakespeare, and her throne is won! And *ours* is Shakespeare.'" Having thus evinced the venue's Shakespearean ori-gins, Corbin turned back to his contemporary moment and remarked to his readers, "By a curious trick of fate, the Old Bowery has remained true for the most part to its traditions."[32] With this, Corbin drew a line from the Anglo-performed Shakespeare productions that graced the theatre's brand-new stage in 1826 to the Yiddish-produced tragedies of the 1890s.

But even as he celebrated the Old Bowery as a site of shared tradition between early (Anglo) American Shakespeare players and (non-Anglo) American immigrant troupes—a shared tradition made all the more poi-gnant by Shakespeare's precarious presence on Broadway—Corbin hedged this moment of intimacy with an italicized claim to Shakespeare as "*ours*" followed by the ironic phrase "curious trick of fate." Fate's trick was curious, of course, because the German, Italian, and Yiddish actors and audiences among whom Shakespeare's muse was reportedly living on the East Side in many ways contradicted Corbin's rigid ideal of what Shakespeare should look and sound like on the American stage. True, the Old Bowery offered Corbin a familiar icon through which to make Lower East Side drama more legible for the *Harper's* half; however, the historic site also highlighted the drastic demographic changes that the neighborhood had undergone in the latter decades of the nineteenth century. Thus, while the Thalia and its attendant Shakespeare traditions offered both literal and figurative grounds for cultural intimacy between Anglo-bourgeois slummers and immigrant theatregoers, the historic space more often surfaced in press commentary as a signifier for critics' usually nostalgic, frequently derogatory, and fundamentally anxious attitudes toward the shifting urban landscape. Perhaps no artifact better evidences this interspatial meaning than a *New York Sun* headline issued one day prior to the historic English-language theatre's becoming a German-language venue: "Exit the 'Old Bowery,'" the headline proclaimed. "After Fifty Years of Citizenship It Becomes an Alien."[33]

Stage luminaries of the Bowery's early (Anglo) American Shakespeare culture thus appeared in critics' coverage of immigrant performance as spectral foils who pointed up immigrant performers' alienness to the Shakespearean stage. Critic Franklin Fyles, acting as a special correspondent to the *Washington Post* in 1905, wrote, "Just around the corner from Chinatown is the Bowery Theatre, the oldest playhouse in America now in use. On its stage Forrest, Davenport, and the elder Booth were tragedians. . . . Now the hallowed house is given over to performances in Yiddish and the audiences are drawn from the Polish Jews, whose crowded quarter is separated from the Chinese by the Bowery only. Thus have the histrionic glories of the neighborhood faded away." Trusting his readers to associate tragedians Edwin Forrest, Edward Loomis Davenport, and Junius Brutus Booth with the roots of American Shakespeare performance, Fyles suggested that the theatre's new clientele degraded its Shakespearean legacy. As late as 1919, Brander Matthews echoed Fyles's sentiment in a *Bookman* piece called "Telescoping Time in the Theatre." "The last time I happened to pass through the Bowery," he recalled, "my heart was saddened by the sight of the Bowery Theatre. . . . Its ample and dignified portico was disfigured by outlandish and unattractive placards, possibly in Italian or more probably in Yiddish. . . . This violent eruption of foreign posters was evidence of the pitiful degradation of a former temple of the drama." Matthews went on to remember "the prime days of [the Bowery Theatre's] youth, when its boards were trodden by Charlotte Cushman and Edwin Forrest, and when its walls echoed the sonorous eloquence of Shakespeare's loftiest dramas." Invoking the nineteenth century's most acclaimed English and American Shakespeareans to parry the image of New York's Yiddish and Italian stages, critics like Fyles and Matthews constructed a "splendor to slum" narrative that began with Shakespeare and ended, quite far from where it began, with immigrant theatre.[34] And their readers—thousands of them, across Washington and New York and beyond—sat with newspaper or magazine in hand, brows furrowed and curiosities lit as they formed a mental impression of Lower East Side players and playgoers, past and present.

Although not mentioned in such narratives, two other nineteenth-century Shakespeare histories thoroughly if troublingly informed Lower East Side theatres' interspatial meaning at the turn of the twentieth century: black and blackface performances. A full treatment of these topics would fill the pages of this book many times over, but a few choice examples are enough to suggest that, as black and blackface Shakespeareans emerged in lower Manhattan throughout the 1800s, so too did patterns of public reception that would shape Anglo-bourgeois critics' late-century associations between the neighborhood's spaces, American races, and Shakespeare. More specifically, these examples show how white Americans marshaled Shakespeare as a way of seeing and securing racial difference.

Histories of Shakespeare on the black American stage inevitably recount the all-black production of *Richard III* staged in the early 1820s at the African Grove Theatre, not far from the Park Theatre (located blocks from the Old Bowery). The African Grove production is especially noteworthy because police reportedly shut it down. English drama scholar Joyce Green MacDonald notes that "[a] condition of [the black actors'] release was the promise never to perform Shakespeare again, as though their black skins marked them as incompetent signifiers for the communication of Shakespearean meanings." She further concludes, "The African Company raid is an early example of the use of Shakespeare as a tool for enforcing cultural and political hegemony. Instead of imperial or colonial power, however, the New York police mounted their defense of Shakespeare on a platform of the cultural authority of whiteness."[35]

As the nineteenth century progressed, black Shakespeareans saw improved if still marginal stage access in lower Manhattan, but white observers continued to use Shakespeare to enforce the color line. In a *Spirit of the Times* article titled "Shakspeare [*sic*] Darkeyized," Mortimer Q. Thompson, a popular humorist who wrote under the pseudonym Q. K. Philander Doesticks, remarked with respect to an 1858 production of *Macbeth* at the Church Street Colored Theatre, "The novelty of seeing a black Macbeth with the entire tragedy done in colors by the best artists, promised to be almost as good a burlesque as the bearded Indian exhibition made by the great American Tragedian at the Broadway; and so with a varied assortment of friends I started to witness the unusual spectacle of a Bowery darky representing a Scottish king." Comparing Shakespeare "done in colors"—that is, performed by black actors—to a racial burlesque and casually referring to a black actor's performance of a Scottish King as an "unusual spectacle," Doesticks made clear to readers that, for him and his friends, this was not *really* Shakespeare, but was nonetheless an entertaining *attempt* to perform the playwright's work. With comparably cruel flippancy, a *New York Times* review of *Othello*, performed by the all-black Astor-Place Tragedy Company at Steinway Hall on East Fourteenth Street in 1885, snidely reported, "The Astor-Place Tragedy Company appeared . . . in a play which they, presuming upon the fact that the Shakespeare family's claim to a copyright of the title has expired, boldly called 'Othello.' The play presented last evening differed from that with which New-York audiences are familiar in many particulars, chief of which was that the characters were all Moors."[36] Like Doesticks, this reviewer refused to recognize the all-black performance as Shakespeare, per se—in fact, this seemed some other play entirely, on which the company had brazenly bestowed the name *Othello*.

In his history of black Shakespearean actors, theatre scholar Errol Hill makes plain that throughout the nineteenth century and into the twentieth, "white audiences in America were unwilling to accept blacks in dramatic portrayals." He shores up this point with a *Washington Post* excerpt from the late 1890s: "It is doubtful that the Negro will ever shine in the Shakespearean drama, excepting possibly the character of Othello. It seems more probable that if the Afro-American proves acceptable in serious roles he will develop a drama of his own, and not content himself with wearing the secondhand attire of the Anglo-Saxon stage." It is no wonder, then, that the famous black sociologist and activist W. E. B. Du Bois wielded Shakespearean imagery to cap a vision for black colleges in his 1903 collection of essays, *The Souls of Black Folk*: "I sit with Shakespeare, and he winces not," he declared, with an air of calm matter-of-factness mixed with provocation toward those who held attitudes like the critics quoted above. "Across the color-line I move arm in arm with Balzac and Dumas . . . and so wed with Truth, I dwell above the Veil. Is this the life you grudge us, O knightly America?"[37]

The American minstrelsy craze also had roots on the Lower East Side, rising to popularity in the Bowery theatres of the 1840s, where blackface performers regularly used Shakespeare to underscore the racial difference represented (and, as many scholars have argued, produced) by minstrel shows.[38] Levine's *Highbrow/Lowbrow* leans heavily on the ubiquity of Shakespearean parody—"short skits, brief references, and satirical songs"— across early nineteenth-century U.S. stage performance to show how Shakespeare was integrated into American culture. But while Levine's discussion sidesteps the social complexities of blackface, his archive is littered with examples from the minstrel stage where the humor in Shakespearean parody did not merely derive from Americans' widespread familiarity with the botched lines and scenes, as Levine argues for the sake of his narrative, but also from the fact that blacked-up bodies performed these malapropisms. Through these Shakespearean missteps—whether they were *Hamlet*-inspired song snippets like "Shuffle off your mortal coil, / Do just so, / Wheel about, and turn about, / And jump Jim Crow," or fully staged burlesque operas such as T. D. Rice's *Otello*—minstrels enacted an imagined incongruity between African Americans and Shakespeare, bringing this ideological difference to life both on stage and in public culture.[39]

These examples of black and blackface Shakespeare in lower Manhattan are not meant to prove any direct causal relation between the ways in which white Americans used Shakespeare to mark, police, and/or caricature blackness throughout the nineteenth century and the ways in which New York's Anglo-bourgeoisie reviewed non-Anglo immigrants' Shakespeare performance in the decades neighboring 1900. Rather, my aim is to illuminate a generative association. To that end, I suggest that a habit of viewing nonwhite Shakespeare performance as racial transgression at worst, racial send-up at best, formed on the Lower East Side and emerged as one of the many insidious ideological imprints that the legacy of blackface minstrelsy stamped on the American public consciousness. This cultural framework for perceiving nonwhite Shakespeareans had potential implications for immigrant-produced Shakespeare at the turn of the twentieth century;

however, full appreciation of these implications requires a short digression to outline more completely what Jacobson calls the "contingent" nature of many European immigrant groups' whiteness between the 1840s and 1920s, as well as the relationship of this contingent whiteness to social perceptions of blackness.[40] Be forewarned: more complete does not mean clear-cut, nor does it mean definitive. In fact, the more one studies the nuances of race during this period, the more complex they appear.

Along with Jacobson, recent critical race scholars have shown how, in the wake of U.S. immigration patterns that saw vastly increased German and Irish populations in the 1840s and '50s and even larger swells of Eastern European Jewish and Southern Italian groups in the decades following 1880, there arose a "profound ideological tension between established codes of whiteness as inclusive of all Europeans, and new, racialist revisions." The rise of phrenology in the early to mid-1800s and eugenics toward the turn of the twentieth century also encouraged a "new visual economy keyed not only to cues of skin color, but to facial angle, head size and shape, physiognomy, hair and eye color, and physique." According to historian Michael Miller Topp, "historians of the construction of whiteness have recognized that . . . the 'whiteness' of these [non-Anglo European] populations was rarely called into serious question; rather, the *quality* of their whiteness was."[41] Further, Jacobson argues convincingly that to label these varying qualities of whiteness as ethnicities is an anachronistic move that overlooks the period's fundamentally racial gloss on cultural difference. "Race is not just a conception," he writes; "it is also a perception."[42] Indeed, over the course of the nineteenth century, American ways of seeing race changed, resulting in fickle ideologies about what whiteness *was* and *meant*, particularly in U.S. cities.

A few telling passages from Riis's *How the Other Half Lives* suggest this new visual economy of race and bear out the hierarchy, albeit a fuzzy one, of white races perceived by Anglo-bourgeois visitors to the Lower East Side in the decades surrounding 1900. Crossing the Bowery into "Jewtown" in his textual tour of the tenement district, Riis drew on a visual (and aural) economy to assure his readers, "No need of asking here where we are. The jargon of the street[,] the signs of the sidewalk, the manner and dress of the people, their unmistakable physiognomy, betray the race at every step." Riis also routinely alluded to different qualities of whiteness, invariably conflating race and class. For instance, sketching an immigrant social ladder of sorts, he wrote, "The Italian comes in at the bottom, and in the generation that came over the sea he stays there. . . . Unlike the German, who begins learning English the day he lands as a matter of duty, or the Polish Jew, who takes it up as soon as he is able as an investment, the Italian learns slowly, if at all." Among those in Riis's social position, Germans were nearly always viewed as racially superior to other non-Anglo European groups, though they were nonetheless commonly classed as racially distinct from Anglo-Saxons. Other groups, however, moved more fluidly along a continuum of whiteness that ranged from desirable to undesirable. For instance, whereas Riis grouped Jews with Germans in the above example, he elsewhere grouped Jews and Italians together in a lowlier class. "The two races," he wrote, "differing hopelessly in much, have this in common: they carry their slums with them wherever they go, if allowed to do it."[43] Linking Jews and Italians by way of their common slumminess, Riis's comment shows how ideas about the slum intersected with ideas about race, and how the spatial and social implications of these ideas intertwined across the period's public discourse. The racial difference represented by immigrant groups who lived in areas deemed slums attached to the term "slum," and the negative connotations of the term "slum" attached to the groups who lived there. The word's racialized meanings ultimately overwhelmed its geographic intentions: for Riis, Jews and Italians "carried their slums with them," as if "slum" were a mode of being as well as a place to live.

The racial undesirability attributed to certain white immigrant groups at the turn of the twentieth century, many of whom lived in slums, has prompted a great deal of analytical labor from historians of race. Jacobson, for one, understands this undesirability as "probationary whiteness." Addressing this vexing question of how groups like Eastern European Jews and Southern Italians, and Germans in rarer instances, were seen as somehow both inside and outside the boundaries of white identity, Eric L. Goldstein posits, "During the initial decades of the [twentieth] century, white Americans often tried to suppress the troubling image of the Jew as they suppressed the distinctiveness of other groups—either by comparing them to blacks or predicting their speedy assimilation into white society." Charles Sprague Smith's and Alice Minnie Herts's reform activities exhibit the latter strategy of speedy assimilation, but the matter of non-Anglo immigrant groups' placement in the American black-white racial structure warrants consideration here, particularly given the association that I wish to draw between lower Manhattan's black, blackface, and immigrant Shake-speare scenes. Throughout the second half of the nineteenth century, tensions around chattel slavery and its eventual abolition resulted in what Goldstein describes as white Americans' "intensifying efforts to assert a clear racial hierarchy organized around the categories of black and white," and scholars like Eric Lott, David Roediger, and Michael Rogin have shown how white American identity and elitism—particularly among working-class immi-grant groups—depended on popular constructions of blackness-as-other. Yet Goldstein maintains that "the discourse concerning European 'races'" and "the black-white understanding of race . . . often interacted, overlapped, and influenced one another." That is, race was relative; groups like Jews appeared "more white," and therefore assimilable, when perceived as "not black," but so too could Anglo-identified groups empower themselves over Jews by perceiving links between Jewishness and blackness. Thomas A. Guglielmo compellingly parses the turn-of-the-twentieth-century U.S. racial land-scape by distinguishing between color, "a social category and not a physical description," and race, "which could mean many things." He accordingly attributes the perplexing coexistence of "Italians' relatively secure white-ness *and* their highly problematical racial status" to the fact that Americans marked non-Anglo immigrant bodies through two systems of difference, one of which afforded them "privileged *color* status as whites," and the other of which condemned them to a "putative *racial* undesirability" in the United States. Like Goldstein, however, Guglielmo acknowledges that "[t]he race/ color distinction was, of course, never absolute."[44]

Thus, as unprecedented numbers of non-Anglo European immigrants moved into New York's slums and complicated social perceptions of whiteness in the final decades of the 1800s, Anglo-bourgeois spectators of immigrant-produced Shakespeare theatre found themselves in an ambigu-ous Shakespearean space on the Lower East Side. In an entertainment zone where white bodies had once performed Shakespeare for early American white audiences, and where nonwhite bodies had bungled Shakespeare in the eyes of midcentury white audiences (who mocked black actors' Shakespearean performances and applauded blackface minstrels' Shake-spearean spoofs), through what racial lens should turn-of-the-century Anglo-bourgeois audiences view Shakespeare performed by the variously and problematically raced, "contingently" white bodies on the German, Yiddish, and Italian stages?

A COMPLEX OF CONTEXTS

As one might expect, the complexities driving the above question compel an inconclusive, although not inconsequential, answer, which we will see play out through close analysis of reviews and commentary written by and for New York's Anglo-bourgeoisie. Across these examples, this answer unfolds as follows: in the Lower East Side spaces where English-language critics engaged with Manhattan's immigrant communities via Shakespeare at the turn of the twentieth century, these critics and their readers perceived German, Yiddish, and Italian Shakespeareans to be performing on the margins of American belonging. On the one hand, familiar Shakespearean repertoire served critics as a vehicle for recognition, for forging a connection across class lines and across "white *races*" ("in the plural," as Jacobson puts it). New York's theatre critics, disappointed by the changing standards of drama under new conditions of production and swept up in the spirit of slumming, saw hope for an otherwise endangered Shakespearean ideal in the city's immigrant theatres. Recognizing Shakespeare in the slums also mollified critics' middle-class fears of proliferating demographic change on the Lower East Side. Haenni calls the turn of the twentieth century "an age when acculturation was thought about through spatializing modes—through pictures and scenes." For Haenni's purposes, acculturation means both immigrants' acculturation to middle-class culture and the middle class's acculturation to a new urban landscape. She uses *pictures* and *scenes* as two distinct concepts to theorize urban social life. "[W]hile a picture places a reified immigrant in a space outside time," she explains, "a scene potentially allows for immigrant, working-class participation." In other words, pictures assign predetermined meaning to social identities and performances, whereas scenes are fluid, enabling participation, exchange, and even improvisation. Haenni's contrast between pictures and scenes proves useful here. Critics' interest in viewing immigrants in Shakespearean scenes, and Shakespeare in immigrant scenes, held the promise of mutual acculturation across social groups.[45]

But the timing was out of joint. Bringing a "Shakespeare is sacred" mindset to the theatre, the primary arbiters of New York's dramatic world demanded onstage portraits rather than performances of the playwright's characters. That is, they imagined Shakespeare's characters as pictures, in Haenni's sense of the term: universal truths, "symbols of life—fixed, immutable," as the *New York Times* put it in 1903.[46] Shakespearean scenes—fluid, dynamic performances that took liberties with Shakespeare and invited audience participation—were out of fashion among elite groups. Yet the popular draw and perceived motley nature of many immigrant performances, particularly those in the Italian and Yiddish theatres where songs, dances, and afterpieces regularly appeared on the program and where audiences were highly engaged with the onstage action, evoked the scenes of early nineteenth-century American Shakespeare culture. Further, despite Shakespeare's association with American whiteness during this period, the cultural work performed in New York's immigrant-run play-houses ran counter to the melting-pot model of assimilation. Embracing, even encouraging immigrant difference, these venues were sites of decidedly non-Anglo identification for immigrant groups—and consequently sites that amplified the probationary status of immigrant whiteness in the eyes of Anglo-bourgeois onlookers. Accordingly, English-language critics who were sure to recognize and identify with the stories, themes, characters, and morals of non-Anglo Shakespeare productions were equally liable to interpret these productions as being in conflict with Shakespearean norms, and, by extension, with norms of American whiteness. Even the Irving Place Theatre—which regularly hosted leading actors from Germany, where Shakespeare performance and scholarship garnered respect from audiences worldwide—was occasionally subject to critics' Anglocentric standards and slights. On top of these ill-fated ideological intersections, a set of spatial meanings converged in the New York neighborhood that, at the turn of the century, simultaneously evoked the seedy thrill of the slums, a bygone Anglo-American Shakespeare tradition, a complex minstrel history, and a rapidly diversifying urban demography, thus further vexing bourgeois reception of immigrant Shakespeare. The result was a body of press coverage that frequently traded in pictures instead of scenes, framing Shakespeare and immigrant culture as fundamentally unassimilable.

"THE SAME VARIETIES OF CHARACTER": IMAGINING SAMENESS
THROUGH SHAKESPEARE

Exiting Maiori's 1898 performance of *Otello* at the Teatro Italiano, Corbin experienced what he initially perceived to be an encounter with a dangerous Bowery type but came to realize was a brush with someone familiar:

Shakespeare's Romeo. "When I left the theatre I was dogged by a swarthy young Italian who carried one hand suspiciously in his breast pocket," Corbin recalled. "As I was new to the Bowery, and had the conventional fear of its ways, I resolved not to be done away with without a struggle." Corbin's response to the "swarthy" body that approached him was suggestive of broader middle-class anxieties, what he called "conventional fear," about Lower East Side racial difference. But the dark figure proved these anxieties unfounded. "What he drew on me was a tintype of himself as Romeo," Corbin continued. "He said he could play a very good Romeo, if he was only given a chance, and was going to make a great deal of fame and money. Wouldn't I take his photograph? It was owing to my stupidity, no doubt, that I was surprised to find the same varieties of character, the same degrees of hope and ambition, I had found in the theatres I was used to." Citing literary scholar Carolyn Porter's work on participant observation, Haenni points to this scene—which she describes as an "Italian villain with a dagger, so familiar from the stage melodramas of the period"—as a source of "power and pleasure" in which Corbin, as observer, "'discovers his participation within the world he has thought to stand outside.'" For Haenni, "although Corbin's theatricalization of the ghetto protects him from a certain version of the everyday, it also enables contact." Indeed, within the broader scope of his essay, Corbin's incidental urban encounter emphasized the possibility of contact, of recognition, where he had initially anticipated a struggle with difference. But rather than tracing this moment of recognition to Corbin's familiarity with a melodramatic archetype, I instead locate it in his sighting of Shakespeare in the slums. Only after reinterpreting the swarthy street figure as Romeo could Corbin perceive in him the "same varieties of character" as he "had found in the theatres [he] was used to."[47] Shakespeare was the common ground that initiated Corbin's contact with the Bowery.

Recall that it was Corbin's discovery of Shakespeare in the slums—"the announcement . . . that 'Othello' and 'Hamlet' were to be brought out in the Italian theatre in the Bowery"—combined with the "dearth of tragedy which has of late fallen on the Broadway theatres" that drew him to the Teatro Italiano in the first place. Here, as with his later Romeo street encounter, Corbin figured Shakespeare as a bridge between him and the city's immigrant scene. That many other English-language critics likewise leveraged Shakespeare as common ground can be seen in the following examples of late nineteenth- and early twentieth-century headlines for announcements and reviews of immigrant Shakespeare: "Othello' in Italian: 'Teatro Italiano' Opens Its Doors—A Large First Night Audience"; "'Otello' in the Bowery"; "Classical and Romantic Drama in East Side Jargon"; "Bertha Kalisch [sic], the Yiddish Favorite, Plays Hamlet"; "Petticoat Hamlet Invades the Bowery: Bertha Kalisch Acts the Dane at the Bowery and Excites the East Side"; "The Jewish King Lear"; "A Bowery Hamlet: Shakespearean Revival on the East Side"; "Jacob Adler—The Bowery Garrick"[48]; "Drama of the Bowery—A Yiddish 'Romeo and Juliet'—Ghetto Life on the Stage—Mr. Thomashefsky and His Company"; "An Italian Shylock"; "The German Shylock"; and "German Players in 'Julius Caesar.'"[49] While various words in these headlines coded social difference (a pattern addressed later on), the Shakespearean terms invited Anglo-bourgeois readers to identify with these East Side events. As a *New York Times* writer put it in a notice about the Maiori-Rapone Company's June 1902 engagement at the People's Theatre, which included *Otello* and *Amleto* among other classic revivals, "The familiar character of the plays of the coming week should make the performances of especial interest." This "familiar character" was key to critics' acts of identification, and it was also key to the cultural work of their articles as slumming narratives. By marking productions staged in immigrant-run playhouses as recognizably Shakespearean, they "[made] the foreign proximate . . . without disturbing middle-class values."[50]

Even when not explicitly reviewing immigrant translations or adaptations of Shakespearean repertoire, critics framed the Lower East Side's dramatic landscape in Shakespearean terms with which their readers could identify. Corbin's "How the Other Half Laughs" called on Shakespeare to emphasize how Yiddish "patronage of art" was "infinitely beyond that of the families uptown," explaining that to rebuff art and artists in the Yiddish community was "the simple and sufficient evidence of villainy, as the lack of music in one's soul was to Shakespeare." Likewise citing Shakespeare to underscore a point about immigrant theatre culture, a 1900 *New York Times* piece on the Teatro Italiano began, "The fact that 'all the world's a stage, and all the men and women merely players,' may be the reason why love of the mimic stage, the portrayal of character, the visible expression of the emotions reduced to the fine art of the Thespian, . . . is inherent in the human breast of all mankind without distinction of class or nationality or race."[51] In these examples, Shakespeare's verse enlightened and endeared Anglo-bourgeois audiences to aspects of immigrant culture. In the first

case, a Shakespearean allusion also underscored the Yiddish community's enviable commitment to the arts, by both Corbin's and Shakespeare's
standards.

Critics who visited or interviewed actors in their Lower East Side homes
even attributed Shakespearean qualities to these offstage spaces, as if Shakespeare might somehow help critics to make sense of performers' foreign
lifestyles. For example, following the performance of *Otello* at the Teatro
Italiano, Corbin visited "the little tenement" where "Othello and Desdemona" (i.e., Maiori and his wife, Concetta Arcamone) lived. Remarking on
Arcamone, he wrote, "Her life on the stage was in sad contrast, to be sure, to
this life at home, for the real Desdemona—poor lady—never lived to have
a parlor, to say nothing of a baby to bathe in it." Crucially, Corbin viewed
Arcamone in relation to some "real," rooted conception of Shakespeare's
Desdemona, betraying his sense of immigrants as performers of difference
and Shakespeare's characters as stable truths to which actors and actresses
might conform. Indeed, Corbin might have remarked on the economic
disparity that separated Arcamone (an actress living in a small New York
tenement flat) from "the real Desdemona" (the daughter of a well-to-do
Venetian senator) or the material conditions that distinguished their lives
at home, but he instead pitied the Shakespearean heroine. For him, Desdemona's realness demanded human compassion whereas Arcamone's
theatricality allowed for emotional and ethical distance.[52]

Tyrrell likewise used Shakespeare to make sense of Maiori's domestic
space. In describing his interview with Maiori for his piece, "Little Italy's
Great Actor," the critic included Shakespearean details that *Theatre* subscribers were sure to appreciate: "[Maiori's] wife was busy arranging and
cataloguing his theatrical library, which contains the standard Italian acting
versions of several hundred repertoire plays, from Goldoni and Shakespeare down to D'Annunzio and Ibsen." As Tyrrell and Maiori talked, "the
tragedian [caught] poor Yorik's skull on the fly, as it was tossed to him
by his three-year-old daughter Marion." Outfitting this depiction of Italian family life with Shakespearean touches—Arcamone straightened up
Shakespearean scripts while little Marion played with an iconic prop from
Hamlet—Tyrrell made the foreign familiar for his readers.[53] By refiguring
tenement rooms as Shakespearean scenes and immigrants as performers in
their own homes, Corbin and Tyrrell made immigrant lives legible—and
theatrical—to an audience that otherwise held itself at a geographic, social,

and moral remove from Lower East Side groups. After all, Arcamone's and Maiori's Southern Italian dialects may have been alien to these writers and their readers, but Shakespeare was a language that the Anglo-bourgeoisie understood well.

Critics also prompted intimacy between their readers and the Lower East Side by linking immigrant stage culture to Elizabethan stage culture. Corbin, in particular, was fond of drawing such parallels. In his March 1898 *Harper's* piece on Maiori, Corbin deemed the Italian theatre "as rude and bare as an Elizabethan playhouse on the bankside"—an analogy that was reprinted in the *Washington Post* later that month. In December of that year, Corbin's "How the Other Half Laughs" made several such comparisons, noting, for example, that "[w]hat we thought worst in the acting of our Bowery Othello may not have been the farthest removed from the Elizabethan spirit." Corbin's March 1899 *Harper's* review of Jacob P. Adler's *Jewish King Lear* likewise remarked that the play's "costume and scenery are as simple and unobtrusive as were those of the original play as presented at the Globe; and the audience of Jewish tailors and shopkeepers is as wholehearted, and no doubt quite as keen and imaginative, as an audience in the little world of Elizabethan London." Writing for the *New York Times* in 1903, Corbin reviewed Thomashefsky's *Jewish Romeo and Juliet*, once again suggesting that "[i]n its [*sic*] native and unabashed expression of the popular taste the Yiddish plays of the Bowery are on the precise plane of the plays that delighted the Bankside under Elizabeth."[54] To be sure, Corbin's Elizabethan analogies asserted social power by portraying immigrant theatres as primitive, but these Shakespearean parallels can also be seen as efforts to overlook—whether in the sense of seeing across or eliding altogether—racial and class difference.

Associating immigrant venues with the "rude and bare," "wholehearted," and "unabashed" scenes of sixteenth-century London, such Elizabethan analogies also grasped at the "excitement and toughness" that, as Gandal suggests, slummers perceived to be lacking in a "feminized" and "overcivilized" middle-class American culture at the turn of the twentieth century. Corbin provides a textbook example of this phenomenon in the above-mentioned review of Thomashefsky's 1903 *Jewish Romeo and Juliet*. "Even Shakespeare we bowdlerize, prettify, and extinguish beneath a load of scenery and costume of the kind which the sensible Elizabethan reserved for the amiable baubles of masques at court," he advised the *Harper's* half,

with a telling "we." "Given a devitalized Shakespeare plus an anaemic drama
on the one hand and an adapted Shakespeare plus a vital drama on the
other, which would a wise man choose?"[55] It would seem that Shakespeare
afforded Corbin and his readers a safe and studied route by which to access
and learn from what they saw to be immigrant virility and vitality—in
contrast to a "prettified" and "bowdlerized" (read: "feminized" and "over-
civilized") dominant culture. But Shakespeare was also sacred territory,
and critics' staunch, Anglocentric ideals of the Bard's canon often turned
opportunity for racial intimacy into occasion for racial scrutiny.

"HAMPERED BY RACIAL LIMITATIONS": MARKING DIFFERENCE THROUGH SHAKESPEARE

For all of their impulses toward intimacy and admiration, critics for the
English-language press were also extremely sensitive to the ways in which
Shakespeare on immigrant stages differed from, and at times even offended,
their idealized notions of what counted as Shakespearean. As a result, their
reviews and commentary foregrounded racial difference through geographic and spatial tropes, linguistic jabs, material descriptions of body
and gesture, characterizations and caricatures of audiences, and a perva-
sive rhetoric of ownership that asserted an Anglo-American "ours" against
an immigrant "theirs" with respect to Shakespearean drama. Collectively
shaping the Anglo-bourgeoisie's perception of How the Other Half Does
Shakespeare, such rhetorical markers signaled territorial borders around
Shakespeare and whiteness, and located immigrant performers on the margins of these borders, if not wholly out of bounds.

Although the list of headlines cited earlier shows how critics leveraged
Shakespeare as a point of identification, it also reveals their preoccupation
with the racially marked geographic locations in which immigrant troupes
performed Shakespeare. Whereas headlines for announcements and reviews
of Broadway productions generally named only actor and character (the
New York Journal's aforementioned 1898 "Miss Ada Rehan as Portia," for
instance), or sometimes play title and venue (as in the *New York Tribune*'s
1905 "Shakespeare at the Garden: 'Macbeth'"), headlines describing productions in immigrant-run theatres signaled race via place in addition to
announcing a Shakespeare play (the *New York Times*'s 1902 "A Bowery
Hamlet," for one). Writers also mapped racial meaning through relative

geographies, as Corbin did in his 1898 coverage of Maiori's *Otello* when he juxtaposed the audience in "the Italian Theater, which is just south of Grand Street," with "our little party from uptown." Writing about Yiddish star Jacob Adler in 1905, Fyles similarly remarked, "People who went Bowerywards in the 'rubberneck' coaches, or any other way, have been coming back for years and telling us of a great actor hidden down there in the lower East Side."[56]

These geographic delineations were not simply accounts of theatregoers' travels to the Bowery district. Rather, as rapidly growing immigrant populations transformed the city of New York, dominant groups responded by rhetorically redetermining the social meaning of this urban space. The relational implications of uptown versus downtown, for example, were socioeconomic as well as directional, and classed expressions of taste were inextricably tied to the city map. Esther Romeyn links geographic boundaries with race, ethnicity, and power, asserting that "[r]ace is made 'visible' in the organization and distribution of social space . . . The apparently 'innocent' spatial organization of social life inscribes structures of power and discipline into human geography." Along similar lines, media studies scholar Kent A. Ono observes how figural borders "travel," insisting that "the border moves with migrants into those social spaces where they live" (just as Jews and Italians, by Riis's measure, carried their slums with them wherever they went). "Think of borders as potential limitations on what we imagine others and ourselves to be," Ono advises.[57] Viewed from this critical perspective, the apparently innocent geographic cues routinely included in mainstream coverage of immigrant Shakespeare were in fact printed performances of power, textually asserted borders that distinguished Shakespeare from the slums and made visible the racial-outsider status of these productions. Corbin's "little party from uptown," for instance, joined others "who went Bowerywards" and subsequently "came back"—back to where, precisely, is unclear, although one senses that the return was less to a precise location than to a normatively Anglo-American cultural space.

Critics for the English-language press also portrayed immigrant translations and adaptations of the Bard's plays to be linguistically un-Shakespearean—an unsurprising trend given American elites' growing preference for "pure" Shakespeare and the melting-pot mentality of "talk and think and be United States."[58] Further, because critics experienced onstage language as sound—particularly when they could not fully comprehend its meaning—their linguistic censures implied that immigrant performances were also sonically at odds with Shakespeare. For instance, to Corbin's ears, at least "as far as [he] could make out," Maiori's 1898 version of *Othello* "was stripped of most of the characteristically Shakespearean passages." Similarly, a *New York Times* critic felt that Ferdinand Bonn's 1903 *Hamlet* suffered from "some shortcoming [that] is of course inevitable as the result of the translation into German." Yiddish proved especially jarring, as it was rendered in the Hebrew rather than Latin alphabet and combined Hebrew, Aramaic, and Slavic components with the Germanic sounds and cognates that English speakers in U.S. cities were more or less accustomed to hearing by the 1890s. Reflecting solemnly on the evolving Bowery district, for example, a *New York Sun* writer declared in 1896 that no change seemed "so significant . . . as the fact that the Old Bowery . . . should now be given over to performances in a tongue so remote from the spirit of our civilization as Yiddish is." Five years later, in his review of Bertha Kalich's *Hamlet*, Dale included a photographic reproduction of the cast list to highlight the "[c]urious spelling of the names of the famous characters in Shakespeare's play." He also described the rest of the playbill, observing that "Shakespeare was ushered in in most riotous Yiddish." Although Joel Berkowitz and a preview article in the *Forverts* point to a Yiddish translation prepared for Kalich's performance, Dale reported that the actress delivered her lines in German, as she "felt that the 'classics' called for German just as pure as they could get it. . . . The consequence," as Dale saw it, "was that the Yiddish audience got its 'Hamlet' in German, without the Polish-Hebrew chowder to which the Thalia audiences are accustomed." Both Kalich's reported choice to perform in German and Dale's relief that Hamlet had "escaped the Yiddish jargon" reflected the common turn-of-the-century perception that German sounded more sophisticated than Yiddish.[59]

Significantly, critics' linguistic jibes went beyond practical matters of translation to suggest a fundamental gap between the nature of German, Italian, or Yiddish and whatever abstract Shakespearean ideal they felt could be expressed in English. Corbin, for instance, heard few "characteristically Shakespearean" speeches in Maiori's Italian *Otello*, the *New York Times* faulted some inevitable shortcoming in Bonn's German, and the *Sun* critic perceived a profound difference between the sound of Yiddish and the "spirit" of American civilization that once graced the Old Bowery. These criticisms were not founded on lexical semantics but on some internalized impression of how Americans and Shakespeareans ought to sound. Across the above examples, charged words like "stripped," "inevitable," and "riotous," not to mention choice phrases like "Polish-Hebrew chowder," drove an ideological wedge between Shakespeare's canon and immigrant speech. In this sense, critics for the English-language press struggled to accept the Lower East Side's diversifying *aural imaginary*, ethnic studies scholar Roshanak Kheshti's term for any "space in which subjects interact through the listening event."[60] What is more, by qualifying the sounds of immigrant Shakespeare performance for their readers, critics promoted a U.S. aural imaginary where non-English sonorities corresponded to racial and cultural difference.

English-language commentary further emphasized racial difference by detailing actors' bodies, gestures, and mannerisms. In fact, critics often seemed more interested in performances of race than in performances of Shakespeare. For example, describing Ophelia in Kalich's 1901 Yiddish *Hamlet*, Dale wrote, "Ophelia, or Affolio . . . was hugely fat and lusty. . . . and her hair was tied back in Grand street style. She was a very beautiful person, but not at all wistful. She might have given cabbages for remembrance and Dutch cucumbers for thought." Whereas Shakespeare's Ophelia gave rosemary and pansies, Dale imagined this "hugely fat and lusty" Affolio to be peddling earthy vegetables, much like a pushcart vendor in the Jewish quarter might have done at the time. As Grand was a Bowery cross street, Dale's comment not only conflated race with body type and occupation but also charted race on the city map. With respect to Bonn's 1903 *Hamlet*, a *New York Times* critic likewise interested in racial types commented, "He has followed the very questionable practice of making Hamlet a blonde, and has made him a very German blonde at that."[61] Another *New York Times* reviewer remarked with respect to Maiori's 1905 Shylock, "He enforces his points with a wink or a nod, and like most of the actors of his race, gesticulates with the utmost freedom." Of Maiori's makeup, the same writer noted that it "came nearer being a duplicate of the roly-poly German images displayed at Christmas time than anything else."[62]

That theatre commentary should address body and gesture is no surprise; after all, theatre is an embodied practice. However, that these articles constructed explicit associations between physicality and identity, representing bodily aesthetic, hair, gesture, and makeup as exaggerated features of race, is noteworthy, especially as critics flagged these physical characteristics as "not at all wistful," "questionable," excessive, and/or clownish. Such critical commentary instantiated what Jacobson calls the "dynamic relationship between visible 'difference' on the one hand, and deep social and political meaning on the other," or the new visual economy of race that emerged in the second half of the nineteenth century. As Ono explains, "From the wink of an eye to the tilt of one's head to the lilt in one's voice, bodies may unknowingly reveal bordered identities. The body itself is a readable text, is discursive, and therefore may be understood to have meanings that need to be controlled, disciplined, deported, imprisoned, or discarded."[63] Given that dramatic criticism richly documents the historical surveillance of bodies on stage, and slum writings document the historical surveillance of bodies in the city, these Anglo-bourgeois accounts of immigrant Shakespeare—read as both dramatic criticism and slum writings—evidence particularly candid efforts to discipline the meaning of immigrant bodies by marking them as foreign to Shakespeare culture.

Critics betrayed an interest in Bowery theatre audiences that, like Charles Sprague Smith's accounts of Shakespeare at the People's Institute, rivaled their concern with the onstage Shakespearean action. The result was a set of commentaries that remarked on performances of race more so than on performances of Shakespeare, in which the audiences as well as those on stage participated as actors. For example, in "How the Other Half Laughs," Corbin prefaced his discussion of *Otello* with a lengthy description of the Teatro Italiano's audience, whom he partially credited with lending the theatre its "curious and very intimate interest." Recalling two playgoers' irate reaction to Iago, Corbin confessed that "the horror with which [Iago's] villainy was resented disturbed my conventional ideas of Italian wickedness." While this confession potentially served to *close* the racial gap between the critic and those seated next to him (albeit backhandedly), Corbin's conventional ideas of Italianness were not so disturbed as to discourage what amounted to racial caricature as he next described the pair's dialogue to his *Harper's* readers. He restaged this overheard conversation as follows: "'If [Otello] knew what man-a [Iago] is, he would-a not trust heem,' said one worthy, with a grave shake of the head. His companion replied, 'Ain't he a son-a gun-a? Ain't he a *son-a gun-a*?'" Corbin then further widened the racial gap he had closed just sentences before by adding, "I am not saying that this gentleness of instinct always went the full length of our moral code; even in the horror at Iago there was a keen spice of delight."

With a pronominal sleight of hand that distinguished the playgoers' "their" from his readers' "our," Corbin rhetorically reassured the *Harper's* half of its moral advantage over the city's Italian American population.[64]

Weighing social similarities and differences by way of Shakespeare, then, Corbin recounted a scene that ultimately affirmed his readers' Anglo-Saxon superiority. Moreover, his divisive rhetoric circulated to an especially wide audience, extending beyond the already formidable *Harper's* readership. The *Washington Post* and the *New York Tribune* each reprinted this material, the former reissuing a fair amount of Corbin's section on the Teatro Italiano, and the latter excerpting only his colorful anecdote about the horrified spectators seated near him. Corbin himself lifted this dialogue from his own earlier profile piece on Maiori, published in *Harper's* nine months prior to "How the Other Half Laughs." The earlier *Harper's* essay described the second spectator's reply as having been delivered "with as just a mingling of horror and delight as Booth ever evoked," going so far as to compare the Italian American playgoer's style of expression directly to that of famed Anglo-American actor Edwin Booth. In this instance, Corbin once again reframed immigrants' everyday practices as theatrical performances—Shakespeare performances even, given Booth's legacy of staging the playwright's repertoire—comparing a playgoer's remark to a tragedian's delivery. All told, with two printings in *Harper's* and reappearances in the *New York Tribune* and the *Washington Post*, Corbin's racialized vignette provided privileged readers across the country with front-row seats to this performance of Italian Americanness.[65]

In an era when American audience behaviors increasingly corresponded to hierarchized categories of taste such as "highbrow" and "lowbrow" repertoire, "uptown" and "downtown" venues, and so on, Italian and Yiddish audiences' highly vocal and participatory style of spectatorship struck critics as incongruent with such unassailably respectable repertoire as Shakespeare's plays.[66] The *Dramatic Mirror* critic who attended Kalich's 1901 *Hamlet* observed how, "with each falling of the curtain the auditors sprang into sudden animation," and the *New York World*, reviewing the same production, remarked that "the bizarre features of the event were all on the audience's side of the footlights." The *New York Sun's* 1904 retrospective of the "memorable production of 'Hamlet'" staged at the Thalia Theatre in 1895 after which the audience relentlessly shouted, "Author, author!" and "Shakespeare, Shakespeare!" (an account reissued in the *Baltimore*

Sun and the *San Francisco Chronicle*) likewise caricatured the playgoers. This Yiddish audience "will thunder for their beloved actors during the presentation of the play," the *Sun* piece remarked, "but at the end there will arise united clamor for the playwright." The writer went on to describe the "rough house," the "clashing of palms [that] made the air rock," "how they howled!" and what ultimately became "an ugly mood," in which fans "were growing decidedly boisterous and obstreperous."[67]

Although some critics described spirited immigrant audiences with an air of admiration (a likely extension of what Gandal calls the middle-class "quest for intense experience"), their ultimately unflattering representations—of Italian and Yiddish audiences in particular—reinforced the stigma toward Old World difference so fundamental to Roosevelt's melting-pot ideal, in turn figuring these playgoers as outsiders to white American culture. As a point of comparison, consider one *New York Sun* writer's take on the audience at a 1905 production of *The Merchant of Venice*, staged at the Knickerbocker Theater on Broadway and West Thirty-eighth Street: "E. H. Sothern and Miss Julia Marlowe last night presented their version of 'The Merchant of Venice' to a fairly well filled house whose enthusiasm never exceeded the bounds of decorum." By contrast, critics routinely portrayed immigrant audiences as unsophisticated and easily excitable, apparently outside the "bounds of decorum." Springing into "sudden animation," these audiences freely announced their reactions to Iago in thick accents. They were "bizarre" and "boisterous." They "howled" and "clamored" like wild animals. The *Sun*'s account of the "Author! Author!" incident not only depicted immigrant playgoers as performers but, what is more, portrayed their performance as farce. While relaying the Yiddish audience's enthusiastic reception of *Hamlet*—among the most widely favored dramas of the long nineteenth century—the writer invalidated this moment of American cultural participation by framing it as a send-up. He recast the Yiddish audience's elated response to Shakespearean drama as an ironic display of difference, leveraging their unfamiliarity with the bard whom James Fenimore Cooper once called the "great author of America" as grounds for a joke between him and his readership.[68]

In general, whether charitable or disparaging toward immigrant Shakespeareans, critics took for granted that "Shakespeare"—that is, the ethos of Shakespearean repertoire rather than Shakespeare the biographical figure—was strictly Anglo-Saxon. Pronoun usage was one telltale indication of such Anglocentrism. For example: Although Winter disapproved of fellow critics' praise for immigrant troupes and rarely found such Lower East Side performances worthy of comment, he did review Shakespeare in Italian when international stars appeared on Broadway stages, and his 1907 rant against one such touring celebrity, Ermete Novelli, made clear the influential critic's conviction that Shakespeare belonged to the Anglo-Saxon group with which he (and, implicitly, his readers) identified. "It is becoming especially wearisome to have foreigners who visit our country instruct us . . . as to the meaning and purposes of our own dramatic literature," he carped.[69] Becoming almost comically agitated, he mocked Italian Shakespeare players: "We—who do not know your language: we—into whose language Shakespeare cannot be translated: in whose language, therefore, Shakespeare does not exist: we—who regard your Anglo-Saxon nature as cold and formal, who do not comprehend it: . . . WE will rescue you from your benighted state: WE will tell you what your Shakespeare means: WE will teach you how to act him, and how to act everything else!"[70] Sardonically inverting and typographically exaggerating his pronouns, Winter drew a stark opposition—on the grounds of language, race, and temperament (all of which he took to be interrelated)—between Italians and Anglo-Americans. For Winter, the brash Italian persona that he subversively ventriloquized for his *Tribune* readers could not possibly understand or even access Shakespeare. Cultural theorist Stuart Hall's notion of "symbolic boundaries" illuminates the performative stakes of pronouns like "we" and "you" in the context of these reviews, as they established "a symbolic frontier between the 'normal' and the 'deviant' . . . what 'belongs' and what does not or is 'Other.'"[71] Distinguishing "us" from "them" and "ours" from "theirs," critics designated non-Anglo performers as outsiders to American Shakespeare culture.

Critics' racial markers were, for the most part, associative. Subtle pronoun choices along with passing references to geography, language, accent, gesture, mannerism, or audience behavior all implicitly signaled immigrant racial difference to Anglo-bourgeois readers. Sometimes, however, writers harnessed Shakespeare to name racial difference outright or named racial difference so as to link the idea of Shakespeare to normative American whiteness. For instance, responding to Novelli's Othello (of all characters), Winter insisted that "Shakespeare's great characters . . . are, essentially, Anglo-Saxon in their nature: the experiences may be those of universal human life: the nature which, in Shakespeare, is subjected to those experiences is not." The *New York Sun*'s review of Novelli's performance noted "a big audience of [Novelli's] self-exiled countrymen" in attendance, with "hardly a Saxon or Semitic face in the audience. Hence the empty seats downstairs." As upper-level seating was less expensive than the "seats downstairs," this last comment implied the Italian American audience's class in addition to naming its race—a race that the *Sun* portrayed as distinct from and socioeconomically inferior to (if seated above) Saxons and Semitics. This same audience likely amplified Winter's ire at how the whole performance violated Anglo-Saxon territory. The *New York Times* reviewer who saw Bonn's 1903 *Hamlet* displayed a similar belief in the fundamental Anglo-Saxonness of Shakespeare's characters—as distinct from the player's and playgoers' German Teutonness. Deeming the actor's performance "Teutonically sentimental in conception," this critic reported that Bonn's "yellow mop of unkempt hair forestalled all possibility of regarding him as the Englishman the poet undoubtedly conceived him to be, or even as a Dane—a type which is still somewhat removed from the Teuton of Herr Bonn's embodiment." The same writer further concluded that "in his interpretation of this broadest and deepest of all parts [Bonn] was hampered by racial limitations," which "in some cases . . . stand between the actor and his author." With like awareness to racial limitations, a *Dramatic Mirror* critic resolved that any crudities in Kalich's *Hamlet* "were crudities born not of negligence but of a temperament alien to that of the characters portrayed." More admiringly but equally attuned to race, Tyrell commended "certain grandly poetic traits which make Majori's Hamlet a revelation to Anglo-Saxon playgoers." And Hutchins Hapgood remarked that Maiori's "Othello . . . breathes passion throughout, and is meat to the dark-browned audience in the Bowery."[72]

Hapgood's reference to the "dark-browned audience in the Bowery" testifies to Jacobson's concept of "variegated whiteness" and the perceptual gap that existed between the legally recognized white identity that granted non-Anglo European immigrants the right to citizenship in the United States, and the socially recognized not-quite-white identity that Hapgood perceived when he surveyed the Italian American theatregoers at Maiori's playhouse. Corbin's depiction of the "swarthy young Italian" who approached him with a "tintype of himself as Romeo" similarly underscored this gap, as did a later passage in "How the Other Half Laughs" wherein Corbin described the prompter for the Teatro Italiano's *Otello*, whose "long brown finger could often be seen indicating where the actors were to stand." Such phrases as "dark-browned audience," "swarthy young Italian," and "long brown finger" recall Guglielmo's observation that "[t]he race/color distinction was . . . never absolute."[73]

What is more, perceptions of whiteness were not just split along legal/social lines. Socially defined whiteness was itself variegated—an inconsistent and unstable mode of seeing others in the world. For the *New York Sun* writer who reviewed an 1897 production of *Otello* at the Teatro Italiano, Maiori's whiteness proved distractingly *opposite* to the blackness of his character. "The effect of his gestures was somewhat marred by the fact that he wore black gloves, instead of stain on his hands," the critic commented, "and the openings showed the white skin beneath with startling whiteness." Compared to those Shakespearean spectators beside whom Hapgood was accustomed to sitting in Broadway venues, the "dark-browned [Italian American] audience in the Bowery" appeared racially alien; but, against a pair of black gloves—and against the memory of those blacked-up Bowery Othellos who *did* wear stain on their hands—Maiori's skin appeared startlingly white. Such conflicting passages evince, and in their own time encouraged, what Jacobson calls the "profound ideological tension" that emerged in the latter half of the nineteenth century "between established codes of whiteness as inclusive of all Europeans, and new, racialist revisions."[74]

———

This profound tension is, finally, the moral of the stories explored here, and it also lays a foundation for how we might fully interpret these stories, as well as the stories to come. On one level, writers for the English-language press used Shakespeare to connect with, understand, and even learn from immigrant culture, while on another level, these critics rhetorically produced and protected a certain ideal of American whiteness by delimiting immigrant bodies as only marginally Shakespearean. But their reviews and commentary ultimately invite a third reading—one that depends on the first two: that is, they show how immigrant troupes' adaptations and translations of Shakespeare simultaneously performed *and defied* critics' ideals of whiteness, exploiting rather than acquiescing to the complex ambiguity of U.S. racial codes at the turn of the twentieth century. Neither of whiteness nor outside it, these immigrant Shakespeareans were "simultaneously inside and outside, dissolving both by mixing them together," to recall Michel de Certeau's imagery.[75]

Indeed, one can read embodied experiences of immigrant stage culture between the recorded lines of English-language press coverage to understand how German, Yiddish, and Italian Shakespeare performances operated both within and against English-language critics' normative claims. Enacting something at once familiar and unfamiliar to Anglo-bourgeois audiences, these performances reconditioned—however subtly—dominant groups' assumptions about how Shakespeare should look and sound on New York stages. Bonn's mop of blonde hair, Maiori's makeup, Rapone's Neopolitan farces, Farfariello's variety performances, Yiddish musical interludes resonant with the timbres of Jewish culture, the sounds of immigrant languages and dialects—all of these physical and aural actualities pushed back against Anglo-bourgeois journalists' ideological quibbles with immigrant translations and adaptations of Shakespeare. As such, critics who marked immigrant difference in the sense of making it visible through their choice of language also marked this difference in the sense of observing it, facing and feeling its reality, even if that reality clashed with the beliefs and attitudes expressed in their writing.

We now track this dynamic to New York's uptown English-language stages, where non-Anglo Shakespeareans appeared alongside English-speaking, Anglo-identified casts. Symbolically crossing into the physical terrain of normative culture, these immigrant actors directly confronted dominant American ideas about space as well as ideas about Shakespeare and race.

CHAPTER FOUR

The Profit of the City Consisteth of All Nations

Yiddish-theatre great Jacob P. Adler made his first appearance on the English-language stage in May 1903, playing Shylock in Shakespeare's *The Merchant of Venice*. The production, which toured Philadelphia, Baltimore, Boston, and finally New York, where it ran for months in multiple theatres, featured Adler delivering his lines in Yiddish while the rest of the cast spoke English. The run was so successful that Adler returned to Broadway in 1905 to play Shylock in a repeat polyglot production, albeit with a different English-speaking cast.[1] Audiences for the New York productions drew from downtown and uptown communities alike. In 1903, the *New York Times* reported that "[t]he spacious auditorium was so crowded with [Adler's] friends, and others who were attracted by his fame, that the reference on the programme to the ordinance against standees seemed a hollow mockery." Reviewing the same performance, *Di yidishe gazeten* (*The Jewish Gazette*), a Yiddish weekly whose front-page banner claimed "the largest circulation of any Jewish paper in the world," confirmed that "[a] mixed public of high tone Americans from the West with the Jewish connoisseurs of art from the East Side occupied every seat and every place to stand in the theatre." Spectators of varying economic means also presumably attended the productions: according to correspondence between Charles Sprague Smith and a New York City press editor, the People's Institute distributed half-price ticket vouchers for Adler's 1905 performance to public schools and social settlements.[2] Thus, as Adler's Yiddish mingled with the surrounding company's English before diverse audiences from around the city, the mainstream theatres in which Adler performed became sites where different social groups intersected along Shakespearean lines.

Adler's memoirs (published serially in a Yiddish newspaper between 1916 and 1919, and then resumed for a short time in 1925) describe the anxious internal monologue that preceded his Philadelphia debut: "What would the world say about this," he asked himself, contemplating his move from the niche Yiddish-theatre circuit to the nation's leading playhouses. "An actor from New York's Lower East Side on an American stage?" Indeed, the world—or at least the New York theatre world—had much to say, as writers for the Yiddish dailies, for the Anglo-Jewish weeklies (published in English by and for the old-immigrant Jewish American communities of Western and Central European descent), and for the mainstream press rallied around Adler's debut on the English-language stage. In April 1903, *Di idishe velt* (*The Jewish World*) announced, "For those who are interested in Yiddish theatre, it will certainly be interesting to hear that Mr. Jacob Adler, the greatest Yiddish actor, will shortly appear on the American stage." Writing that May for Philadelphia's *Jewish Exponent*, Louis Lipsky, an American-born Jewish journalist based in New York, likewise braced himself and his Jewish American readers for Adler's upcoming performance. "That the Yiddish actors have been striving to obtain wider recognition and have failed is known to the writer, and the fact is to be deplored," he lamented. "But I have in mind one notable exception who will, in the next four weeks, attempt to break through the barriers of his own limited public and endeavor to reach an American audience." And as early as the fall of 1902, having confirmed rumors of Adler's engagement (although apparently misinformed about the language in which Adler would perform), Henry Tyrrell announced to *Theatre* subscribers "that Jacob Adler, the great Hebrew actor, who for twelve years has been the idol of the Jewish masses of New York, will shortly emerge from the Bowery—the scene of all his triumphs—and take his place on the American stage as an English-speaking tragedian of the first rank."[3]

Across these passages and numerous other descriptions of this production from Yiddish- and English-language sources alike, phrases like "American stage" and "American audience" qualified where and for whom Adler was to perform in May 1903. But such phrases presented a rhetorical paradox where ideological and empirical realities clashed with one another. Used colloquially, these expressions denoted a gap—or a barrier, as Lipsky

138   HERE IN THIS ISLAND WE ARRIVED

put it—between the Anglo-identified English-language stage and the immigrant-run Yiddish-language stage, where the former was "American" and the latter was something else. Yet Adler himself identified as "an actor from New York's Lower East Side," and both Lipsky and Tyrrell acknowledged the public in the Bowery to whom Adler had played in New York for over a decade. The Lower East Side was U.S. ground, after all, and the Bowery's immigrant audiences built lives there as Americans. Nevertheless, the term "American stage" idiomatically excluded the East Side's Yiddish, Italian, and German venues despite geographic and demographic evidence to the contrary. So when Adler "emerged from the Bowery" to "take his place on the American stage," public discourse from the period suggested a scenario in which he was *on*, but not necessarily *of*, the latter cultural space.

Adler's story, along with others like it, prompts us to examine the definitional stakes of labels like "American stage" and shows how appearances by immigrant Shakespeareans in Anglo-identified (and largely Anglo-populated) theatres influenced ideas about American social difference and belonging. Along with Adler, a number of foreign-born actors trafficked New York's English-language stages in the late nineteenth and early twentieth centuries. International stars like Italy's Tommaso Salvini and Germany's Bogumil Dawison toured the United States in the 1880s, teaming up with English-speaking casts to give polyglot Shakespeare performances. While not immigrants themselves, these celebrities set an important precedent for foreign-born American actors, popularizing a niche Shakespearean soundscape wherein multiple languages shared the stage. Polish-born actress Helena Modjeska, who immigrated to the United States in the 1870s and performed across the country thereafter, played Shakespeare's heroines in English, gaining great renown as an American actress. Ukrainian-born Bertha Kalich, a multilingual performer who had a successful American career on the English-language stage, was reportedly first recruited to Broadway following her Yiddish performance of *Hamlet* at the Thalia Theatre in 1901. And Antonio Maiori, known for his Shakespearean roles, secured funding from the Four Hundred—the group of slummers who had "discovered" the Italian American tragedian in their travels to the Lower East Side—to perform with his Italian-speaking company at the Carnegie Lyceum for a week in 1903.[4] Across these examples and others, Shakespeare served as a bridge that connected foreign-born actors with the so-called American stage. Some, like Adler and Modjeska, played Shakespearean roles when they crossed over; others, like Kalich and Maiori, gained visibility among leading producers or wealthy investors on account of their Shakespearean successes, but rarely if ever performed Shakespeare for predominantly English-speaking audiences. In all cases, however, Shakespeare hovered in the vicinity of these cultural crossings.

Given how major economic and demographic shifts in U.S. cities threw into question what it meant to be "distinctively American" at the turn of the twentieth century (to recall Jacob Riis's phrase), it seems important to ask how a term like "American stage" shaped the significance of performances like Adler's—and vice versa.[5] The same question goes for "Shakespearean stage," the theatrical versus physical space that Adler occupied. Of course, various cases yield diverse interpretations, and each of the above-named actors could occupy a book-length study. Adler's example, however, is similar to others in multiple respects and therefore makes for a particularly rich and representative focus. His polyglot performances recalled Salvini's and Dawison's, while his geographic trajectory paralleled that of other American immigrant actors like Kalich and Maiori, who performed in uptown theatres after making their start on the Lower East Side. Further, Adler's appearances before polyglot and polyracial audiences in the role of Shylock, one of Western drama's best-known racial outsiders, underscored questions about social difference and belonging more urgently than, say, Modjeska's appearances as Juliet in English-language Shakespeare revivals. Adler's Shylock, then, bears out the complex significance of immigrant actors' Shakespearean star turns in English-language venues. Public ideas about Shakespeare and U.S. belonging undoubtedly influenced Adler's reception; but Adler just as surely bent public assumptions about Shakespeare on the American stage.

Indeed, Adler's Shylock can be seen as a historical prism, enabling different readings depending on how one examines it. Previous scholarship tends to prioritize Adler's significance to Yiddish theatre historiography, and to Jewish American culture more broadly. But "characterizations of social reality are not 'given,'" warns communications scholar David Zarefsky; rather, they are defined by elements of framing, contextualization, and association.[6] By setting Adler's Shylock against other backdrops—its production history, the cultural history of Shylock and contemporary performances of the role that contextualized it in its own time, the press reception that responded to it, the visual artifacts that mark its memory, and so on—we can extend the significance of his performances into new realms, both past and present.[7] For instance, many spectators, Anglo and non-Anglo alike, interpreted Adler's Broadway debut as the ultimate melting-pot victory: the foreign-born performer had transcended immigrant difference and "made it" as both an actor and a citizen on the American stage. For others, however, the production's mainstream context, along with Adler's appearance as one of Western drama's best-known racial outsiders, underscored the actor's social difference—difference begrudged by some audiences and hailed by others. Adler thus simultaneously performed and disrupted conventions of national belonging, and it was precisely because of this ambiguous scenario that his appearances on New York's English-language stage ultimately debunked the fixed ideological meanings of words like "American" and "Shakespearean."

SURPASSING SOCIAL DIFFERENCE

The material conditions of Adler's polyglot performances—particulars of venue, costume, and scenery—garnered considerable public attention and proved one frame of reference by which audiences attributed significance to Adler's English-language-stage debut. According to advertisements in *Dos abend blat* (*The Evening News*), a Socialist Yiddish daily, Adler first performed Shylock with his Yiddish-speaking company at the Lower East Side People's Theatre in December 1901. Two years later, reportedly after much negotiation, Broadway producer Arthur Hopkins persuaded Adler to make his debut with an English-speaking company as Shylock in an East Coast tour that would conclude in Times Square.[8] Although European celebrities had for decades crossed the Atlantic to star in polyglot performances staged by leading playhouses across the United States, a Yiddish actor's appearance in such productions and venues was unprecedented. Yiddish- and English-speaking audiences alike therefore expressed great excitement about this tour, often fixating on its production details: Where would Adler perform? Alongside whom? What would the costumes and scenery entail?

Of course, such material matters had social implications. Writing for *Theatre* subscribers—a readership with the means to purchase the magazine and the leisure time to enjoy its considerable coverage of New York's theatre scene—Tyrrell staked his claim that Adler would "shortly emerge from the Bowery […] and take his place on the American stage" on a perception that the so-called American stage marked the star's arrival in a space of greater social value. When Lipsky declared that Adler would "[break] through the barriers of his own limited public and endeavor to reach an American audience," he presumed a similar set of assumptions among his audience of old-immigrant Jews. Tyrrell, however, noted Adler's ascent as a cultural novelty, whereas Lipsky framed it as a cultural triumph—one to be taken personally by his readers. Yiddish-language papers also broadcast Adler's rise as triumphant. *Di yidishe gazeten* (*The Yiddish Gazette*), for one, announced, "Mr. Jacob P. Adler triumphs at the American Theatre," and proudly relayed that buzz about "Mr. Adler of the People's Theatre" had traveled from Philadelphia, Baltimore, and Boston, stirring anticipation of the New York performance that ultimately earned "applause, applause, and applause."[9] The Yiddish paper's investment in these mainstream appearances was slightly different than Lipsky's: rather than breaking away from a "limited public," Adler was breaking new ground for Yiddish culture in an American setting.

The venues where Adler appeared as Shylock, then, carried a range of meanings that shaped the significance of his performances. Theatre spaces, explains dramaturge and theorist Ric Knowles, are "full of histories, ghosts, pressures, opportunities, and constraints, of course, but most frequently they are full of ideology."[10] Following Marvin Carlson, Knowles emphasizes the significance of "'urban semiotics'—the ways in which the inhabitants of a city intellectually structure their surroundings and hence symbolically position various areas and buildings, including theatres, within the urban landscape." Relatedly, performance historian Susan Bennett stresses how audiences make meaning of performances in part based on the location of the venue. Whereas Adler's "usual Bowery theatres," his "own limited public," and his affiliation with the People's Theatre symbolized Manhattan's immigrant communities—communities that, according to Riis, lacked any "distinctively American" character—phrases like "American audience" and "American stage" represented Adler's "emergence" or "breaking through" into normative culture, an opportunity to surpass immigrant difference, and a chance to claim U.S. national belonging in his native Yiddish tongue, to great applause.[11]

In New York, especially, the Forty-second Street address of the venue where Adler performed alongside an English-speaking cast signified the

actor's social mobility. The *New York Sun* succinctly expressed this significance in a headline that read, "A Yiddish 'Shylock': The Bowery Actor
Jacob P. Adler Plays at an Uptown Theatre." Readers were sure to associate
the term "uptown theatre" with high ticket prices and quality production
value, and the fact that Adler literally journeyed north from the tenements
to Times Square underscored his figurative social ascent. A *New York
Times* critic (likely John Corbin) rather crassly linked theatre geography to
audience makeup, with the added implication that certain audiences held
more cachet than others. Instead of straightforwardly announcing Adler's
upcoming appearance in *The Merchant of Venice*, the critic labeled the event
"[the] transition of the Yiddish tragedian, Jacob P. Adler, from his east-side
environment to one less essentially associated with the Ghetto population."
The same writer further conveyed a widespread belief that Broadway was a
conduit to levels of fame and glory unknown to the East Side, explaining,
"There were many who contended that in exhibiting his talents elsewhere
Mr. Adler would not only add to his own fame, but would in some sense
glorify the people whom he represented."[12] Indeed, Adler's appearance on
Broadway represented his step across the threshold of dominant U.S. theatre culture—a border-crossing that took on especially pointed significance
given that the Times Square venue where he performed in both 1903 and
1905 was the aptly named American Theatre.[13] Moreover, his Boston debut
took place at the Columbia Theatre, a site whose name similarly asserted
Adler's newfound national belonging.

Jewish American audiences for whom Adler's Broadway debut marked
a triumph spoke in terms of elevated rank and class when discussing the
production details of Adler's 1903 tour, as if the actor were poised to trade
in his racial outsider status for the economic advantage imbricated in normative white American identity. The *Jewish Exponent* remarked that Adler's
Philadelphia appearance "demands attention for several reasons, the most
important being the fact that Mr. Adler will be surrounded for the first
time in his career by an English-speaking company of players, who have
been selected from the first rank of the dramatic profession." While the
phrase "first rank" most immediately referred to the surrounding company's presumed level of artistic talent, it also implied a social hierarchy
within the dramatic profession and suggested that Adler would be joining
this upper echelon by way of association. Similarly, an announcement in
the *Forverts* cried out, "Extra! Astonishing! Extra! Mr. Jacob P. Adler plays

with a first-class English artistic company in just a week," adding that the "equipment, scenery, and costumes were all especially newly made and cost ten thousand dollars." Proud to identify with Adler's racial and cultural difference in the wake of his success, the city's Jewish community nonetheless expressed widespread attitudes about social power at the turn of the twentieth century: that is, since white, Gentile America set the nation's terms of taste-making and social belonging, Adler's collaboration with a reputed English-language company and his access to expensive equipment, costumes, and scenery were meaningful indications of his improved social status. Mainstream newspapers certainly stressed the social import of Adler's appearance with an English-language company but did not so baldly emphasize the rank or class of the actors; in fact, many mainstream press reviewers found Adler's supporting casts lacking. The *New York Tribune*, for instance, stated in 1905 that, "as on the previous occasions of [Adler's] Broadway appearances," the actor's return to the American Theatre featured "poor support."[14]

Although the *Forverts* advertised that these costly production materials were new, they had in fact been built for an 1898–1899 production of *The Merchant of Venice* at Daly's Theatre, located at Thirtieth Street and Broadway—a provenance that arguably invested them with even more clout than if they had been created expressly for Adler (at least among the Anglo-bourgeois audiences who were mostly likely privy to Augustin Daly's oeuvre). In May 1903, the *New York Times* announced that "Jacob Adler, who has for many years been known as the great Yiddish tragedian of the Bowery, appeared as Shylock last night at the American Theatre, speaking his part in Yiddish, with an English-speaking support, and the magnificent production used four years ago by the late Augustin Daly." Using the present perfect to qualify Adler's prior reputation "as the great Yiddish tragedian of the Bowery," the *Times* implied that Adler's appearance in a scenic revival of the renowned and recently deceased impresario's "magnificent production" signaled a shift into new symbolic territory for the Yiddish-speaking actor. Philadelphia's *Jewish Exponent* likewise recognized the significance of the Daly scenery, reporting that Adler was to "be supplied with a scenic environment, the elaborateness of which has seldom, if ever, been equalled in this country. . . . [H]e has acquired all of the scenery, costumes and accessories used by the late Augustin Daly upon the occasion of his production of 'The Merchant of Venice' at Daly's

Theatre, New York, which has repeatedly been cited as the best example of the scenic artists' skill shown in America in recent years."[15] In other words, when Adler first stepped on stage with an English-speaking company, he crossed into one of the most iconic American Shakespeare scenes of his day. Indeed, it seems hardly coincidental that Hopkins's 1903 production paired Daly's legacy with Adler's mainstream-stage debut as its two primary selling points, as if to couch Adler's potential alienness to uptown theatregoers in the beloved Broadway director's signature style.

Daly was among the most powerful and popular figures in American Shakespeare culture when he died in June 1899. As Virginia Mason Vaughan has shown, the North Carolina native for whom "Shakespeare provided a gateway to the American dream of upward mobility and increased status" was indebted to, representative of, and in part responsible for the turn-of-the-twentieth-century shift by which Shakespeare became "a source of American cultural capital, and knowledge of his plays a mark of gentility" among dominant social groups. Throughout the late 1900s, Daly collaborated with the most visible Anglo-bourgeois figures in Victorian era U.S. Shakespeare theatre, including actor Edwin Booth and critic William Winter. In an 1895 article titled "Shakespeare at Daly's: A Long Series of Memorable Achievements," the *New York Tribune* lauded Daly's "ludicrously simple method . . . of doing things just as Shakespeare wrote them, instead of in some other way that somebody else fancied might be an improvement." In this sense, Daly's Shakespearean style hewed to the purist trend that Lawrence W. Levine and others associate with Shakespeare's late nineteenth-century transformation from popular into polite culture.[16] Given this, Adler's appearance as Shylock against the scenic backdrop that was used in Daly's 1898–1899 production of *The Merchant of Venice*, which ran six months prior to the actor-manager's death, symbolized Adler's assimilation into the upper crust of white American Shakespeare culture.

This symbolic assimilation surely registered for those playgoers and critics who attended Adler's 1903 performance having seen the Daly production in 1898–1899. Indeed, a trip to the Folger Shakespeare Library to view photographs of the two productions side by side yields a kind of experiential evidence for such historical speculation. Both sets of black-and-white photographs—eleven of Daly's production and thirteen of Adler's—were taken by the Byron Company, a leading New York studio that specialized in stage photography.[17] The images across both series thus rhyme stylistically

FIGURE 12 Photograph of Ada Rehan as Portia in Augustin Daly's 1898–1899 production of *The Merchant of Venice*. By permission of the Folger Shakespeare Library.

and feature like signatures penned in silver along their bottom margins. The costumes, set pieces, and painted scenery depict nearly identical stage worlds: the ship sails and domed buildings visible beyond the water-side Doge's palace; Bassanio's two-toned bloused sleeves and Antonio's horizontal-striped pantaloons; the elaborate frescoes and ornate molding along the walls and ceilings of the courtroom set; and the orientation of the courtroom columns, benches, and doorways (figs. 12, 13). Whereas press coverage by the likes of John Corbin and Brander Matthews revealed how ghosts of Anglo-American Shakespeareans past haunted Lower East Side venues and cast immigrant difference into relief for Anglo-bourgeois crit-ics, these photographs show how Hopkins resurrected the Daly materials to cloak Adler's immigrant difference in borrowed robes and set pieces. Hunched over a library table, studying the photographic evidence of these long-past productions, one experiences the Adler scenes as an eerie echo of the Daly images. Alongside the 1898–1899 photographs, the 1903 prints have

FIGURE 13   Photograph of Jacob Adler as Shylock in a 1903 revival of Augustin Daly's production of *The Merchant of Venice*. By permission of the Folger Shakespeare Library.

the quality of a palimpsest, where traces of the earlier production—traces both symbolic and material—can be felt even more than a century later.[18]

But Adler did not blend in entirely. He was the star of the show, after all, and his own costume differed considerably from that worn by actor Sidney Herbert as Shylock in the Daly performances. Whereas Herbert wore a simple black frock of a uniformly matte, dark fabric, Adler was costumed in what appears to have been an embellished vest and layered skirt of variously patterned, stiff satin. At first glance, then, the pomp of Adler's costume relative to Herbert's may be seen to have accentuated the Yiddish-speaking actor's difference. But such a conclusion results from faulty comparison, as Daly's Portia, played by the company's star actress Ada Rehan, is the more suitable analogue for Adler. Indeed, the luster of Adler's costume most closely resembles that of Rehan's attire, a resemblance in accord with the fact that Rehan, not Herbert, headlined the 1898–1899 performances. Examining the trial-scene photographs, for example, one sees how Rehan's courtroom robe, which appears to have been made of a heavy satin, stood out against the duller fabric of Herbert's belted coat. In the Adler production, the comparatively lesser-known actress Meta Maynard donned a plainer judge's robe as Portia, ensuring that all eyes would fall on Adler, whose lavish skirt-folds, enhanced by the stage light, must have swished impressively as he walked. The photographs' composition also re-creates the productions' respective publicity dynamics, wherein Rehan and Adler received more audience attention and critical acclaim than their surrounding casts. Four of the images in the Daly photograph set feature Portia's casket scenes, and four in the Adler set picture Shylock alone on a street by his home, mourning the loss of his money and his daughter. Further, in the respective trial scenes, the 1898–1899 camera angle focuses on Rehan while the 1903 angle favors Adler. Of course, Adler's Shylock could not have worn the same costume as Rehan's Portia, but his attire did assert equal grandeur and claimed comparable command of a stage that was outfitted in the best equipment any U.S. Shakespeare theatre had to offer.

In 1903, at a time when Shakespeare had something to do with "making good Americans" on the Lower East Side, when the phrase "American stage" seemingly stood in for any English-language theatre in uptown Manhattan, and when Augustin Daly had set the gold standard in New York for Shakespeare on the American stage, Adler's Broadway debut as Shylock launched him into a scenic melting pot where he was transformed into an American celebrity, on dominant culture's terms. At least, this was one way to see it.

THE JEW THAT SHAKESPEARE DREW

For some critics, the material significance of the venues, scenery, and costumes that framed Adler's Shylock did not equip the actor to fully transcend his immigrant difference. Namely, a cohort of self-identified Shakespeare aficionados, primarily those among the Anglo-bourgeoisie as opposed to those among the Lower East Side intelligentsia, gauged whether Adler's Jew of Venice accurately and stirringly staged what was long imagined by scholars and performers to be the playwright's ideal—an ideal often referenced by an eighteenth-century epithet attributed to Alexander Pope, "the Jew that Shakespeare drew." The *New York Times* critic who reviewed Adler's 1903 debut at the American Theatre, for instance, listed Shylock among the

Shakespearean figures who were "fixed, immutable" "symbols of life" that could not "be tampered or juggled with." The writer was therefore disappointed when Adler's performance deviated from this preconceived portrait of the character. "Mr. Adler takes this remarkable personage and brings him to the level of everyday life," the critic complained. "Shakespeare's characters . . . are great largely by reason of their universality, and the actors who have come nearest to realizing the full measure of their significance have been those who most nearly approximated the conditions of intellectual life which has enabled them to get into the heart of Shakespeare's mood and reproduce it by their technical mastery." In short, he continued, "Mr. Adler's Shylock . . . is not the representation of a type; it is the narrow presentment of one individual Jew, conceived upon the lines of a personal conception rather than upon the broad scale of the poet's universal conception." Other critics echoed this sentiment, although most found merit in Adler's performance even if it stood apart from an established Shakespearean ideal. The *New York Daily Mirror*, for instance, called Adler's Shylock "an artistic and dignified representation, whether or not it was 'the Jew that Shakespeare drew,'" and *Theatre*'s Henry Tyrrell, while an admirer of Adler's interpretation, charged that "[w]hether or not it be 'the Jew that Shakespeare drew,' is open to discussion."[19]

Drama critics also measured Adler's performance relative to a cadre of famous actors who had performed Shylock on the English-language stage throughout the nineteenth and early twentieth centuries. Leading English tragedian Edmund Kean and American celebrity Edwin Booth held chief acclaim as Shylock during the mid- to late 1800s, while American actor-manager Richard Mansfield's Shylock was significant in the early 1900s; but perhaps the most proximate and influential performance for Adler was that of British luminary Sir Henry Irving, who introduced a uniquely sympathetic Shylock to the stage in the 1880s, delivering "the definitive English-language performance of the role for well over a generation," according to theatre historian Harley Erdman.[20] Many critics mentioned these other Shylocks when discussing Adler. *Forverts* critic Morris Vintshevski called Adler's Shylock "even higher than Irving's, for however great the latter may be, he can never sufficiently understand the Venetian Jewish merchant's pride . . . Adler's heart speaks where Irving's art paints." Lipsky remarked in the *Jewish Exponent*, "The limitations of Mr. Adler are not so vital as Irving's and his robustness not so imposing as

Mansfield's." Even Adler felt that "Irving is the greatest actor I have seen. . . .
But, strongly as I was impressed with the Englishman's Shylock, I felt all the
more conviction in my own conception of the Jew of Venice."[21]

But unlike Vinshevski, Lipsky, and Adler, who referenced Irving and
others only to situate Adler as a superlative Shylock, Anglo-bourgeois
reviewers often held Adler's performance *accountable* to previous interpretations. For instance, one *New York Times* critic wrote, "In attitude
and demeanor [Adler] was the Jewish money lender—dignified, but in
a manner that was matter-of-fact and unimaginative. The grim austerity
of Irving and the malignancy of Mansfield were alike absent." Along similar lines, the *New York Tribune's* announcement that Adler would play at
the American Theatre conveyed a somewhat smug reserve in remarking,
"[T]he Bowery tragedian, Jacob Adler, who has become more or less of a
fad, but is said to possess great, if crude, force in spite of that, will appear as
Shylock in 'The Merchant of Venice.' . . . It is said that his interpretation is
quite different from that of Sir Henry Irving."[22]

To be sure, Adler's portrayal of Shylock *was* a departure from previous performances. After all, he had first developed the role for the Lower
East Side's growing Jewish American community and, in turn, played to
that audience's artistic and cultural sensibilities. Joel Berkowitz aptly characterizes how the Yiddish-stage production, and Adler's performance in
particular, responded to its Lower East Side surroundings. Even more than
Henry Irving, who had popularized a sympathetic Shylock in the late nineteenth century, the Yiddish star embraced the tragic over the comic in *The
Merchant of Venice*. "[A]s problematic as Shylock is to a Jewish audience,"
Berkowitz explains, "a Jewish daughter abandoning her father and convert-
ing to Christianity is the stuff of tragedy, not comedy. After all, this was
the culture that produced Sholem Aleykhem's Tevye the Dairyman, who
went into mourning when a far more devoted daughter married a Gentile."
Indeed, after returning home to find Jessica gone, Adler "tore his garment
in a symbolic gesture of mourning" and sighed, "'oy, oy,' according to the
stage directions." Adler also restored unprecedented dignity to the Jewish
moneylender. To his daughter Stella, "Adler's Merchant, above all, was a
man of power." Recalling the end of the courtroom scene, she describes
how Adler threw back the Venetians who had forced him to the ground
and "slowly rose again—and to those watching, all Judaism rose with him.
Erect, with a backward glance of burning scorn for this court and its justice,

in the full pride of his race, he slowly left the hall." Putting this noble exit in context, Lulla Rosenfeld—Adler's granddaughter, his biographer, and the translator of his memoirs—explains, "At the People's Theatre, Adler's innovation was accepted without question. A murderous Jew lusting for blood would have aroused only the scorn of an audience that still remembered the pogroms of Russia."[23]

In mainstream theatres, however, Adler's innovation met with frequent question, and critics who doubted the Shakespearean authenticity of Adler's Shylock often faulted, whether implicitly or explicitly, the Yiddish-speaking star's immigrant difference. This reception may strike modern-day readers as counterintuitive given that Adler made his Broadway debut as Western drama's most famous stage Jew, a role that would seemingly absorb or at least suit Adler's perceived social alterity. However, in 1903, the popular image of Shylock's Jewishness had little to do with Adler's Jewishness, especially for non-Jewish spectators. Rather, Shylock's Jewishness was more analogous to and as definitively circumscribed as Hamlet's Hamlet-ness, that allegorical hoop through which "every eminent actor was bound to jump," as Alan Dale put it. Shylock, after all, was Shakespearean above all else, and as earlier chapters have shown, many Anglo-bourgeois critics viewed immigrant difference to be at odds with the Shakespearean tradition. "If [Adler] failed to command a place among the greatest interpreters of the part," a *Times* critic mused, "this was largely, no doubt, due to the fact that to make Shylock fully sympathetic to a Jewish audience is virtually impossible." In other words, for this reviewer, Adler's embodied Jewishness, and the embodied Jewishness of many who attended his performances, stood between the actor and Shakespeare's portrait of the Jew.[24] Whereas "Shylock the Jew" was fixed as a symbolic Shakespearean type, Adler's Jewishness was particular to New York's Lower East Side. Unable to square their conception of a universal Shylock with the local Yiddish star, some critics found that Adler's performance fell short.

Comparing a single newspaper's response to concurrent performances of Shylock further shows how cultural biases and racial ideologies conditioned some reviewers' reception of Adler. Take, for example, three *New York Times* headlines for reviews of *Merchant of Venice* productions staged in Manhattan during the spring of 1905. In late March of that year, Mansfield appeared as Shylock at the New Amsterdam Theatre on Forty-second Street between Seventh and Eighth Avenues. In May, Adler returned to the American Theatre as Shylock, and that same month, Antonio Maiori opened his season at the People's Theatre as Shylock. The *Times* reviewed these performances under the following headlines: "Mansfield's Shylock Is a Figure of Power: Actor's Lucid Portrayal Seen at New Amsterdam Theatre"; "The Yiddish Shylock of Jacob P. Adler: East Side Favorite Appears with Fawcett Company"; and "An Italian Shylock: Antonio Maiori Plays the Role at the People's Theatre." While the newspaper's coverage of Mansfield, a British–born actor-manager who built his successful career in the United States, occasioned a racially neutral headline (although, as a white American male, Mansfield certainly was a figure of power), the reviews of Adler and Maiori qualified the actors' Shylocks on racial terms. Although the words "Yiddish" and "Shylock" may *seem* more sensibly linked than the terms "Yiddish" and "Italian" given the first pair's shared association with Jewishness, these headlines show how "Yiddish" and "Italian" were in fact more kindred signifiers for Anglo-bourgeois critics writing in 1905. By appending "Yiddish" or "Italian" to "Shylock," the *Times* headlines betrayed an assumption that Adler and Maiori had somehow racialized a character who was otherwise racially unmarked.[25]

Further, by the *Times*'s estimate, Mansfield's performance was more *Shakespearean* than Adler's. Mansfield's Shylock was "in short, an individual Shylock—Mr. Mansfield's Shylock—which is by no means a reflection on its quality. The actor has evidently sought to represent, as he conceived him, the one particular Jew of Shakespeare." Recall that the *Times* criticized Adler's 1903 performance on the grounds that "Mr. Adler's Shylock . . . is not the representation of a type" but "the narrow presentment of one individual Jew, conceived upon the lines of a personal conception." In Adler's case, then—at least as a *Times* critic portrayed it in 1903—the actor's personal conception impeded his realization of Shakespeare's "universal conception," whereas Mansfield's individual conception represented the playwright's "one particular Jew." Of course, two years' time separated these reviews, but their direct comparison nonetheless invites the conclusion that Adler's impediment, so far as the *Times*'s theatre section was concerned, was not so much his personal conception of Shylock as his personal connection to Jewishness. The *Times* critic who reviewed Adler's 1905 appearance was more complimentary but likewise felt that Adler's conception of Shylock had missed the mark. "There is something almost grotesque about the Shylock of Jacob P. Adler," the writer began, "and, though it is reasonably certain that the Jew as he reveals him is not the Jew of whom Pope wrote the famous couplet, he is an interesting figure for all that, and one that will probably continue to win the favor of many discriminating theatregoers both in and out of the zone where Yiddish alone is spoken." In the spring of 1905, then, *Times* readers learned that Mansfield's (Anglo) Shylock was a "figure of power," and Adler's (non-Anglo) Shylock was an "almost grotesque" figure. Readers further gathered that Mansfield had ably represented Shakespeare's Jew, while Adler had failed to render the Jew that Shakespeare drew. At bottom, the 1905 *Times* reviewer, like the same paper's 1903 critic, could not reconcile Adler's Shylock with the Shakespearean character, however praiseworthy playgoers might deem his performance.[26]

Unsurprisingly, critics also pinned their criticism of Adler's Shylock on the *sound* of immigrant difference. As Berkowitz observes, "[T]he Yiddish dialogue of Adler's Shylock amid the English of the rest of the cast both challenged the actor's ability to make himself understood, and further underscored his character's Jewishness." Perhaps more so, the sound of Yiddish underscored *Adler's* Jewishness. (And to those who did not know the language, Adler's lines were merely sound, delivered with emphasis, emotion, and gesture that, combined with many spectators' knowledge of the play, ensured some measure of comprehension.) To be sure, many playgoers, Yiddish-speakers and non-Yiddish-speakers alike, found Adler's polyglot performance to be effective. But for some spectators, Adler's use of Yiddish proved so striking that even Shylock, one of Shakespeare's most iconic outsiders, sounded alien to their rigid conception of the part. In 1903, a *New York Times* critic complained that Adler's "colloquial patois" robbed "the lines of all semblance of blank verse, though enabl[ed] the actor to color his playing with many realistic touches that [we]re highly effective if not too closely analyzed and studied in connection with the original text." In 1905, a *New York Evening World* critic—who was generally complimentary of Adler's performance—expressed a similar sentiment more bluntly, calling Adler's Yiddish "a mixture of the Hebrew and German tongues that sounded like a sacrilege of Shakespeare." Thus, even critics who appreciated aspects of Adler's playing regretted his choice of language, faulting the sound of this "colloquial patois" for his failure to approximate "the original text"—or, put in stronger terms, for his sonic "sacrilege of Shakespeare." A *New York Tribune* critic, sounding an awful lot like a cranky William Winter, went so far as to deem all polyglot performance "unnatural and inartistic, and, although a display of impersonation can be made in it, every such performance is a bore. Mr. Adler gives a conventional, prosy performance of Shylock, presenting him as a turbulent, vociferous East Side Jew."[27] This last sentence captured in especially crass yet direct terms what arose as a theme across dissatisfied reviews of Adler's performance—namely, that Shakespeare's Shylock had for centuries attuned English-speaking playgoers to a sound of Jewishness that was altogether distinct from the sound of Jewishness that New Yorkers increasingly heard at the turn of the twentieth century: the Yiddish of East Side Jews.

SHYLOCK'S TYPE REVOLUTIONIZED

Whereas mainstream newspapers published mixed reviews of Adler's Shylock—many English-language reviews were considerably more positive than those cited above—the period's Anglo-Jewish and Yiddish newspapers, so far as I have found, unanimously praised the performance. For communities of old-immigrant Jews who by and large adopted an Anglo-American habitus and championed reform efforts that assimilated Eastern European immigrants to the same social milieu, Adler's move from the Yiddish-language to the English-language stage was a win. For new immigrant Jews on the Lower East Side, Adler's visibility before a broad public meant wider acceptance of Yiddish culture and language. For both groups, a Jewish actor's appearance as Shylock posed an opportunity to right the wrongs that the character had for centuries wreaked on cultural ideas about Jewishness. Across their reviews, Jewish American writers lauded Adler's innovative interpretation, declaring "a new Shylock," to quote a 1903 *Yidishe gazeten* review, or, "Shylock's Type Revolutionized," as critic M. Katz headlined a 1903 *Idishe velt* article.[28] Whereas the Daly scenery visually assimilated Adler into dominant U.S. Shakespeare culture, and the cohort of Anglo-bourgeois critics felt that Adler's performance did not assimilate to their idea of Shakespeare's Jew, Jewish American critics commended Adler for assimilating the popular image of Shylock to a new idea of Jewishness. Key to such praise, however, was the fact that this Jewishness, while new to the so-called American stage, was familiar to Jewish American spectators. Adler's interpretation of the role was originally conceived for a Yiddish-speaking demographic, and of course, many Jewish spectators were explicitly familiar with Adler's Shylock, having attended one (or more) of his frequent Lower East Side appearances, or read about his popular portrayal in Yiddish dailies or Anglo-Jewish weeklies (the latter of which covered the so-called Hebrew stage along with the "American" theatre scene). But even for Jewish New Yorkers who first heard of Adler's Shylock in the spring of 1903, the actor's offstage embodiment of Jewishness made his onstage performance all the more true.

While Adler's social difference was apparent and meaningful to these Jewish American audiences, then, they did not feel that it hindered his ability to render a true Shakespearean portrait. That is, they did not view the actor's Yiddishness as mutually exclusive with Shylock's Shakespearean-ness. Rather, Adler's performance revolutionized the "Shylock" category, imbuing it with new and improved meaning from within its bounds. An insightful writer for the *American Hebrew and Jewish Messenger*, New York's English-language Jewish weekly, put it this way: "Shylock, as Shakespeare must have conceived him, died with the performers instructed by him. Since then, the players of Shylock have put into the character the prejudices of their own time, varying from ridicule when Shylock was a comic character, to dislike, when he became a money-lender. The Shylock presented by Jacob P. Adler," he continued, "was 'the Jew that Shakespeare drew,' at least in outlines, which Mr. Adler filled in with great intelligence; it was the Jew which Shakespeare would have constructed had he known more of the details of Jewish life." Attuned, perhaps unconsciously, to the historical context and social agency that produce (and reproduce) Shylock's meaning, this reviewer's perspective anticipated Stuart Hall's theory of ideological struggle: "A particular ideological chain becomes a site of struggle," writes Hall, "not only when people try to displace, rupture or contest it by supplanting it with some wholly new alternative set of terms, but also when they interrupt the ideological field and try to transform its meaning by changing or re-articulating its associations." He goes on, "Often, ideological struggle actually consists of attempting to win some new set of meanings for an existing term or category."[29] For the *American Hebrew* reviewer, then, Adler at once inhabited, interrupted, and reconstituted the ideological terrain of Shylock, outlining a new set of associations and meanings for Shakespeare's Jew.

Titling the review "The True Shakespeare's Jew," this *American Hebrew* writer conveyed that Shylock at his truest was precisely *not* a "fixed, immutable" "symbol of life." A true Shylock yielded to historically and geographically specific cultural forces. A true Shylock was locally relevant rather than universally applicable. A true Shylock performed Jewishness in a manner that resonated with turn-of-the-twentieth-century Jewish American audiences. "Mr. Adler has revived the Jewish Shylock," the same critic stated. "He takes a place in the synagogue; not among the nobility, but among these who are typical." Whereas the *New York Times* faulted Adler for failing to "represent a type," the *American Hebrew* praised his portrayal of a typical modern Jew. Similarly, an *Idishe velt* article published the April prior to Adler's May 1903 tour claimed that Adler "puts into Shylock all the power of the Jewish diaspora, of Jewish suffering, and of the emotions that this suffering elicits. And he can do this better than a Christian actor because he is a member of that persecuted, subjugated race." Quoting the better part of Shylock's "Hath not a Jew eyes?" speech in Yiddish translation, the article resolved, "No, this cannot issue as it should from a Christian mouth. To groan like this, one has to have a Jewish heart. For such despairing feelings, one has to have a Jewish soul, and such gnashing—Jewish teeth. This is why Mr. Adler's appearance as Shylock on the American stage for Christians is most important." Katz, writing for *Di Idishe velt* the following month, also felt that Adler had revolutionized Shylock's type by portraying a Jew true to nature. "This is not one of those picturesque marble-figure carvings with classically polished scenes, which impresses the eyes, and sends the head into extreme reflection, but which speaks little to one's heart and in which we, the spectators, see more artifice than nature," he advised. "No. In Adler's Shylock there are very few classically-realized character-scenes. He gives us more nature than art or put correctly, more nature in the art."[30] For Katz, Adler's Shylock was not a motionless marble figure or predetermined portrait; his Shakespearean Jew was fluid, more true to lived expression than to a dramatic ideal.

Along with Adler's innovative representation *of* Shylock, Jewish American critics celebrated what this new Shylock represented *to* the American public. In a 1903 review headlined "Shylock the Jew: Jacob Adler Astounds America with a New Character of Shakespeare's Jew," a *Yidishe gazeten* writer declared that "[t]he English world, which is used to seeing in Shakespeare's Shylock an ugly, hateful person, a usurer who wants the flesh of the man who borrows money from him, is now astounded by a new translation of Shakespeare's drama and a new presentation of Shakespeare's Jew." Focused on how definitively Adler's performance had reshaped the wider public's understanding of Shylock, this critic went so far as to summarize the English-language press's response by way of prosopopoeia (a rhetorical device whereby the speaker assumes the voice of an absent other), writing, "'We are used to believing'—now cry all the English newspapers—that Shylock represents the ugly characteristic of the Jews. We are used to seeing him from the horrible side and it is a conventional idea that Shakespeare hated Jews. Mr. Adler has shown us our mistake." The implication, here—conveyed most overtly in the phrase, "We are used to believing . . . that Shylock represents the ugly characteristic of the Jews"—was that conventional American understandings of Shylock had conditioned not only expectations for actors in the role but also public perceptions of Jewishness and, further, that Adler's performance had undone certain negative perceptions. Communicating a similar sentiment, the *Jewish Exponent* reported in 1903 that "Mr. Adler's characterization of Shakespeare's Jew . . . presented Shylock in a new phase, and it afforded the public an opportunity of seeing the role enacted by a Jew in a language which is the only one known to millions of Jews throughout the world."[31] Surrounded by the Daly scenery, in a role encrusted with centuries-old ideas about what Shakespeare and Jewishness should look like on the English-language stage, Adler went beyond winning a new set of meanings for Shylock and interrupted the ideological field of racial difference itself.

While both abovementioned writers used the word "seeing" (i.e., "we are used to seeing him" and "an opportunity of seeing the role"), the *Jewish Exponent* review also underscores the aural effects of Adler's performance: his Shylock changed how Shakespeare's Jew sounded on the English-language stage. The reviewer elaborated on this sonic effect, writing:

> [I]t was a language which many of those who had heard it in the past had deemed harsh and raucous, but which seemed, as uttered by this actor, replete with gentle cadences and harmonies. It did not obtrude itself grotesquely, as many had feared it would, into the immortal English of Shakespeare, but proved a telling vindication of a language which is not only the mother tongue of great numbers of people, but which contains many gems of literature, both poetry and prose. That its use was not a mistake last evening was again and again attested throughout the play by the applause and enthusiasm with which the star was greeted.[32]

Katz expressed a similar observation in his *Idishe velt* review. "Most wonderful of all," he wrote of the performance, "is the Yiddish language, when it melts together with the English. At first glance it can seem that it must result in ridiculousness, when the surrounding speakers give their cues in English and the main role interrupts with Yiddish. But remarkably, one doesn't even feel a hair's worth of discomfort from the difference in the languages." These reviews re-create an aural arena where the intersection, or "melting together," of Yiddish and English produced an unexpectedly effective Shakespearean soundscape. Although both critics reported that Adler's Yiddish had not "obtruded into" or "interrupted" Shakespeare's English as many predicted it might, his performance, at least by their accounts, did interrupt conventional ideologies about the sound of Jewishness in turn-of-the-twentieth-century U.S. cities. Such records of Adler's positive reception suggest that many who previously found Yiddish "harsh and raucous," for instance, may have gained an appreciation for the language's "gentle cadences and harmonies" in viewing Adler's performance.[33] What is more, listeners who formerly associated Yiddish with New York's East Side may have left *The Merchant of Venice* having forged new associations between Yiddish and Shakespearean verse, which in turn would have encouraged a transitive link between the East Side and Shakespeare, overriding the ideological barrier that many Americans—Yiddish newspaper writers, Lipsky, Tyrrell, and even Adler himself—perceived between these two cultural spaces.

Indeed, Jewish American reception illuminates with particular clarity how Adler's debut on the so-called American stage, in a production designed by none other than Augustin Daly, was not so much an entry into normative U.S. Shakespeare culture as it was an interruption of this tradition. The Folger's Adler photographs may eerily echo the Daly images, but their resonance is uncanny, resounding with the radical as well as the familiar qualities of Adler's Shylock.[34] Elaborating on how ideas about race take shape, Hall writes, "Meaning is not a transparent reflection of the world in language but arises through the differences between the terms and categories, the systems of reference, which classify out the world and allow it to be in this way appropriated into social thought, common sense."[35] Ideological formations are restructured, then, and terms are invested with new social meaning when historical actors dispute or disaffirm differences between cultural categories or create new points of association between them. In the case of Adler's Shylock, widely perceived differences between "immigrant" and "Shakespeare," or "Yiddish theatre" and "American stage," or "East Side audience" and "American audience"—which not only categorized what, where, and for whom actors performed in the United States around 1900 but also implicated ideas about identity, race, class, and national belonging—lost ground when a Yiddish-speaking New Yorker performed Shakespeare for combined Anglo- and non-Anglo-identified audiences, in venues that mainstream discourse classified as "American." (Plus, Adler twice appeared in a venue literally named the American Theatre!)

Such a reading of Adler's Shylock recalls Angela G. Ray's analysis of Frederick Douglass's late nineteenth-century lyceum lectures, in which Douglass "rhetorically accepted premises long familiar to lyceum participants . . . and then adapted them to correspond to the lived experience of black Americans, changing the foundation of these premises in the process." Like Douglass, Adler stepped into a space and a role long familiar to white American theatregoers and adapted the figure of Shylock to correspond to the lived experience of Yiddish-speaking Americans, changing the meaning of the American stage and redrawing Shakespeare's Jew in the process. Also like Douglass, Adler's "exertions in redefining hegemonic concepts . . . disturbed the idea of these concepts as immutable." Finally, Adler's Shylock undermined beliefs that certain cultural categories were mutually exclusive (i.e., "American stage" and "immigrant") and, moreover, challenged the presumed uniformity of such categories by showing that empirical differences—in language, birthplace, neighborhood residence, and so on—could thrive *within* them.[36] In other words, Adler's performances insisted that such categories need not index some homogeneous ideal of U.S. culture but could instead reference a dynamic mode of national belonging that comprised difference rather than defending and/or defining itself against it.

A *New York Herald* review of Adler's 1905 appearance as Shylock at the American Theatre subtly reveals the actor's success in waging such ideological change: like many reviews of Adler, the piece begins with a summary rave: "That rare dramatic experience on Broadway—the coincidence of a great actor and a great play—was provided at the American Theatre last night in the appearance there of Mr. Jacob P. Adler, a well known Yiddish actor, as Shylock in 'The Merchant of Venice.'"[37] But while seemingly customary if high praise, this sentence in fact demonstrates a shift in popular perspective between 1903, when Adler debuted Shylock on Broadway, and 1905, when he returned to the American Theatre in the same role. Significantly, the *Herald* writer specified that the "rare dramatic experience on Broadway" was "the coincidence of a great actor and a great play," not the spectacle of a Yiddish-speaking actor on an English-language stage, as it had been for so many critics—non-Jewish and Jewish alike—two years prior.

THE PROFIT OF THE CITY CONSISTETH OF ALL NATIONS

Frederick Douglass "imagined a national identity transformed through incorporation of difference," writes Ray. Adler's Shylock helps us imagine something similar. Insofar as terms like "American stage" and "Shakespeare" carried connotations of national belonging, Adler's performances encouraged precisely such a transformation of national identity. Ray associates this type of transformation with philosopher John P. Pittman's concept of social assimilation, which involves shedding rather than conforming to the customs, behaviors, and beliefs of a powerful group, therein revising and broadening the terms of national identity and inclusion. My own associations call up W. T. Lhamon Jr.'s characterization of assimilation as a process of "combination and transaction" versus cultural substitution, "negotiated in a moving ratio that always retains traces of the previous identity."[38] While Daly's 1898–1899 production of *The Merchant of Venice* initially served to frame Adler's Shylock as his symbolic assimilation into dominant American Shakespeare culture, certain records of Daly's production can also point up the opposite: namely, that Adler's Shylock helped to form an American Shakespeare culture that incorporated rather than erased difference.

As a collector of theatre and Shakespeare memorabilia, Daly commissioned extra-illustrated copies of ten of his Shakespeare revivals—large folio albums, inlaid with souvenir acting editions, playbills, cast lists, watercolor portraits, photographs, costume design drawings, scene sketches, and newspaper clippings. The collection for his 1898–1899 *Merchant of Venice* production, which spans two volumes, is available for restricted viewing in the Folger Shakespeare Library. A specialist librarian accompanies it to the reading room and sets one of the hulking volumes atop doubly stacked foam wedges, where it towers above whatever other materials lie on the shared reader desks (in my case, Samuel Mencher's handwritten Yiddish translation of *Macbeth* and the playbill for Antonio Maiori's *Amleto*), just as Daly himself towered over New York's Shakespeare scene. This added height demands that a researcher stand while handling the album, that she rise in respect toward it and therein tower along with it, drawing a degree of attention from fellow readers that befits such a supposedly significant artifact of American Shakespeare history.[39]

When I began to page through the first album, I expected to find yet more evidence of how New York's cultural elite perceived and promoted ideological differences between categories like "immigrant" and "Shakespeare." Daly's Broadway renown, his scholarly approach to Shakespearean drama, and his close association with Winter, who wrote the prefatory matter for Daly's *Merchant of Venice* acting edition, all pointed toward an Anglo-bourgeois perspective consistent with that of critics like John Corbin, Henry Tyrell, and the Hapgoods—one that held Shakespeare to be sacred ground, and Anglo-identified Americans its rightful property owners. The albums' extravagance also fed my preconceived notions. Each is several inches thick, with half goatskin binding, marbled paperboard, and the words "MERCHANT OF VENICE, SHAKESPEARE ... AS PRODUCED AT DALY'S THEATRE N.Y., 1898" stamped in gold along its embossed leather spine.[40] Indeed, Anglo-Shakespearean ghosts haunt the first album's opening pages, as a stage history of *The Merchant of Venice* unfolds in portraits, sketches, photographs, and clippings. Rehan's Portia looks out from the inside cover, Daly claims the facing page, and Shakespeare himself commands page 2. A series of Shylocks follows: Richard Burbage, the first to play Shylock in Shakespeare's own company; late eighteenth-century British actor John Henderson; early nineteenth-century British tragedian Edmund Kean; and Anglo-American actor and theatre owner J. W. Wallack occupy pages 3–6.[41]

But page 7 introduces a plot twist into the visual narrative when Germany's Bogumil Dawison enters the scene ahead of early nineteenth-century American stars Edwin Loomis Davenport and Edwin Forrest. Several pages later, a woodcut captioned "Reception behind the Scenes" remembers the evening that Fon Chong Mai, a famous Chinese actor who performed with the Lower East Side's Choy Ting Quoy theatre company, attended Daly's *Merchant of Venice*, reportedly Mai's first-ever Shakespeare play, and met Rehan backstage following the performance. From here on out, a polyglot and multinational fleet of Shylocks and Portias takes shape—Adolf Sonnenthal, Ernst Possart, Philippe Garnier, Helena Modjeska. And there among them, rendered in watercolor, are Jacob Adler and, about seventy pages later, his wife, Sara Levitsky Adler. The album is a veritable lookbook of Shakespeare-themed border-crossings and cultural exchanges.[42]

The Adlers' portraits resemble dozens of others featured in the extra-illustrated edition. Painted by the relatively obscure late nineteenth-century artist Victor Moblard, the watercolor series captures actors costumed as Shylock or Portia, each portrait captioned by a handwritten note that indicates where, and sometimes when, a performance occurred, followed by a quoted line from the play. For example, Possart glowers in a gold-striped tunic, combing his long gray beard with his right hand and gripping a sleek wooden staff with his left over the words, "Ernst Possart as Shylock. (Munich &c New York) Shylock: How like a fawning publican he looks!" Garnier takes a wide stance in a heavy, red fur-trimmed coat, knife in his right hand and scale in his left, atop the text, "Mons. Garnier as Shylock. (Paris) Shylock: A sentence! Come, prepare." Jacob Adler, draped in a chartreuse robe that complements his feathery red curls, hunches over a knobbed walking stick above the phrase, "Herr Adler as Shylock. (New York 1890) Shylock: For three months,—well." And a bust of Sara Adler in a black judge's gown lined in red satin, sporting a neat black mortarboard, is captioned, "Mme. Adler as Portia. (New York 1890) Portia: Is your name Shylock?"[43] The portraits are vivid yet soft, with figures drawn in clear strokes and deep shades against smoky, mottled backgrounds (figs. 14, 15). According to the Folger's online catalog, the portraits' sources remain unknown, although they likely trace to earlier prints or photographs.

The sight of the Adlers in Daly's extra-illustrated edition prompts a double take. Press announcements, reviews, and advertisements, along with memoirs and history books, unanimously hail 1903 as the year in which Adler's Shylock exchanged the anonymity of the Bowery for the spotlight of the so-called American stage. But here in the Folger Reading Room, set into the brittle leaves of this commemorative volume, is hard evidence that Daly counted Adler among history's top roster of Shylocks four years earlier. What is more, Sara Adler's inclusion in the album means that these portraits reference a Yiddish-language production, staged at one of the Lower East Side venues where the Adlers routinely appeared together in starring roles during the 1890s. The American-made album thus captures a Shakespeare tradition where Yiddish-, German-, French-, and English-speaking companies are represented on equal terms—free of

FIGURE 14 Victor Moblard's watercolor portrait of Jacob Adler as Shylock. By permission of the Folger Shakespeare Library.

equivocation, geographic rhetoric (e.g., "Bowery" versus "uptown"), racial qualifiers, or divisive pronouns. Adler, Burbage, Dawison, Forrest, Garnier, Modjeska, Possart—all appear in like fashion in this material history of *The Merchant of Venice*. Without stating so directly, then, the Daly collection asserts that the meaning of Shakespeare's plays and characters at the turn of the twentieth century was not fixed or universal at all; rather, it was the fluid composite of an ever-growing set of local uses and interpretations.

Adler's Shylock, especially in the context of this extra-illustrated volume, keenly exemplifies how a "*repertoire* of embodied practice/knowledge (i.e., spoken language, dance, sports, ritual)" can live within and push against an "*archive* of supposedly enduring materials (i.e., texts, documents, buildings, bones)," to revisit Diana Taylor's concepts. The archive at hand consists of the Daly albums themselves, of course, but it also comprises the character roles that were doubly scripted by the physical inlaid *Merchant of*

FIGURE 15 Victor Moblard's watercolor portrait of Sara Levitsky Adler as Portia. By permission of the Folger Shakespeare Library.

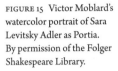

Venice play text and by the cultural traditions and expectations that attached to that text over time. Together, repertoire and archive account for the full Adler-as-Shylock *scenario,* in Taylor's sense of the italicized term: "a paradigmatic setup that relies on supposedly live participants, structured around a schematic plot, with an intended (though adaptable) end." Historical analysis that privileges scenarios over traditional forms like text or narrative is more apt to "draw from the repertoire as well as the archive," explains Taylor. "Whether it's a question of mimetic representation (an actor assuming a role) or of performativity, of social actors assuming socially regulated patterns of appropriate behavior, the scenario more fully allows us to keep both the social actor and the role in view simultaneously, and thus recognize the areas of resistance and tension." As we have seen, Adler's Shylock certainly underscores that to appear on the so-called American stage in any Shakespearean role around 1900—particularly such an ideologically freighted role as Shylock—was to perform both mimetic representation and socially regulated behavior. But this same historical scenario has also shown how appearances like Adler's enacted tension and change. As Taylor observes, "Social actors may be assigned roles deemed static and inflexible by some. Nonetheless, the irreconcilable friction between the social actors and the roles allows for degrees of critical detachment and cultural agency."[44]

The meaning of these roles—be they Shakespearean, or social, or both— is therefore always up for grabs. While certain voices deemed the categories of "Shylock" and "American stage" inflexible at the turn of the twentieth century, other voices—and bodies—begged to differ. Of course, that Daly presumed to chronicle these voices and bodies in an expensive, leather-bound collection further evidences the Anglo-bourgeoisie's presumed ownership of Shakespeare during this period; but the albums themselves nevertheless illustrate a deeply diverse New York stage scene wherein Shakespearean scenarios formed (and re-formed) by incorporating a repertoire of social difference.

POSTSCRIPT: HISTORICAL DOUBLE TAKES

The Adlers' watercolor portraits elicit a double take for a second reason as well: both Berkowitz and Lulla Adler Rosenfeld cite 1901 as the year Adler first performed Shylock with a Yiddish-speaking company. Berkowitz traces the inaugural performance to December 5, and newspapers from the period corroborate this date.[45] As early as November 10, 1901, *Dos abend blat* announced that Adler's "testimonial performance" would take place Thursday, December 5, and would feature, "for the first time on the Yiddish stage . . . 'Shylock, or the Merchant of Venice.' By William Shakespeare." Reviews in the *Forverts* and *Dos abend blat* from late December 1901 wonder at Adler's recent interpretation of Shylock, further supporting Berkowitz's and Rosenfeld's chronology.[46] Finally, English-language critics writing about Adler prior to 1901 emphasized his dramatic achievements in *The Jewish King Lear, Uriel Acosta*, and *Der Wilde Mensch* but did not mention *Shylock; or, The Merchant of Venice* (as the Yiddish-stage version was titled). Nor does Adler's memoir mention Shylock as a role that he took up during his early years in New York.[47] Yet penned on the Adlers' respective watercolor portraits in the extra-illustrated volume is "New York 1890." Granted, the faultiness of this date is simple enough to explain—Moblard's portraits do not trace to any particular playbill, photograph, or program and could have been mislabeled. But the Daly volume itself is stamped 1898, and records date its sale at auction (to Henry and Emily Folger) to 1900.[48] Adler's Shylock may not have been made to appear out of place relative to other actors pictured in Daly's commemorative volume, but the actor's portrait does strike a contemporary scholar of Yiddish theatre as out of place in time. Seen in the context of this extra-illustrated album, Adler's Shylock is not only a historical prism but also a historical puzzle.

For my purposes, the matter of this puzzle—that is, the archival discrepancy that the Daly volume brings to light—yields more historical insight than the date itself. For some historians of Yiddish theatre, however, and certainly for Adler's biographers, the precise date *is* meaningful: it plots a significant moment in Adler's career and in the development of the American Yiddish stage on a temporal continuum, and it positions that moment relative to other significant moments. Adler's appearance in the Daly extra-illustrated edition disrupts this timeline and therein topples one of the standard building blocks of historical investigation (and presumed historical truth)—the "when." Perhaps Adler experimented with *The Merchant of Venice* on the Yiddish stage prior to 1901, earning little notice from Lower East Siders but attracting attention from Daly, one of the city's foremost Shakespeare connoisseurs. Perhaps the Yiddish press's 1901 build-up of a never-before-seen *Merchant of Venice* was a strategic media ploy that drew large crowds and therefore cemented that year in public memory. The challenge that the Adlers' watercolor portraits pose to other historical records certainly invites such informed speculation in an effort to reclaim the "when." But remember, this book is more concerned with history's "hows" than its "whens." More significantly than revealing a questionable timeline, then, this discrepancy invites the reminder that archived materials are not data points; rather, they themselves are historical acts that do not so much report on the past as they do represent, or simply express, some aspect of it.[49] To be sure, they often express some aspect of the past very persuasively, leading historians to frame "what happened" in one way or another and claim that version as truth. As such, archives determine how we characterize earlier social realities, which in turn influences how we understand ourselves in the present. And so in order to better understand ourselves, we can approach old archives with new questions.

Such was my aim throughout *Here in This Island We Arrived*: to expand our knowledge of marginalized pasts by shifting from the common focus on Shakespeare as a source of cultural capital, authority, and/or resistance for Americans in the 1890s and early 1900s toward a slightly different focus on Shakespeare as an arena for social exchange—from the culture-shaping force of Shakespeare's words to the culture-making force of Shakespearean activity. For example, as I researched this final chapter, Daly's spectral role in Adler's 1903 *Merchant of Venice* performances (to the extent that the deceased director's influence and authority attached to the revived production) compelled my looking beyond conventional Yiddish-history archives—actors' papers, Yiddish newspapers, directors' memoirs, and so on—to seek new perspectives on Adler in the Folger Library's Daly collection. The pursuit of this Shakespearean social node led to another, unanticipated point of intersection between the uptown theatre world that Daly stood for and Adler's Lower East Side stage scene: Jacob and Sara Adler's inclusion in Daly's album of Shylocks and Portias, an improbable and problematic discovery by previous accounts of Yiddish stage history. This experience calls to mind a wise warning from performance scholar Gay Gibson Cima: "If [carefully preserved artifacts housed in well-organized archives] are not dislocated from their overdetermined status and remapped in new coordinates, they will not yield new insights."[50] And so here, in the supremely organized Folger Shakespeare Library, between the pages of the well-preserved extra-illustrated copy of Daly's 1898–1899 *Merchant of Venice*, I encountered a stark challenge to previously accepted theatre chronologies and a rich example of how alternative archives—combined with alternative repertoires of engaging well-worn archives—unveil alternative histories.

Conclusion

This Island's Mine

In January 1917, the U.S. Congress passed an act that banned immigration by individuals from most Asian countries, along with all individuals over age sixteen who could not demonstrate literacy in any language. Widely considered to be the most significant limitation on American entry up to that point, the impact of this 1917 legislation was trumped shortly thereafter by the 1921 Emergency Quota Act and the 1924 Johnson Reed Act, which further slashed U.S. immigration, especially for groups outside of northern and western Europe.

Of course, these unprecedented caps on immigration responded to the equally unprecedented wave of immigration that preceded them. Between 1880 and 1900, New York City's foreign-born population more than doubled, jumping from 478,670 to 1,270,080. By 1910, it reached 1,944,357. Although immigration numbers peaked around 1907, between 750,000 and just over 1 million immigrants entered the United States (most by way of Ellis Island) each year through 1914, when World War I broke out in Europe. In short, the Progressive Era was a period of singular demographic change in the country's urban settings. At the same time, American cities throbbed with industrial development, technological advancement, economic shifts, and socioeconomic rifts. Such a fast-changing U.S. landscape incited "ideological ambivalence at the core of the concept of Americanness," as Coppélia Kahn aptly puts it—ambivalence deeply rooted in matters of race and class.[1] Within the nation's policymaking spheres, by late

1916 this ambivalence had festered into anxiety that, along with economic and wartime considerations, led Congress to legally redraw the terms of national belonging.

The year 1916 also marked the three-hundredth anniversary of Shakespeare's death, which sparked an array of tributes around the world.[2] For New York's part, the city sustained a yearlong Shakespeare Tercentenary Celebration that encompassed thousands of commemorative events and culminated in a sweeping "community masque" titled *Caliban by the Yellow Sands*, written and directed by playwright Percy MacKaye. The spectacle premiered at the Stadium of the College of the City of New York, convening thirty speaking actors and more than two thousand chorus members, dancers, and artists from civic and ethnic groups across the city in an effort to fulfill "the desire . . . of democracy consistently to seek expression through a drama of and by the people," as MacKaye framed it. Translated into Yiddish, German, and Italian, the *Tempest*-inspired masque represented the theme "of Caliban attempting to learn the art of Prospero—'the slow education of mankind through the influence of cooperative art.'"[3] Given its occurrence at the close of the Progressive Era, its proximity to a period of radical immigration restriction, and its resonance with the four-hundredth Shakespeare anniversary celebrations that overlapped with my work on this book a century later, MacKaye's masque also offers a fitting culmination to *Here in This Island We Arrived*. Indeed, the masque beautifully figures how Shakespeare linked different social groups from around the city in a scene of social exchange.

That said, the masque is just as easily construed as an Anglo-American claim to Shakespeare. Close analysis of MacKaye's script alongside English-language press coverage of the masque and the event's official program booklet leads one to conclude, as Shakespeare scholar Thomas Cartelli has, that "MacKaye was selectively attempting to privilege and promote a construction of Shakespeare that was consistent with the paternalist ideology of his own caste." Or, as Kahn puts it, "Drawing from . . . a [Progressive reform] model inflected with the idea of Anglo-Saxon racial superiority, MacKaye call[ed] upon Shakespeare to resolve" the "ideological ambivalence at the core of the concept of Americanness."[4] Despite MacKaye's pluralistic ambitions, then, recorded accounts taken at face value reveal his masque to have been an Anglocentric cultural event—Cultural with a capital "C," where Culture may be understood to stand in for an idealized body of knowledge, obtained through exposure to (largely Western) art and literature, and generally associated with moral value and social advantage. Charles Sprague Smith, for one, drew on this sense of "Culture" in his vision that the People's Institute would bring unity to Manhattan's "world of culture" and its "world of labor." Unlike Shakespeare's Caliban, whose defiant assertion against Prospero (and by extension, against the unquestioned authority of Western thought that Prospero represented) inspires the title of this chapter—"This island's mine by Sycorax my mother"—MacKaye's Caliban reverently kneels at Prospero's feet in the masque's final stage directions; or, rather, at Shakespeare's feet, as the Bard himself appears as a surrogate to deliver Prospero's closing lines. Here, according to the event program, Caliban is surrounded by the thousands-strong ensemble, now arranged in "national groups" to represent the "Theatres of the World." An orchestra accompanies this last scene, finally transitioning into "strains of the national anthem, in which all the assembled Pageant, Participants [sic], and the Spectators in the audience join."⁵ The message is clear: as anxiety about foreign-born populations peaked among U.S. elites, Shakespeare made manifest the American melting pot in immigrant New York—at least, insofar as the program notes dictate—assimilating thousands of different social groups in a unison show of national belonging.

Imagining the lived rather than scripted experiences of the masque's participants and spectators, however, conjures a cultural encounter in a messier, everyday sense of the word "cultural."⁶ Thousands of individuals from across New York gathered in an actual arena to celebrate the three-hundredth anniversary of the famous playwright's death and, in the act of coming together, forged new associations between Shakespeare, race, and national belonging. For example, many spectators could not hear the English verse spoken from the stage, as Kahn points out, and others simply did not understand English well enough to follow aurally, hence the foreign-language translations of the production. Certainly, then, informal (and inform*ing*) side conversations took place among the "thousands of auditors" who, Kahn notes, "sat as far away as 'the distance of two city blocks.'" Moreover, hundreds of amateur performers—many recruited from settlement house clubs—participated in dance and choral interludes, likely inventing a step or fudging a cue from time to time. And despite "MacKaye's central role as *auteur*," which Kahn amply demonstrates, those in attendance from the Lower East Side Yiddish community doubtless felt personal pride and ownership over the event when they turned to page 2 of their programs and saw "Jacob P. Adler" listed fourth among the hundred-plus public figures appointed to the Tercentenary Celebration's Honorary Committee by Mayor John Purroy Mitchell (in company with fellow committee members Brander Matthews and Norman Hapgood, as well as Emma Sheridan Fry and Isabelle Dwight Sprague Smith—or "Mrs. Charles Sprague Smith," as the program put it—both of whom gained mention farther down the page).[7] All such scenarios suggest that, however tainted MacKaye's democratic intentions may have been by his Anglocentric nationalism and Prospero-like control over the masque's choreography, *Caliban by the Yellow Sands* nonetheless pulsed with unscripted performances. Indeed, the Shakespearean masque occasioned countless opportunities for New Yorkers to assert, in all manner of expressions, "This island's *ours*."

Introduction

1. "Dr. Joseph Adams, Authority on Bard: Head of Folger Shakespeare Library Dies—Wrote on Life and Work of Dramatist," *New York Times*, 11 November 1946, 26.

2. "About the Folger," Folger Shakespeare Library (website), accessed 3 March 2018, https://www.folger.edu/about.

3. James Waldo Fawcett, "Folger Library, Memorial to Shakespeare, Dedicated," *Washington Post*, 24 April 1932, 1.

4. Adams, "Shakespeare and American Culture," 418, 421; Painter, *History of White People*, 107; see "Ellis Island History: A Record Year for New Americans," The Statue of Liberty—Ellis Island Foundation (website), accessed 3 March 2018, https://www.libertyellisfounda tion.org/ellis-island-history/.

5. Adams, "Shakespeare and American Culture," 431–33, 428.

6. "Macbeth [manuscript], 1904/translated and arranged by Samuel Mencher," W.a.269, Folger Shakespeare Library, Washington, D.C. (hereafter cited as Folger Library). The Folger's catalog entry for the *Macbeth* manuscript indicates that the play was translated and arranged for a 1904 production at the Thalia Theatre in New York City. There is some ambiguity about the date on the manuscript itself, however, where the "4" in "1904" appears to be written atop another number, perhaps a "1" or a "2." While I have not located any other printed records of this production and therefore cannot confirm the year in which the translation was produced, Mencher's grandson, Judge Bruce S. Mencher, relayed that the manuscript is in his grandfather's hand and that the performance, according to two versions of his grandfather's memoirs, ran for a handful of nights at most, more likely closing after a preview performance; conversation with the author, 10 November 2014.

7. "Teatro Italiano ... Amleto Principi Danimarca [playbill]," 262733 PLAYBILL, Folger Library; "Two great Hamlets, Booth and Sonnenthal [graphic] / C. de Grimm," ART Vol. b2 no. 377, Folger Library.

8. We might view such historical scenarios as what Mary Louise Pratt calls *contact zones*, or "social spaces where cultures meet, clash, and grapple with each other, often in contexts of highly asymmetrical relations of power." Like Pratt, I aim to "foreground the interactive, improvisational dimensions" of such encounters. See Pratt, "Arts of the Contact Zone," 34; Pratt, *Imperial Eyes*, 7.

9. See Brown, "Uses of Shakespeare in America," 230–38; Gustafson, "Eloquent Shakespeare," 81–83; Shapiro, introduction to *Shakespeare in America*, xxvii; and Sturgess, *Shakespeare and the American Nation*, 191–98.

10. Huang, *Chinese Shakespeares*, 30.

11. Sorin, *Time for Building*, 70–71; Rosenwaike, *Population History*, 95; Haenni, *Immigrant Scene*, 4; Berkowitz, *Shakespeare on the American Yiddish Stage*, 4. Between 1890 and 1910, the city's foreign-born population more than tripled, from just under 650,000 to nearly 2 million, with the total population increasing from about 1.5 million to over 4.5 million; see "Total and Foreign-born Population: New York City, 1790–2000" (website), accessed 3 March 2018, https://www1.nyc .gov/assets/planning/download/pdf/data -maps/nyc-population/historical-population /1790-2000_nyc_total_foreign_birth.pdf.

12. Jacobson, *Whiteness of a Different Color*, 9, 11, 72, 137; Painter, *History of White People*, ix.

13. Levine, *Highbrow/Lowbrow*, esp. chap. 1.

14. "The Drama: Herr Sonnenthal as Hamlet," *New York Tribune*, 20 March 1885, 5.

15. See Levine, *Highbrow/Lowbrow*, esp. chap. 1; Shattuck, *Shakespeare on the American Stage*; Vaughan and Vaughan, *Shakespeare in America*; Sturgess, *Shakespeare and the*

American Nation; Cartelli, *Repositioning Shakespeare*, esp. part 1; Kahn, Nathans, and Godfrey, *Shakespearean Educations*.

16. For example, see Antonio Maiori, "Italian Actor on 'Shylock': Antonio Maiori Thinks His Ideas Better than Adler's," *New York Times*, 28 May 1905, 22.

17. See Aleandri, *Italian-American Immigrant Theatre* (2006); Berkowitz, *Shakespeare on the American Yiddish Stage*; Carlson, *Italian Shakespearians*; Koegel, *Music in German Immigrant Theater*; Moon, *Yellowface*; and Williams, *1586–1914*.

18. Scobey, *Empire City*, 13, 21, 22 (quotation of Cooper).

19. Shattuck, *Shakespeare on the American Stage*, xiv; Haenni, *Immigrant Scene*, 18.

20. Kennedy, "Introduction," 16; Shakespeare, *Tempest*, 1.2.171.

21. Benedict Anderson characterizes nation-states as "imagined communities" in his landmark work, *Imagined Communities*. The study is premised on Anderson's conviction that "nationality, or, as one might prefer to put it in view of that word's multiple significations, nation-ness, as well as nationalism, are cultural artefacts of a particular kind. To understand them properly, we need to consider carefully how they have come into historical being, in what ways their meanings have changed over time, and why, today, they command such profound emotional legitimacy" (13–14).

22. Paolucci, preface to *Italian-American Immigrant Theatre*, ii; Dionne and Kapadia, "Introduction," 2–3.

23. Massai, "Defining Local Shakespeares," 6.

24. "What Does It Mean to Be American Now? We Went to Every State to Find Out," *Washington Post Online*, 18 January 2018; George F. Will, "Who's Worthy of Immigrating Here? We May Never Decide," *Washington Post Online*, 19 January 2018.

25. This approach is deeply informed by Angela G. Ray's definition of *rhetoric* as "the broad, neutral sense of symbolic action as culture-making practice." Summarizing Kenneth Burke's emphasis on the identificatory powers of rhetoric, Ray explains that "it is through the use of symbols that human beings represent themselves as selves, band together in groups, and create and destroy boundaries among

those groups. It is by rhetorical action that cultures are made." See Ray, *Lyceum and Public Culture*, 2.

26. Thompson, *Passing Strange*, 17.

27. Jackson, *Lines of Activity*, 201.

28. Taylor, *Archive and the Repertoire*, 19 (italics original).

29. Bill Clinton, foreword to *Shakespeare in America*, xviii.

30. "Public Works: About Public Works; Theater of, by, and for the People," The Public, accessed 2 April 2018, https://www.publicthe ater.org/Programs--Events/Public-Works/.

Chapter 1

1. "A Foreword," *Theatre*, May 1901, 1.

2. Smith, *Working with the People* (1904), xii; Lubove, *Progressives and the Slums*, 8–9, 261–62; L. S., "Twenty-Five Cent Shakespeare for the People," *Theatre*, July 1904, 179–80.

3. Spiegelberg, *Souvenir Book of the Fair*, 19, Educational Alliance Records, RG-312, folder 19, YIVO Institute for Jewish Research, New York, NY (hereafter cited as YIVO); "Brewing of the 'Tempest' in New York's Ghetto," *Theatre*, August 1904, 207–8.

4. "Brewing of the 'Tempest,'" 207–8.

5. Leviatin, "Introduction," 6.

6. For representative images, see Riis, *How the Other Half Lives*, ed. Dominguez, 53, 99, 262, 268.

7. Twigg, "Performative Dimension of Surveillance," 306.

8. "Structure of national feeling" refers to Raymond Williams's concept of "structures of feeling," the "social experiences in solution" that characterize and influence "human cultural activity" at a given historic moment as distinct from the "fixed forms" that are too often the object of historical analysis; see Williams, *Marxism and Literature*, 128–35, esp. 128, 133. See also Eric Lott's discussion of "structures of racial feeling" in *Love and Theft*, 6.

9. Pittenger, "World of Difference," 28; Riis, *How the Other Half Lives*, ed. Dominguez, 17.

10. Riis, *How the Other Half Lives*, ed. Dominguez, 17; Painter, *History of White People*, 107; Dominguez, "Editor's Epilogue and Author Biography," 245.

11. Here I have in mind Pierre Bourdieu's concept of *habitus*, summarized by Randal Johnson as a socially instilled "set of dispositions which generates practices and perceptions"; see Johnson, "Editor's Introduction," 4–6.

12. Dominguez, "Editor's Epilogue and Author Biography," 246.

13. Riis, *Making of an American*.

14. The metaphorical term "melting-pot" was made popular in the United States by British playwright Israel Zangwill's play *The Melting Pot*, which premiered in Washington, DC, in 1908. The tenor of this metaphor, that is, what Gary Gerstle calls the "central and enduring myth . . . that the United States was a divine land where individuals from every part of the world could leave behind their troubles, start life anew, and forge a proud, accomplished, and unified people," dates back to the early days of the Republic and intensified as the country grew increasingly diverse throughout the nineteenth century. See Gerstle, *American Crucible*, 3.

15. On Roosevelt's "civic nationalism," see Gerstle, *American Crucible*, 45, 53; Jacobson, *Whiteness of a Different Color*, 40, 12.

16. Ngai, "Race, Nation, and Citizenship," 123; Jacobson, *Whiteness of a Different Color*, 72, 176.

17. Kahn, "Caliban at the Stadium," 258.

18. Lubove, *Progressives and the Slums*, 50.

19. Jacobson, *Whiteness of a Different Color*, 43.

20. Bonfiglio, *Race and the Rise of Standard American*, 192.

21. For a characterization of national conditions leading into the Progressive Era, see Diner, *Different Age*, 14–29.

22. Haenni, *Immigrant Scene*, 3; Romeyn, 3–4.

23. Noting how Riis "ignit[ed], and just barely controll[ed], spectacular and potentially lethal bursts of artificial light" to "expos[e] and fram[e] the Other Half while straddling a society in the throes of transition," Leviatin emphasizes Riis's literal exposure of one source of this public anxiety; see Leviatin, "Introduction," 9.

24. Diner, *Different Age*, 6; Recchiuti, *Civic Engagement*, 67–68; Spiegelberg, *Souvenir*,

13–19; Minutes of the Education Alliance, "Regular Meeting of the Board of Directors," 2 November 1905, p. 10, in Educational Alliance Records, RG-312, box MK342, folder 3745, YIVO; Bliss and Binder, *New Encyclopedia of Social Reform*, 1108.

25. Mary Simkovitch cited in Recchiuti, *Civic Engagement*, 89; on the "ultimately untenable equilibrium between cultural autonomy and social assimilation," see Carson, *Settlement Folk*, 109; Wild, "Americanization Movement," 29–30. For more on settlement house activities, see also Davis, *Spearheads for Reform*, 40–60.

26. Hill, "Americanization Movement," 613–24.

27. Davis, *Spearheads for Reform*, 41; Hecht, "Social and Artistic Integration," 176; Carson, *Settlement Folk*, 116.

28. Chansky, *Composing Ourselves*, 52; "People's Institute Plays: Sixteen Hundred Girls Enjoy 'Merchant of Venice'—Appreciative Letter," *New York Tribune*, 22 May 1904, A4; "To Give the 'Tempest': A Whole Neighborhood Absorbed in the Work of Production," *New York Tribune*, 28 February 1904, A4; "Shakespeare on the East Side: Several Nationalities Represented in 'Taming of the Shrew,'" *New York Tribune*, 22 May 1904, A5; Ben Greet, "Shakespeare and the Modern Theatre," *Harper's Weekly*, 11 November 1904, 1605; Kahn and Nathans, introduction to *Shakespearean Educations*, 22; Hecht, "Social and Artistic Integration," 175.

29. Bliss and Binder, "Smith, Charles Sprague," in *Encyclopedia of Social Reform*, 1125.

30. Smith, *Working with the People* (1904), 13.

31. Smith, *Working with the People* (1904), 1–2.

32. Smith, *Working with the People* (1904), 11, 62, 14, 11, xiv–xv.

33. Lecture Programs, The People's Institute Records, 1883–1933, Series III: Cooper Union Activities, 1897–1926, box 9, folder 3: "Lectures: 1897–1926," New York Public Library Manuscripts and Archive Division, New York (hereafter cited as NYPL).

34. Charles Sprague Smith, "A Theatre for the People and the Public Schools," *Charities*, 4 February 1905, 427.

35. "Drama Banished from Cooper Union," *New York Times*, 6 January 1905, 16.

36. Letter from Charles Sprague Smith to unnamed associate, 16 February 1905, in the People's Institute Records, 1883–1933, Series VIII: Drama Department, 1905–1918, box 14, folder 2: "General Correspondence: 1905–1911," NYPL.

37. "What Is the People's Institute?: Its Work Explained," *New York Times*, 22 April 1906, SM4.

38. For Smith's frequent use of the word "experiment," see Smith, *Working with the People* (1904), 36, 39, 42, 62, 80, 84, 106, 118, 131.

39. Smith, *Working with the People* (1908), 38.

40. "Shakespeare for the People's Institute: Ben Greet's Company Play 'The Merchant of Venice' at the Cooper Institute," *New York Times*, 14 May 1904, 6; "People's Institute Plays"; "Notes of the Stage: Mr. Greet to Play Shakespeare on the East Side," *New York Tribune*, 2 October 1905, 7; "Notes of the Stage: The People's Institute to See Mantell at Reduced Rates," *New York Tribune*, 11 December 1905, 9, "Give 'Romeo and Juliet,'" *New York Times*, 5 March 1905, 9.

41. L. S., "Twenty-Five Cent Shakespeare," 180.

42. L. S., "Twenty-Five Cent Shakespeare," 181; "Notes of the Stage: Mr. Greet to Play Shakespeare on the East Side"; "Good Drama: Cheap Seats: Movement to Introduce the Masses to the Best Plays," *New York Tribune*, 10 February 1907, B8.

43. Wilson, *Labor of Words*, 14–15, 39.

44. Schudson, *Discovering the News*, 68.

45. In his work *American Journalism*, Frank Luther Mott writes that the "intellectual plane" of the *New York Tribune* "was definitely higher than most of its competitors" and credits the *New York Times* as being "a high-class paper" that contributed to the decline of yellow journalism around 1900 (425, 549). Importantly, the *Tribune* and the *Times* resisted the sensationalist, picture-heavy style of yellow journalism popular at the turn of the century; as Mott explains, "[T]he yellow journal, with its pictures, sensation, and easy editorials, brought the immigrant more and more into the newspaper audience" in the early 1900s (598), whereas the *Times* and *Tribune* certainly invoked, and likely drew, a privileged readership.

46. For information on *Harper's Weekly*, see Henry Mills Alden, "Reminiscences of Fifty Years of 'Harper's Weekly': 1857–1907," *Harper's Weekly*, 5 January 1907, 8–12. Alden writes, "*Harper's Weekly* has never been merely a weekly newspaper. From its connection with the history of the country at its most critical moments it has had, more than any other journal of its class, the character of a national institution" (11). For circulation information on *Theatre*, which distributed more than 50,000 copies across the United States in the summer of 1904, see "A Word to Our Readers," *Theatre*, July 1904, 183(?).

47. Jackson, *Lines of Activity*, 7.

48. Spiegelberg, *Souvenir*, 25; "Brewing of the 'Tempest,'" 207; Herts, *Children's Educational Theatre*, 3–4.

49. Herts, *Children's Educational Theatre*, xi, 4–5.

50. Herts, *Children's Educational Theatre*, 113–21.

51. Speigelberg, *Souvenir*, 19; Minutes of the Education Alliance, "Regular Meeting of the Board of Directors," 8 May 1905, p. 5, in Educational Alliance Records, RG-312, box MK342, folder 3745, YIVO; Minutes of the Education Alliance, "Regular Meeting of the Board of Directors," 10 April 1905, p. 5.

52. Fisher, "Writing Immigrant Aid," 84; Minutes of the Education Alliance, "Regular Meeting of the Board of Directors," 8 May 1905, p. 3.

53. Herts, *Children's Educational Theatre*, 10, 27, 25.

54. Herts, *Children's Educational Theatre*, 24, 5.

55. Herts, *Children's Educational Theatre*, 59, 66–67, 150.

56. "Educational Value of Plays: Reproduction of Dramas Have Far Reaching Results on East Side," *New York Tribune*, 20 July 1904, 5.

57. Foreword to *Educational Theatre for Children and Young People*.

58. *Educational Theatre for Children and Young People*.

59. *Educational Theatre for Children and Young People*.

60. "To Give the 'Tempest'"; Shakespeare, *Tempest*, 2.2.162–63.

61. "To Give the 'Tempest.'"

62. Thompson, *Passing Strange*, 15, 130.

63. See Levine, *Highbrow/Lowbrow*; Vaughan and Vaughan, *Shakespeare in America*; Kahn, "Caliban at the Stadium," 265–84; Cartelli, *Repositioning Shakespeare*, esp. part 1; and Sturgess, *Shakespeare and the American Nation*.

64. Levine, *Highbrow/Lowbrow*, 38, 21–22, 23; Kahn and Nathans, introduction to *Shakespearean Educations*, 20, 21; Cooper, quoted in Levine, *Highbrow/Lowbrow*, 20; "Shakespeare: Dedication of the Statue in the Central Park," *New York Tribune*, 24 May 1872, 1.

65. Levine, *Highbrow/Lowbrow*, 56; Vaughan, "Shakespeare in the Gilded Age," 333; Kahn, "Caliban at the Stadium," 263; Scheil, *She Hath Been Reading*, 141n2, xi, xii.

66. "Sothern as Hamlet: A Vigorous and Dignified Interpretation of the Most Difficult Shakespearean Role," *New York Times*, 31 December 1902, 9; "The Drama: Ada Rehan as the Shrew," *New York Tribune*, 19 January 1904, 9; "Shakespeare for the People's Institute"; Levine, *Highbrow/Lowbrow*, 33.

67. Pierre Bourdieu, *Distinction*; Smith, "Contingencies of Value," 1–35; Taylor, *Reinventing Shakespeare*; Ray, *Lyceum and Public Culture*, 2.

68. Pollock, "Introduction: Making History Go," 8; Jackson, *Lines of Activity*, 247.

69. *Forverts*, 28 February 1905, 2; 26 March 1905, 2.

70. *Forverts*, 21 February 1905, 8; 28 February 1905, 8; 13 May 1905, 8.

71. "To Give the 'Tempest'"; L. S., "Twenty-Five Cent Shakespeare," 180; De Certeau, *Practice of Everyday Life*, 166.

72. "To Give the 'Tempest.'"

73. De Certeau, *Practice of Everyday Life*, 174.

74. J. Garfield Moses, "The Children's Theatre," *Charities and the Commons* 18, no. 1 (6 April 1907): 26.

75. Here I borrow the differentiation between reform efforts that "focus on exposure" and those that focus on "a deep engagement" from Thompson, *Passing Strange*, 140.

76. "Shakespeare for the People's Institute"; Smith, "Theatre for the People," 425; "People's Institute Plays"; and Smith, "Theatre for the People," 426–27; Greet, "Shakespeare and the Modern Theatre," 1604; Herts, *Children's Educational Theatre*, 5.

77. "Brewing of the 'Tempest,'" 208; "People's Institute to See Mantell"; Haenni, *Immigrant Scene*, 23.

78. Lhamon, *Raising Cain*, 108; Lhamon himself borrows the image of a "moving ratio" from anthropologist Paul Rainbow; see Lhamon, *Raising Cain*, 77.

79. See Koegel, *Music in German Immigrant Theater*, 117; Adler, *Life on the Stage*, 310; "The Timeline," The Thomashefskys: Music and Memories of a Life in the Yiddish Theatre (website), accessed 3 March 2018, http://www.thomashefsky.org/timeline.html; Kessler, "Reminiscences of the Yiddish Theatre," 41–43; "Dramatic Lion Discovered: Mrs. H. O. Havermeyer and Her Friends Have Found Him: His Name Is Maiori, and He Is an Italian Tragedian," *Boston Herald*, 31 August 1902, 6, in HTC Clippings 14, Newspaper Clippings: Persons in the Theater, ca. 1800–2010, Antonio Maiori, Harvard Theatre Collection, Cambridge, MA; Daniel Soyer, "Bertha Kalich," in *Jewish Women: A Comprehensive Historical Encyclopedia*, Jewish Women's Archive (website), accessed 3 March 2018, https://jwa.org/encyclopedia/article/kalich-bertha.

Chapter 2

1. "Thalia Theatre / Bowery near Canal Str. / Friday, the 5th of February 1892: / Guest Performance by / Josef Kainz / and / Gustav Kober. / "Hamlet" / Prince of Denmark. / Tragedy in five acts by William Shakespeare"; "Thalia Theatre 46–48 Bowery. / Madame Bertha Kalich / Wednesday evening 30 January / Comes a performance of / Shakespeare's famous drama / Hamlet"; "201 Bowery. People's Theatre, 201 Bowery / Monday evening, the 18th of November, 1901 / Through great effort and expense is presented / Shakespeare's undying tragedy, Mr. Thomashefsky's unparalleled success / Hamlet / The Prince of Denmark"; "Teatro Italiano / Guilia Hall 196 Grand Street. / Italian Comic-Dramatic

Company / A. Maiori and P. Rapone / This evening / Friday, August 30, exactly 8pm / Give you / Hamlet / Prince of Denmark / Tragedy in 6 acts by the immortal W. Shakespeare." Sources for these excerpts are as follows: "Josef Kainz und Gustav Kober: Hamlet," Bowery Theatre 1873–1897, bpf TCS 65, Playbills and programs from New York City theatres, ca. 1800–1930, Harvard Theatre Collection, Cambridge, MA (hereafter cited as Harvard Theatre Collection); "Hamlet: Madam Bertha Kalish als Hamlet," January 30, 189–(?), Yiddish theater placards / New York Yiddish theater placards, New York Public Library Digital Collections, Dorot Jewish Division (hereafter cited as NYPL Digital, Dorot), accessed 18 March 2018, http://digitalcollec tions.nypl.org/items/510d47db-1488-a3d9 -e040-e00a18064a99; "Hamlet, der prints fon Denemark," 18 November 1901, NYPL Digital, Dorot, accessed 18 March 2018, http://digital collections.nypl.org/items/510d47da-dc52 -a3d9-e040-e00a18064a99; "Teatro Italiano . . . Amleto Principi Danimarca [playbill]," New York: New York, c1901, Folger Shakespeare Library Digital Image Collection (hereafter cited as Folger Digital), accessed 18 March 2018, http://luna.folger.edu/luna/servlet /detail/FOLGERCM1~6~6~62155~104750 :Teatro-Italiano—Amleto-Princi.

2. Charles Sprague Smith used the phrase "intelligent use of the ballot" in Working with the People (1908), 1. Brander Matthews used the phrase "making good Americans" in a letter to Alice Minnie Herts, reprinted in Educational Theatre for Children and Young People (1908), n.p.

3. Haenni, Immigrant Scene, 97; Maffi, Gateway to the Promised Land, 8.

4. The image of assimilation as a "moving ratio" comes from Lhamon, Raising Cain, 108.

5. Maffi, Gateway to the Promised Land, 91; Haenni, Immigrant Scene, 97–98. Among Haenni's interlocutors are Emelise Aleandri, see "History" and Italian-American Immigrant Theatre (1999), and Nahma Sandrow, see Vagabond Stars.

6. Approaching nation-ness as a historically constructed cultural artifact, Benedict Anderson proceeds through a multistep analysis of the emergence of the modern conditions in which humans could "think" nationalism. Common language emerges in Anderson's work as a crucial mechanism by which power groups assert national identity. He argues that capitalism drove the print industry to consolidate vernacular languages across politically bound regions, "setting the stage" for imagined communities around shared language and the knowledge made available in that language. Whereas this mode of nation making demands common language, some of the community-building activities I address in this chapter occurred in multiple languages, as different immigrant groups connected and collaborated via Shakespeare theatre. See Anderson, Imagined Communities, 49.

7. Levine, Highbrow/Lowbrow, 255.

8. The best-known account of this shift is Levine's Highbrow/Lowbrow. See also Taylor, Reinventing Shakespeare, 193–204.

9. Levine, Highbrow/Lowbrow, 56, 29.

10. Chansky, Composing Ourselves, 8.

11. Levine, Highbrow/Lowbrow, 22–23.

12. Levine, Highbrow/Lowbrow, 33; Carlson, "Development of the American Theatre Program," 101–14.

13. "E. H. Sothern and Virginia Harned, special production of Hamlet," Library of Congress, Theatrical poster collection, Prints and Photographs Division, Washington, DC, POS-TH-1900.H35, no. 2 (hereafter cited as Library of Congress, Theatrical Poster Collection); "Rob't B. Mantell assisted by Miss Marie Booth Russell and a company of players in classic and romantic productions," Library of Congress, Theatrical poster collection, POS-TH-POR.M35, no. 1.

14. Levine, Highbrow/Lowbrow, 50–51.

15. Haenni, Immigrant Scene, 65–67; Aleandri, Italian-American Immigrant Theatre (2006), 181. For histories of the Yiddish theatre that detail tensions between "low" and "high" tastes, see Warnke, "Reforming the New York Yiddish Theatre; Berkowitz, Shakespeare on the American Yiddish Stage, esp. 14–17, 32–39; and Howe, World of Our Fathers, 460–96.

16. Haenni, Immigrant Scene, 65–72; "Freitag, den 27. Oktober 1899, und Samstag, den 28. Oktober, Matinee, zu ermäßigten Breisen: Othello," Irving Place Theatre, found in Institute Hall–Italian Opera House, bpf TCS

65, Playbills and programs from New York City theatres, ca. 1800–1930, Harvard Theatre Collection.

17. "Teatro Italiano . . . Amleto Principi Danimarca [playbill]," Folger Digital; Levine, *Highbrow/Lowbrow*, 22; Haenni, *Immigrant Scene*, 124.

18. "Hamlet: Madam Bertha Kalish als Hamlet," NYPL Digital, Dorot; "Hamlet, der prints fon Denmark," NYPL Digital, Dorot; Thomashefsky, *Mayn lebens-geshikte*, 296, 300.

19. As Berkowitz puts it, Yiddish theatre audiences consisted mainly of "recent immigrants from eastern Europe who, when Yiddish theatre began to be performed in the United States in the early 1880s, by and large knew little of Shakespeare and the three centuries' worth of cultural baggage his name carried"; Berkowitz, *Shakespeare on the American Yiddish Stage*, 1. Reflecting on his decision to translate and perform *Hamlet* in November 1893, Thomashefsky likewise explains, "The majority of the audience knew as much about Hamlet the prince of Denmark as a religious Jew knew of the taste of gentile delicacies. They thought that this was a new operetta"; see Thomashefsky, *Mayn lebens-geshikhte*, 298. However, Yiddish audiences were not necessarily ignorant of Shakespeare's work. The same autumn, a series of abridged Yiddish Shakespeare translations ran in *Di yidishe gazeten*, a popular New York–issued Yiddish-language daily, recurring more or less weekly through the winter of 1894. The inaugural entry in the series, printed about a month prior to Thomashefsky's debut of *Hamlet*, was "Der keniglikher yosem: Hamlet, prints fun Denmark" ("The Royal Orphan: Hamlet, Prince of Denmark"); see "Shekspir oysgepregilt," *Di yidishe gazeten*, 18 October 1893, 5.

20. For variations on this Yiddish theatre anecdote, see "Shakespeare's Very Last Appearance," *New York Sun*, 17 April 1904, 11; "Call for Shakespeare: New York Theatre Audience Wanted Author of 'Hamlet,'" *Baltimore Sun*, 12 May 1904, 9; "Shakespeare's Last Appearance on Any Stage," *San Francisco Chronicle*, 1 May 1904, 5; Howe, *World of Our Fathers*, 466; Berkowitz, *Shakespeare on the American Yiddish Stage*, 80; Ricciardi, quoted in Aleandri, "History of Italian-American Theatre: 1900–1905,"

26. Aleandri recounts the Italian theatre anecdote on 26–27.

21. Levine, *Highbrow/Lowbrow*, 23; de Certeau, *Practice of Everyday Life*, 166. See Sturgess's *Shakespeare and the American Nation* for an extended treatment of what he calls the "paradox" whereby early nineteenth-century Americans "declared . . . cultural independence" from England but nonetheless "embraced and consumed" Shakespeare (47).

22. Kahn and Nathans, introduction to *Shakespearean Educations*, 22.

23. Berkowitz, *Shakespeare on the American Yiddish Stage*, 2; "Der yudisher kenig Lier," 13 October 1898, NYPL Digital, Dorot, accessed 18 March 2018, http://digitalcollections .nypl.org/items/510d47db-1487-a3d9-e040 -e00a18064a99.

24. Berkowitz, *Shakespeare on the American Yiddish Stage*, 41.

25. Berkowitz, *Shakespeare on the American Yiddish Stage*, 41.

26. Gay, "Inventing a Yiddish Theater in America," 86–87.

27. Rhetorical scholars might also use the term "polysemy" to denote this manner in which a text, object, image, or act can convey two or more meanings at once. Leah Ceccarelli's concept of polysemy as "strategic ambiguity" seems especially apt. This form of polysemy, she explains, "result[s] in two or more otherwise conflicting groups of readers converging in praise of a text"; see Ceccarelli, "Polysemy," 395–415.

28. Taylor, *Archive and the Repertoire*, 49, 46.

29. See Berkowitz, *Shakespeare on the American Yiddish Stage*, 94, 42, 161; John Corbin, "Drama of the Bowery—A Yiddish 'Romeo and Juliet'—Ghetto Life on the Stage—Mr. Thomashefsky and His Company," *New York Times*, 26 April 1903, 25.

30. Thomashefsky, quoted in Berkowitz, *Shakespeare on the American Yiddish Stage*, 2; Heskes, "Music as Social History," 73; Bharucha, *Theatre and the World*, 244; Wolitz, "*Shulamis* and *Bar Kokhba*," 88.

31. Heskes, "Music as Social History," 80, 81.

32. "The Jewish King Lear," arr. H. Russotto, 1899, Hebraic Section, Yiddish Sheet Music, Box 1–33, Library of Congress,

Washington, DC, accessed 18 March 2018, http://lcweb2.loc.gov/diglib/ihas/loc.natlib.ihas.200154853.

33. Louis Friedsell and Bores Thomashefsky, "Prayer for the Dead," in the Yiddish Theatre Digital Archives, 2nd Avenue Archive, 2nd Avenue Online, accessed 18 March 2018, http://2ndave.nyu.edu/handle/123456789/13234. The YIVO Institute for Jewish Research Sound Archives also holds several recordings of Friedsell's *Kaddish* performed by actors other than Thomashefsky.

34. Maffi, *Gateway to the Promised Land*, 8.

35. "'Hamlet' im jüdischen Theater aufgeführt," *New York German Journal*, 31 January 1901, Bertha Kalich Papers, *T-Mss 1991–005, series VI, box 14, folder 1, Reviews and Clippings (1895–1904), Billy Rose Theater Division, New York Public Library for the Performing Arts (hereafter cited as Billy Rose); Alan Dale, "Bertha Kalisch, the Yiddish Favorite, Plays Hamlet," *New York Morning Journal*, 31 January 1901(?); Bertha Kalich Papers, *T-Mss 1991–005, series VI, box 14, folder 1, Reviews and Clippings (1895–1904), Billy Rose; Berkowitz, *Shakespeare on the American Yiddish Stage*, 102; "Hamlet in Thalia Theater: Madam Kalich in di hoipt-rol," *Forverts*, 15 December 1900, 2; *Hamlet*, prompt copy with handwritten finale, Bertha Kalich Papers, *T-Mss 1991–005, series IV, box 8, folder 8, Billy Rose; "Madame Kalisch as Hamlet," *New York Dramatic Mirror*, 9 February 1901, Bertha Kalich Papers, *T-Mss 1991–005, series VI, box 14, folder 1, Reviews and Clippings (1895–1904), Billy Rose; Carlson, *Speaking in Tongues*, 3. At another point in his study, Carlson details a 1998 production titled the *Secret History of the Lower East Side*, which he calls "a playful re-creation of a performance in one of [New York's immigrant] theatres which presupposed actors drawn from Italian, German, and Yiddish backgrounds working together to create a melodramatic spectacle in which each actor spoke his own language and acted in his own conventionalized style." Carlson goes on to claim that such a scenario would have been "unthinkable at that time," as the "languages of the surrounding communities were as unknown to the audiences of these theatres as their own language was to the stages of the majority population in

the city center" (*Speaking in Tongues*, 48–49). The examples studied herein, however, suggest otherwise.

36. Berkowitz, *Shakespeare on the American Yiddish Stage*, 29. Berkowitz notes that Yiddish translators worked from Russian Shakespeare editions as well.

37. *Di arbeyter tsaytung*, quoted in Berkowitz, *Shakespeare on the American Yiddish Stage*, 113.

38. Berkowitz, *Shakespeare on the American Yiddish Stage*, 77.

39. "Der eyntsiger Hamlet, Der eyntsiger Otelo," 11 June 189-(?), NYPL Digital, Dorot, accessed 3 March 2018, http://digitalcollections.nypl.org/items/510d47db-1486-a3d9-e040-e00a18064a99; "Our New York Letter," *Jewish Exponent*, 4 March 1904, 7; "The Drama," American Hebrew and Jewish Messenger, 15 April 1910, 640.

40. Berkowitz, *Shakespeare on the American Yiddish Stage*, 118. In addition to Morrison, German star Rudolph Schildkraut—who appeared in Max Reinhardt's 1905 production of *The Merchant of Venice* at the Berlin Deutsches Theater—performed Shylock in Yiddish for Lower East Side audiences in 1911; see Berkowitz, *Shakespeare on the American Yiddish Stage*, 184.

41. For a concise history of Shakespeare in Germany, see Williams, *1586–1914*.

42. Thomashefsky, *Mayn lebens-geshikhte*, 299; Koegel, *Music in German Immigrant Theater*, 11.

43. Aleandri, "History of Italian-American Theatre," 63; "People's Theatre, 201 Bowery, apposite [*sic*] Spring St.: One week only, Sig. Antonio Majori with his entire company [program]," ART Vol. e260, Folger Shakespeare Library, Washington, DC (hereafter cited as Folger Library); *L'Araldo Italiano*, quoted in Aleandri, "History of Italian-American Theatre," 63.

44. While it would be difficult to determine the precise motives behind Maiori's choice to address the editor of the *New York Times* on May 26 (his editorial was published two days later), it may be that he was posturing for the *Times*'s drama critics, who had reviewed Adler's performance on May 15 and would attend Maiori's on May 29, reviewing it in the

following day's newspaper; see "The Yiddish Shylock of Jacob P. Adler: East Side Favorite Appears with Fawcett Company," *New York Times*, 16 May 1905, 6; and "An Italian Shylock: Antonio Maiori Plays the Role at the People's Theatre," *New York Times*, 30 May 1905, 7.

45. Antonio Maiori, "Italian Actor on 'Shylock': Antonio Maiori Thinks His Ideas Better than Adler's," *New York Times*, 28 May 1905, 22.

46. Berkowitz, *Shakespeare on the American Yiddish Stage*, 118; Haenni, *Immigrant Scene*, 93, 101–3.

47. Courtney and Mercer, introduction to *Globalization of Shakespeare*, x; Peter Holland, foreword to *Globalization of Shakespeare*, iii; "Hamlet, der prints fon Denemark," NYPL Digital, Dorot.

48. "People's Theatre, 201 Bowery, apposite [*sic*] Spring St.," Folger Library; "Teatro Italiano . . . Amleto Principi Danimarca [playbill]," Folger Digital.

49. Aleandri, "History of Italian-American Theatre," 61; William Sartain, "'Hamlet' in Italian," *New York Times*, 23 March 1902, 6; Maud McDougall, "Brilliant Dramatic Star, Playing in an Unknown Italian Theater, Discovered by the Four Hundred," *Brooklyn Eagle*, 27 August 1902, 6, Antonio Maiori, HTC Clippings 14, Newspaper Clippings: Persons in the Theater, ca. 1800–2010, Harvard Theatre Collection; "Dramatic Lion Discovered: Mrs. H. O. Havemeyer and Her Friends Have Found Him," *Boston Sunday Herald*, 31 August 1902, Antonio Maiori, HTC Clippings 14, Newspaper Clippings: Persons in the Theater, ca. 1800–2010, Harvard Theatre Collection.

50. Aleandri, "History of Italian-American Theatre," 63; "People's Theatre, 201 Bowery, apposite [*sic*] Spring St.," Folger Library; McDougall, "Brilliant Dramatic Star." "Majori" is often seen as an alternate spelling of "Maiori."

51. Painter, *History of White People*, 107; Carlson, *Speaking in Tongues*, 3.

52. "The Jewish King Lear, by Jacob P. Adler and His Company," Programmes, Billy Rose.

53. "The Jewish King Lear," Billy Rose; "The City," *American Hebrew*, 3 May 1901, 716; "The Jewish King Lear: Yiddish Play to Be Presented for the Benefit of a Playground,"

New York Tribune, 29 April 1901, A10; "Local News in Town," *Jewish Messenger*, 26 April 1901, 9. The *American Hebrew* and the *Jewish Messenger* merged in 1903; see "Jewish Messenger, The," in *Jewish Encyclopedia: The Unedited Full-Text of the 1906 Jewish Encyclopedia* (website), accessed 18 March 2018, http://www.jewishencyclopedia.com/articles/8644-jewish-messenger-the.

54. "Der yudisher kenig Lier," NYPL Digital, Dorot; People's Theatre Advertisement, *Di arbeyter tsaytung*, 1 December 1901, 3.

55. "The Jewish King Lear," Billy Rose; "Federation of East Side Clubs," *New York Tribune*, 25 January 1902, 7; Jacob Riis, "Playgrounds for City Schools," *Century Magazine*, September 1894, 660.

56. Brander Matthews to Alice Minnie Herts, in *Educational Theatre for Children and Young People*.

57. "The Jewish King Lear: American Audience Acknowledges the Merit of the Play," *New York Times*, 26 May 1901, 19.

58. Levine, *Highbrow/Lowbrow*, 255, 243–44. Levine published *Highbrow/Lowbrow* at the dawn of the American culture wars that raged throughout the 1990s, which pitted progressive against conservative views and stirred controversies in the academy as to what should count as "canonical" literature—a historic moment that undoubtedly colored the somewhat black-and-white terms of his analysis.

59. "Jewish King Lear: American Audience Acknowledges the Merit," 19.

60. Berkowitz, *Shakespeare on the American Yiddish Stage*, 3; de Certeau, *Practice of Everyday Life*, 166. I use "Culture" with a capital "C" to signal the *idea* of culture that Raymond Williams aptly describes as "an abstraction and an absolute: an emergence which, in a very complex way, merges two general responses—first, the recognition of the practical separation of certain moral and intellectual activities from the driven impetus of a new kind of society; second, the emphasis of these activities, as a court of human appeal, to be set over the processes of practical social judgment and yet to offer itself as a mitigating and rallying alternative." Williams recognizes this idea of culture as "a complex and radical response to the new problems of social class"

in the nineteenth century and contrasts it to another sense of culture as "a whole way of life, not only as a scale of integrity, but as a mode of interpreting all our common experience, and, in this new interpretation, changing it." It is the reciprocally informing relationship between these two definitions of culture—the idea of "Culture" as "an abstraction and an absolute" and culture as "a whole way of life"—that I am concerned with here; see Williams, *Culture and Society, 1780–1950*, xvi.

61. Huang, *Chinese Shakespeares*, 5–6.

Chapter 3

1. John Corbin, "How the Other Half Laughs," *Harper's New Monthly Magazine*, December 1898, 30.

2. Fox and Lears, introduction to *Culture of Consumption*, x.

3. My approach, here, draws on Raymond Williams's work on cultural formation throughout *Marxism and Literature*, wherein he holds that a hegemonic, dominant perspective is always in "dynamic interrelation" with residual and emergent cultures (121). Hegemony, for Williams, can be understood as "a whole body of practices and expectations, over the whole of living. . . . It is a lived system of meanings and values—constitutive and constituting—which as they are experienced as practices appear as reciprocally confirming. It thus constitutes a sense of reality for most people in the society, a sense of absolute because experienced reality beyond which it is very difficult for most members of the society to move, in most areas of their lives. It is, that is to say, in the strongest sense a 'culture,' but a culture which has also to be seen as the lived dominance and subordination of particular classes" (110). However, "[i]n authentic historical analysis," he stipulates, "it is necessary at every point to recognize the complex interrelations between movements and tendencies both within and beyond a specific and effective dominance. It is necessary to examine how these relate to the whole cultural process rather than only to the selected and abstracted dominant system" (121).

4. Around 1900, William Randolph Hearst's *New York Journal* was the only one of these publications to practice so-called yellow journalism, a combination of sensational stories, large-print headlines, ample use of pictures, Sunday comics, and "more or less ostentatious sympathy with the 'underdog,'" as Frank Luther Mott puts it, "with campaigns against abuses suffered by the common people" (Mott, *American Journalism*, 539). This type of journalism addressed a more mixed audience, including new immigrants (598), than the respectable *New York Times*, *New York Sun*, and *New York Tribune*, which campaigned against yellow journalism (549). Yet the *Journal* had top circulation numbers, reaching its height at the turn of the century (539). It also employed British-born writer Alan Dale as its highly influential if controversial dramatic critic. Dale's tone and taste, while playful and welcoming of lower-brow entertainments, nonetheless implied, more often than not, a socially privileged Anglo-identified persona and audience. In fact, Dale's real name was Alfred J. Cohen, but the writer exchanged this bit of insight into his Jewish background for a pseudonym that referenced the character of Alan-a-Dale from the Anglo legend *Robin Hood* (Miller 70). I have thus included Dale's output in this chapter as representative of a bourgeois perspective, although his work no doubt reached readers in the lower classes as well as those in the middle and upper echelons of U.S. society. *Harper's* was among the leading "quality" magazines at the turn of the century, and *The Bookman: A Review of Books and Life*, primarily a literary magazine, reached a circulation of more than 40,000 by 1907 (Mott, *American Magazines*, 43, 436). *Forum* was an intellectually rigorous magazine that began as a weekly and shifted to a quarterly model in 1902 (511–18). The *New York Dramatic Mirror* was perhaps the leading theatre periodical at the turn of the century, and *Theatre* was established in 1900 as an illustrated monthly that Mott calls "quite the most ambitious attempt in American theatrical history to present adequate representation of the stage in a periodical" (260–61). See Mott, *American Journalism*; Miller, "Hearst Critic," 74; and Mott, *American Magazines*.

5. "Franklin Fyles Is Dead: Dramatic Critic of The Sun for Thirty Years and Playwright," *New York Times*, 5 July 1911, 11; Clark, "John

Corbin," v; Miller, *Bohemians and Critics*, 72; Hart, *Oxford Companion to American Literature*, s.v.v. "Norman Hapgood" and "Hutchins Hapgood."

6. My understanding that public address can produce group subjectivities is premised on rhetorical criticism's notion of "constitutive rhetoric," the development of which is perhaps most often attributed to Maurice Charland's essay, "Constitutive Rhetoric," 133–50.

7. Corbin, "How the Other Half Laughs," 30, 43; Epp, "Imprint of Affect," 55.

8. Levine, *Highbrow/Lowbrow*; Winter, *Shakespeare on the Stage*, 41–43.

9. Levine, *Highbrow/Lowbrow*, 78–79.

10. Henry Tyrrell, "The Drama," *Forum*, January 1904, 402; Winter, *Shakespeare on the Stage*, 1:44.

11. "Shakespeare and the Theatre," *Harper's Weekly*, 18 April 1903, 655; Alan Dale, "Miss Ada Rehan as Portia: Alan Dale Reviews 'The Merchant of Venice,'" *New York Journal*, 19 November 1898, "Scrapbooks of Alan Dale (i.e., Alfred J. Cohen) containing his dramatic criticism of plays performed in New York, 1891–1928," vol. 6, n.p., Folio CRT (Dale) (YCAL), the Beinecke Rare Book & Manuscript Library, Yale University, New Haven, CT (hereafter cited as Beinecke); "The Drama: Miss Crosman as Rosalind. Manhattan Theatre,'" *New York Tribune*, 8 September 1903, 9; John Corbin, "How Shakespeare Spells Ruin," *New York Times*, 7 February 1904, 26.

12. Keith Gandal, *Virtues of the Vicious*, 10. On Winter's career, see McGaw, "William Winter as Dramatic Critic," 121; and Miller, *Bohemians and Critics*, 98–99. On Dale's career, see Miller, "Hearst Critic," 74.

13. Winter, *Shakespeare on the Stage* 1:44; Alan Dale, "Some Dramatic Surprises," *Ainslee's*, January 1905, 150, Robinson Locke, "Collection of Dramatic Scrapbooks," vol. 140, p. 68; Billy Rose Theater Division, New York Public Library for the Performing Arts (hereafter cited as Billy Rose).

14. W. W., "The Drama: Signor Novelli as Macbeth," *New York Tribune*, 3 December 1907, 15 December 1907, 7; Alan Dale, "'Henry VIII,'" no publication title, 10 October 1892(?), "Scrapbooks of Alan Dale (i.e., Alfred J. Cohen) containing his dramatic criticism of

plays performed in New York, 1891–1928," vol. 1, n.p., Folio CRT (Dale) (YCAL), Beinecke.

15. "Yiddish Shylock Viewed from Ghetto Standpoint," *New York Times*, 31 May 1903, 10; Alan Dale, "Alan Dale Reviews Sothern's Portrayal of 'Hamlet,'" no publication title, 17 September 1900, "Scrapbooks of Alan Dale (i.e., Alfred J. Cohen) containing his dramatic criticism of plays performed in New York, 1891–1928," vol. 7, n.p., Folio CRT (Dale) (YCAL), Beinecke. According to Michael Pennington's *Hamlet: A User's Guide*, Dale's choice quotation can be traced to British writer Max Beerbohm (185).

16. Norman Hapgood, "The Foreign Stage in New York: II The German Theatre," *Bookman: A Review of Books and Life*, July 1900, 452, 454, 457–58; John Corbin, "A Clever German Character Comedian," *Harper's Weekly*, 13 January 1900, 42.

17. Haenni, *Immigrant Scene*, 60–61.

18. Corbin, "How the Other Half Laughs," 37; Hutchins Hapgood, "The Foreign Stage in New York: I The Yiddish Theatre," *Bookman: A Review of Books and Life*, June 1900, 348; "Development of the Hebrew Drama in America," *Washington Times*, 28 January 1906, 5.

19. On Yiddish playwrights' use of *daytshmerish*, see Sandrow, "Romanticism and the Yiddish Theatre," 50. To be clear, these ties between Yiddish and German theatre predated American Yiddish theatre. What is known as the "Jewish Enlightenment" began in eighteenth-century Germany when philosopher Moses Mendelssohn led a movement to reconcile "German culture with the traditions of Jewish learning." This movement spread to Eastern Russia, where advocates of Western scholarship and scientific advancement clashed with religious traditionalists. Abraham Goldfaden, widely regarded as the founder of the Yiddish theatre, was born into a family of Enlightenment thinkers. Further, in imperial Russia in the 1880s, when the deputy minister of internal affairs imposed a ban on all theatre performed in conversational Yiddish, Jewish troupes shrewdly sought police approval for plays spoken in "German Jewish," submitting Germanized play scripts that were ultimately (and subversively) performed in Yiddish. See Gay, "Inventing a Yiddish Theater in America,"

74; and Klier, "'Exit, Pursued by a Bear,'" 165–67.

20. Corbin, "How the Other Half Laughs," 46.

21. Corbin, "How the Other Half Laughs," 37, 35; Hutchins Hapgood, "The Foreign Stage in New York: III The Italian Theatre," *Bookman: A Review of Books and Life*, August 1900, 546; Jacobson, *Whiteness of a Different Color*, 41.

22. H. T., "Little Italy's Great Actor," *Theatre*, June 1902, 25.

23. John Corbin, "Shakspere [*sic*] in the Bowery," *Harper's Weekly*, 12 March 1898, 244.

24. Dorothy Chansky, *Composing Ourselves*, 54; Epp, "Imprint of Affect," 54; Kaplan, *Social Construction of American Realism*, 1.

25. See Dowling, *Slumming in New York*; Herring, *Queering the Underworld*; and Gandal, *Virtues of the Vicious*.

26. Haenni, "Visual and Theatrical Culture," 495, 496; Haenni, *Immigrant Scene*, 1; Gandal, *Virtues of the Vicious*, 13, 10.

27. Corbin, "How the Other Half Laughs," 30; Gandal, *Virtues of the Vicious*, 21.

28. Kaplan, *American Realism*, 1.

29. Corbin, "How the Other Half Laughs," 30.

30. Jackson, *Lines of Activity*, 24.

31. Ferrara, *Bowery*, 53–57.

32. Corbin, "How the Other Half Laughs," 45.

33. "Exit the 'Old Bowery': After Fifty Years of Citizenship It Becomes an Alien," *New York Sun*, 6 July 1879, 5.

34. Franklin Fyles, "Queer Gotham Playhouses and Their Players," *Washington Post*, 21 May 1905, R6; Brander Matthews, "Telescoping Time in the Bowery," *Bookman: A Review of Books and Life*, November/December 1919, 467.

35. MacDonald, "Acting Black," 236.

36. "Shakspeare Darkeyized—Macbeth in High Colors. From 'Doesticks: What He Says,'" *Spirit of the Times*, 11 August 1855, 303–4, quoted in Wolter, *Dawning of American Drama*, 147–51; "An Othello Without a Rival: The Astor-Place Tragedy Company at Steinway Hall," *New York Times*, 11 November 1885, 5.

37. Hill, *Shakespeare in Sable*, 77; Du Bois, *Souls of Black Folk*, 67.

38. Toll, *Blacking Up*, chap. 2, esp. 31–33. Studies of how blackface performance produced racial difference in the United States include Roediger, *Wages of Whiteness*; Lott, *Love and Theft*; and Rogin, *Blackface, White Noise*.

39. Levine, *Highbrow/Lowbrow*, 23, 14; Rice, "Otello: A Burlesque Opera," 110–58. Lhamon's analysis of *Otello* makes the compelling case that "every aspect" of Rice's adaptation "is heightened to call attention to and trouble [the period's] racism." However, whether or not one finds Lhamon's case persuasive, Rice's intentions could not control for audience reception, and Rice's Otello character is as comical as he is subversive. My own experience of seeing Matt Stone and Trey Parker's *Book of Mormon* at Chicago's Bank of America Theatre in 2013 convinced me that well-to-do white audiences with little investment in a production's comically subversive political undertones will nonetheless laugh heartily at bodies performing exaggerated blackness on a mainstream stage.

40. Jacobson, *Whiteness of a Different Color*, 12.

41. Jacobson, *Whiteness of a Different Color*, 72, 46; Topp, "Racial and Ethnic Identity," 67.

42. Jacobson, *Whiteness of a Different Color*, 9. In fact, literary theorist Walter Benn Michaels has shown how race still fuels any affective attachments we may invest in culture, despite contemporary claims that culture, commonly associated with ethnicity, displaced race in twentieth-century American discussions of identity. See Michaels, "Race into Culture," 655–85.

43. Jacob Riis, *How the Other Half Lives*, ed. Dominguez, 82, 39–40, 20; on Germans' being perceived as racially distinct from Anglo-Saxons, see Jacobson, *Whiteness of a Different Color*, 47.

44. Jacobson, *Whiteness of a Different Color*, 176; Goldstein, *Price of Whiteness*, 2, 41; Guglielmo, *White on Arrival*, 8–9. On the relationship between white identity and blackness-as-other, see Roediger, *Wages of Whiteness*; Lott, *Love and Theft*; and Rogin, *Blackface, White Noise*.

45. Jacobson, *Whiteness of a Different Color*, 41; Haenni, "Visual and Theatrical Culture," 519, 507.

46. "Yiddish Shylock Viewed from Ghetto Standpoint."

47. Corbin, "How the Other Half Laughs," 35; Haenni, "Visual and Theatrical Culture," 505, 504.

48. "Garrick" refers to David Garrick, the eighteenth-century British actor, manager, and producer whose Shakespeare performances were wildly popular and highly influential.

49. "'Othello' in Italian: 'Teatro Italiano' Opens Its Doors—A Large First Night Audience," *New York Sun*, 9 November 1897, 7; "'Otello' in the Bowery," *New York Tribune*, 27 November 1898, C19; "Classical and Romantic Drama in East Side Jargon," *New York Tribune*, 14 January 1900, B6; Alan Dale, "Bertha Kalisch, the Yiddish Favorite, Plays Hamlet," *New York Morning Journal*, 31 January 1901(?), Bertha Kalich Papers, *T-Mss 1991–005, series VI, box 14, folder 1, Reviews and Clippings (1895–1904), Billy Rose; "Petticoat Hamlet Invades the Bowery: Bertha Kalisch Acts the Dane at the Bowery and Excites East Side," *New York World*, 31 January 1901(?), Bertha Kalich Papers, *T-Mss 1991–005, series VI, box 14, folder 1, Reviews and Clippings (1895–1904), Billy Rose; "Jewish King Lear: American Audience Acknowledges the Merit," 19; "A Bowery Hamlet: Shakespearean Revival on the East Side—Maeterlink in Broken English," *New York Times*, 7 September 1902, 35; Henry Tyrrell, "Jacob Adler—The Bowery Garrick," *Theatre*, November 1902, 18–19; John Corbin, "Drama of the Bowery—A Yiddish 'Romeo and Juliet'—Ghetto Life on the Stage—Mr. Thomashefsky and His Company," *New York Times*, 26 April 1903; "An Italian Shylock: Antonio Maiori Plays the Role at the People's Theatre," *New York Times*, 30 May 1905, 7; "The German Shylock," *New York Times*, 29 December 1910, 9; "German Players in 'Julius Caesar,'" *New York Times*, 16 March 1916. "Kalisch" is often used as an alternate spelling of "Kalich."

50. "Repertory of Drama in Italian," *New York Times*, 1 June 1902, 30; Haenni, "Visual and Theatrical Culture," 496.

51. Corbin, "How the Other Half Laughs," 47; "At the Teatro Italiano: A Primitive Temple of Tragedy on the East Side," *New York Times*, 28 January 1900, 20.

52. Corbin, "How the Other Half Laughs," 35–36.

53. H. T., "Little Italy's Great Actor," 25.

54. Corbin, "Shakspere in the Bowery," 244; Corbin, "How the Other Half Laughs," 35; John Corbin, "Drama," *Harper's Weekly*, 18 March 1899, 261; Corbin, "Yiddish 'Romeo and Juliet.'"

55. Gandal, *Virtues of the Vicious*, 10; Corbin, "Yiddish 'Romeo and Juliet.'"

56. Dale, "Miss Ada Rehan as Portia"; "Shakespeare at the Garden: 'Macbeth,'" *New York Tribune*, 14 November 1905, 7; "Bowery Hamlet"; Corbin, "Shakspere in the Bowery"; Fyles, "Queer Gotham Playhouses and Their Players."

57. Romeyn, *Street Scenes*, xxi; Ono, "Borders That Travel," 31.

58. Theodore Roosevelt, quoted in Gerstle, *American Crucible*, 53.

59. Corbin, "Shakspere in the Bowery," 244; "Bonn in Role of Hamlet: An Interesting But on the Whole Disappointing Performance," *New York Times*, 2 January 1903, 9; "Live Topics About Town," *New York Sun*, 10 September 1896, 7; Dale, "Bertha Kalisch, the Yiddish Favorite." See Berkowitz, *Shakespeare on the American Yiddish Stage*, 102; "Hamlet in Thalia Theater: Madam Kalich in di hoipt-rol," *Forverts*.

60. "The Yiddish Theatres: Three Thriving Playhouses in the Jewish Quarter," *New York Sun*, 18 October 1896, 7; Corbin, "Shakspere in the Bowery," 244; Brooks and Kheshti, "Social Space of Sound," 334. In this *Theatre Survey* article, Brooks and Kheshti engage in a dialogue, moderated by Patrick Anderson.

61. Dale, "Bertha Kalisch, the Yiddish Favorite"; "Bonn in Role of Hamlet." Hamlet's hair color preoccupied Alan Dale as well, as he described Sarah Bernhardt's 1899 Hamlet as "wearing a fuzzy, Titian-tinted wig" and noted that Kalich wore "a long black wig" since the blonde hue of Bernhardt's Dane was "not popular in Division street." See Alan Dale, "Alan Dale Describes Sarah Bernhardt as Hamlet," no publication title, 1 June 1899(?), "Scrapbooks of

Alan Dale (i.e., Alfred J. Cohen) containing his dramatic criticism of plays performed in New York, 1891–1928," vol. 6, n.p., Folio CRT (Dale) (YCAL), Beinecke; and Dale, "Bertha Kalisch, the Yiddish Favorite."

62. "Italian Shylock: Antonio Maiori."

63. Jacobson, *Whiteness of a Different Color*, 173; Ono, "Borders That Travel," 30.

64. Corbin, "How the Other Half Laughs," 30, 31–32.

65. "Shakespeare in the Bowery: Original Italian Performance of 'Othello' Near Grand Street," *Washington Post*, 27 March 1898, 22; "'Otello' in the Bowery"; Corbin, "Shakspere in the Bowery," 244.

66. Levine, *Highbrow/Lowbrow*, esp. 76–78.

67. "Madame Kalisch as Hamlet," *New York Dramatic Mirror*, 9 February 1901; "Petticoat Hamlet"; "Shakespeare's Very Last Appearance," *New York Sun*, 11; "Call for Shakespeare: New York Theatre Audience Wanted Author of 'Hamlet,'" *Baltimore Sun*, 12 May 1904, 9; "Shakespeare's Last Appearance on Any Stage," *San Francisco Chronicle*, 1 May 1904, 5.

68. Gandal, *Virtues of the Vicious*, 10; "'The Merchant of Venice': Sothern as Shylock and Miss Marlowe as Portia," *New York Sun*, 31 October 1905, 7; Cooper, quoted in Levine, *Highbrow/Lowbrow*, 20.

69. Clark, "John Corbin," 244; W. W., "Drama: Signor Novelli as a Moor," 7.

70. W. W., "Signor Novelli as a Moor."

71. Hall, *Representation*, 258.

72. W. W., "Signor Novelli as a Moor"; "Novelli Visits Us Again," *New York Sun*, 3 December 1907, 7; "Bonn in Role of Hamlet"; "Madame Kalisch as Hamlet"; H. T., "Little Italy's Great Actor," 25; Hapgood, "Foreign Stage in New York: III," 549.

73. Jacobson, *Whiteness of a Different Color*, 41; Corbin, "How the Other Half Laughs," 35, 33; Guglielmo, *White on Arrival*, 8.

74. "'Othello' in Italian"; Jacobson, *Whiteness of a Different Color*, 72.

75. De Certeau, *Practice of Everyday Life*, 174.

Chapter 4

1. Berkowitz, *Shakespeare on the American Yiddish Stage*, 180. The title of this chapter is

a phrase spoken by Antonio in Shakespeare, *Merchant of Venice*, 3.3.30–31.

2. "The Yiddish Shylock: Jacob Adler and the Augustin Daly Production," *New York Times*, 26 May 1903, 9; "Der Nayer Shaylok," *Di yidishe gazeten*, 29 May 1903, 1, 16; Letter from Charles Sprague Smith to City Editor, 25 April 1905, the People's Institute Records, 1883–1933, Series VIII: Drama Dept. 1905–1918, box 14, folder 2: "Corres. 1905–09," Manuscripts and Archive Division, New York Public Library, New York, NY.

3. Adler, *Life on the Stage*, xxiv, 347; "A Yidishe Shaylok far Goyim," *Di idishe velt*, 27 April 1903, 4; Louis Lipsky, "Acting and Jacob P. Adler," *Jewish Exponent*, 8 May 1903, 7; Henry Tyrrell, "Jacob Adler—The Bowery Garrick," *Theatre*, November 1902, 18.

4. On Kalich, see, for example, Harrison Grey Fiske, "Mme. Kalich and the Brilliant Years," *New York Times*, 11 January 1931, 104. On Maiori, see, for example, "Topics of the Theatres: Fifth Avenue in Little Italy and Little Italy in Fifth Avenue," *New York Times*, 19 March 1903, 9; or "New York Stage and Stage Folk," *Baltimore Sun*, 22 February 1903, 7.

5. Riis, *How the Other Half Lives*, ed. Dominguez, 17.

6. For previous discussions of Adler's Shylock appearances, see Berkowitz, *Shakespeare on the American Yiddish Stage*, chap. 4; Berkowitz, "'True Jewish Jew'"; and Rosenfeld's commentary in Adler, *Life on the Stage*, 341–50; Zarefsky, "Presidential Rhetoric," 611.

7. To study an instance of public address as a multidimensional phenomenon, as I am suggesting here, rather than an isolated exchange between speaker/actor and audience is to take what Michael Calvin McGee calls a materialist approach to rhetoric; see McGee, "Materialist's Conception of Rhetoric," 23–48.

8. People's Theatre advertisement, *Dos abend blat*, 10 November 1901, 3; Berkowitz, *Shakespeare on the American Yiddish Stage*, 180; Adler, *Life on the Stage*, 342–44.

9. Tyrrell, "Jacob Adler," 18; Lipsky, "Acting and Jacob P. Adler"; "Der nayer Shaylok," 16.

10. Knowles, *Reading the Material Theatre*, 63.

11. See Knowles, *Reading the Material Theatre*, 79, citing Carlson, *Places of Performance*;

Bennett, *Theatre Audiences*, 127–29; Riis, *How the Other Half Lives*, ed. Dominguez, 17.

12. "A Yiddish Shylock: The Bowery Actor Jacob P. Adler Plays at an Uptown Theatre," *New York Sun*, 26 May 1903 (?); "Yiddish Shylock Viewed from Ghetto Standpoint," *New York Times*, 31 May 1903, 10.

13. Bertha Kalich also made her English-language-stage debut in 1905 at the American Theatre. See Fiske, "Mme. Kalich and the Brilliant Years."

14. "Adler in Shylock at Academy of Music," *Jewish Exponent*, 8 May 1903, 11; Columbia Theatre advertisement, *Forverts*, 15 May 1903, 3(?); "The Drama: Jacob Adler as Shylock, American Theatre," *New York Tribune*, 16 May 1905, 5.

15. "Yiddish Shylock: Jacob Adler"; "Adler in Shylock at Academy of Music."

16. Vaughan, "Shakespeare in the Gilded Age," 344, 333; "Shakespeare at Daly's: A Long Series of Memorable Achievements," *New York Tribune*, 3 March 1895, 14; Levine, *Highbrow/Lowbrow*, esp. chap. 1.

17. Robert R. Macdonald, foreword to *Gotham Comes of Age*, 7.

18. Photographs cataloged under "Merchant of Venice [graphic]: [11 photographs of Augustin Daly's production at the Daly Theatre, New York, 1898]/Byron, ART File D153.7m3 no.1–11 PHOTO, Folger Shakespeare Library, Washington D.C." (hereafter cited as Folger Library); and "[A production of] The Merchant of Venice [starring] Jacob P. Adler [graphic]/Byron, ART File A237 no.1–13 PHOTO," Folger Library. Images of these photographs are also available through the Folger's Digital Image Collection.

19. "Yiddish Shylock Viewed from Ghetto Standpoint"; *New York Daily Mirror*, quoted in Adler, *Life on the Stage*, 349; Tyrrell, "Jacob Adler," 19.

20. Erdman, *Staging the Jew*, 28.

21. Vinshevski, quoted in Berkowitz, *Shakespeare on the American Yiddish Stage*, 178; Lipsky, "Acting and Jacob P. Adler"; Adler, quoted in Tyrrell, "Jacob Adler," 19.

22. "Yiddish Shylock: Jacob Adler"; "Theatrical Incidents and News Notes: Oscar Hammerstein as a Prophet—Shakespeare by Bellew and Adler—Comforts of Coney," *New York Tribune*, 24 May 1903, A7.

23. Berkowitz, *Shakespeare on the American Yiddish Stage*, 176 and 177; Stella Adler, introduction to Adler, *Life on the Stage*, xiv; Rosenfeld's commentary in Adler, *Life on the Stage*, 345.

24. "Yiddish Shylock Viewed from Ghetto Standpoint"; Alan Dale, "Alan Dale Reviews Sothern's Portrayal of 'Hamlet,'" no publication title, 17 September 1900, "Scrapbooks of Alan Dale (i.e., Alfred J. Cohen) containing his dramatic criticism of plays performed in New York, 1891–1928," vol. 7, n.p., Folio CRT (Dale) (YCAL), the Beinecke Rare Book & Manuscript Library, Yale University, New Haven, CT; "Yiddish Shylock: Jacob Adler."

25. "Mansfield's Shylock Is a Figure of Power: Actor's Lucid Portrayal Seen at New Amsterdam Theatre," *New York Times*, 26 March 1905, 5; "The Yiddish Shylock of Jacob P. Adler: East Side Favorite Appears with Fawcett Company," *New York Times*, 16 May 1905, 6; "An Italian Shylock: Antonio Maiori Plays the Role at the People's Theatre," *New York Times*, 30 May 1905, 7.

26. "Mansfield's Shylock Is a Figure of Power"; "Yiddish Shylock Viewed from Ghetto Standpoint"; "Yiddish Shylock of Jacob P. Adler."

27. Berkowitz, *Shakespeare on the American Yiddish Stage*, 182; "Yiddish Shylock of Jacob P. Adler"; C. D., "Adler's Shylock Racially True: Jewish Tragedian's Conception of the Character Is Thoroughly Semitic, Plausible and Consistent," *Evening World's Home Magazine*, 16 May 1905, 13(?); "Shakespeare at the American: Mr. Adler as Shylock," *New York Tribune*, 26 May 1903, 9.

28. "Der nayer Shaylok"; M. Katz, "Shaylok's tip revolutsyionirt," *Di idishe velt*, 29 May 1903, 4.

29. L., "The True Shakespeare's Jew," *American Hebrew and Jewish Messenger*, 15 May 1903, 870; Hall, "Signification, Representation, Ideology," 112.

30. L., "True Shakespeare's Jew"; "Yiddish Shylock Viewed from Ghetto Standpoint"; "Yidishe Shaylok far Goyim"; Katz, "Shaylok's tip revolutsyionirt."

31. "Shaylok der yid: Jacob Adler iberasht Amerike mit a nayem kharakter fun Shekspir's yid," *Di yidishe gazeten*, 15 May 1903, 11; "Mr. Adler's Shylock: Commended by Press and Public as a Masterpiece of Characterization," *Jewish Exponent*, 15 May 1903, 7.

32. "Mr. Adler's Shylock."

33. Katz, "Shaylok's tip revolutzyionirt."

34. I apply the term "uncanny" with a light touch here, intending to cite the basic dynamic of Freud's definition—where the novel and the familiar coexist in a single image—without the grim effects (cognitive dissonance, fear, repulsion, etc.) that attend the term in its psychological context. See Freud, *Uncanny*.

35. Hall, "Signification, Representation, Ideology," 108.

36. Ray, *Lyceum*, 139, 141.

37. "Mr. Adler Scores in Shylock Role," *New York Herald*, 16 May 1905, 12.

38. Ray, *Lyceum*, 139, 114; Lhamon, *Raising Cain*, 108.

39. Extra-illustrated copy cataloged under "The Merchant of Venice/by William Shakspere [*sic*]; a comedy in five acts; as arranged for representation at Daly's Theatre by Augustin Daly; and there produced for the first time on Saturday, November 19th, 1898; with a few prefatory words by William Winter," ART vol. b26–27, Folger Library. For an informative discussion of the Daly extra-illustrated copies, see Erin Blake, "A Perfect Ten," The Collation: A Gathering of Scholarship from the Folger Shakespeare Library, 8 March 2013, accessed 18 March 2018, http://collation.folger.edu/2013/03/a-perfect-ten.

40. See description of extra-illustrated copy in online catalog record, accessed 18 March 2018, http://shakespeare.folger.edu/cgi-bin/Pwebrecon.cgi?BBID=302495.

41. Page numbers here refer to vol. 1 (cataloged as vol. b26).

42. Page numbers in vol. 1 (cataloged as vol. b26) for these actors' portraits are: Dawison, 7; Davenport, 8; Forrest, 9; Mai, n.p. (located between 21 and 22); Sonnenthal, 43; Possart, 60; Garnier, 126; Modjeska, 139; J. Adler, 64; S. Adler, 136.

43. Page numbers in vol. 1 (cataloged as vol. b26) for these actors' portraits are: Possart, 60; Garnier, 126; J. Adler, 64; S. Adler,

136. Incidentally, the line attributed to Sara Adler's Portia—"Is your name Shylock?"—is excerpted from Daly's slightly adapted version of *The Merchant of Venice*, which curiously substitutes this question for the more commonly seen: "Which is the merchant here? And which the Jew?" (4.1.173). In a late nineteenth-century "visual economy keyed not only to cues of skin color, but to facial angle, head size and shape, physiognomy, hair and eye color, and physique," Daly seemingly imagined that his Portia would have no trouble identifying the Jewish man in the courtroom. See "The merchant of Venice: a play in five acts/by William Shakespere [*sic*]; as re-arranged for the stage by Augustin Daly for production at Daly's Theatre; with a prefatory chapter by William Winter," 249112, Folger Library. On the new visual economy that developed in the latter half of the nineteenth century, see Jacobson, *Whiteness of a Different Color*, 46.

44. Taylor, *Archive and the Repertoire*, 19 ("repertoire" and "archive" italicized in the original), 13, 30, 29.

45. Berkowitz, *Shakespeare on the American Yiddish Stage*, 175; Rosenfeld's commentary in Adler, *Life on the Stage*, 342.

46. People's Theatre Advertisement, *Dos abend blat*; Kh. Aleksandrov, "Shaylok af der yidishe bine," *Dos abend blat*, 28 December 1901, 4; M. Vinshevski, "Shaylok: A yidisher yid," *Forverts*, 28 December 1901, 4.

47. See, for example, John Corbin's piece on Adler, "Drama," *Harper's Weekly*, 18 March 1899: 260–61; or Hutchins Hapgood's "The Foreign Stage in New York: I The Yiddish Theatre," *Bookman: A Review of Books and Life*, June 1900, 348. For Adler's reflections on his early years in New York, see Adler, *Life on the Stage*, 310–28. Marcus's *United States Jewry*, is one known outlier among the examples listed, citing 1893 as Adler's earliest appearance as Shylock (411).

48. Blake, "Perfect Ten."

49. Speaking on a panel entitled "Communication's Intellectual Boundaries with Related Disciplines" at the 2014 annual convention of the National Communication Association, Susan Zaeske underscored rhetoricians' reluctance to see historical texts as "data points" (Chicago, 22 November 2014).

50. Cima, "Minstrelsy and Mental Metempsychosis," 107.

Conclusion

1. "Total and Foreign-Born Population: New York City, 1790–2000" (web), accessed 28 July 2018, https://www1.nyc.gov/assets /planning/download/pdf/data-maps/nyc -population/historical-population/1790-2000 _nyc_total_foreign_birth.pdf; "No. HS-8. Immigration—Number and Rate: 1900 to 2001," U.S. Census Bureau (web), accessed 18 March 2018, http://www2.census.gov/library /publications/2004/compendia/statab/123ed /hist/hs-08.pdf; Kahn, "Caliban at the Stadium," 258.

2. Clara Calvo and Coppélia Kahn's *Celebrating Shakespeare: Commemoration and Cultural Memory* includes essays about a number of worldwide Tercentenary celebrations, including those in England, Ireland, and Australia.

3. "Using Shakespeare's Tercentenary to Awake the Spirit of Civic Cooperation," *Current Opinion*, June 1916, 408.

4. Cartelli, *Repositioning Shakespeare*, 82; Kahn, "Caliban at the Stadium," 275–76, 258.

5. Shakespeare, *Tempest*, 1.2.332; "Using Shakespeare's Tercentenary," 409; "Caliban" Program, 'Papers of MacKaye Family,' ML-5, box 42, folder 9, Rauner Special Collections Library, Dartmouth College, Hanover, NH, pp. 22–23.

6. As at the end of chapter 2, I am thinking of Raymond Williams's distinction between culture as "an abstraction and an absolute" and culture as "a whole way of life"; see Williams, *Culture and Society*, xvi.

7. Kahn, "Caliban at the Stadium," 272, 275; "Caliban" Program, Rauner Special Collections Library. To be sure, not all members of the Yiddish-speaking community could read English, but many could, and Adler's name appeared in English on posters and marquees along the Bowery such that even those with minimal English reading skills may well have recognized the local star's name.

BIBLIOGRAPHY

Archival Collections

The Beinecke Rare Book and Manuscript
Library, Yale University, New Haven,
Connecticut
Billy Rose Theater Division, New York Public
Library for the Performing Arts, New York
Folger Shakespeare Library, Washington, D.C.
Harvard Theatre Collection, Cambridge,
Massachusetts
Library of Congress, Washington, D.C.
  Hebraic Section, Yiddish Sheet Music
  Prints and Photographs Online Catalog
New York Public Library, New York
  Digital Collection, Dorot Jewish
  Division
  Manuscripts and Archive Division
  The People's Institute Records
Rauner Special Collections Library, Dartmouth
College, Hanover, New Hampshire
  Papers of MacKaye Family
The Yiddish Theatre Digital Archives, 2nd
Avenue Archive, 2nd Avenue Online
YIVO Institute for Jewish Research, New York

Newspapers and Periodicals

ENGLISH-LANGUAGE PUBLICATIONS

Ainslee's, 1905
American Hebrew, 1901
American Hebrew and Jewish Messenger, 1903
Baltimore Sun, 1903–4
Bookman: A Review of Books and Life, 1900–19
Boston Herald, 1902
Brooklyn Eagle, 1902
Century Magazine, 1894
Charities, 1905
Charities and the Commons, 1907
Current Opinion, 1916
Evening World's Home Magazine, 1905
Forum, 1904
Harper's New Monthly Magazine, 1898
Harper's Weekly, 1898–1907
Jewish Exponent, 1903–4

Jewish Messenger, 1901
New York Dramatic Mirror, 1901
New York Herald, 1905
New York Journal, 1898
New York Morning Journal, 1901
New York Sun, 1879–1907
New York Times, 1885–1946
New York Tribune, 1872–1907
New York World, 1901
San Francisco Chronicle, 1904
Theatre, 1902–1904
Washington Post, 1898–1905
Washington Post Online
Washington Times, 1906

YIDDISH-LANGUAGE PUBLICATIONS

Forverts, 1900–1905
Di arbeyter tsaytung, 1901
Di idishe velt, 1903
Di yidishe gazeten, 1893–1903
Dos abend blat, 1901

GERMAN-LANGUAGE PUBLICATION

New York German Journal, 1901

Books, Articles, and Dissertations

Adams, Joseph Quincy. "Shakespeare and
  American Culture." In *Shakespeare in
  America: An Anthology from the Revo-
  lution to Now*, edited by James Shapiro,
  418–35. New York: Library Classics of
  the United States, 2013.
Adler, Jacob. *A Life on the Stage: A Memoir.*
  Translated by Lulla Rosenfeld. New
  York: Applause, 2001.
Adler, Stella. Introduction to *A Life on the
  Stage: A Memoir*, by Jacob Adler,
  xiii–xx. Translated by Lulla Rosenfeld.
  New York: Applause, 2001.
Aleandri, Emelise. "A History of Italian-Amer-
  ican Theatre: 1900–1905." Ph.D. diss.,
  City University of New York, 1983.

———. *The Italian-American Immigrant Theatre of New York City*. Charleston, S.C.: Arcadia, 1999.

———. *The Italian-American Immigrant Theatre of New York City, 1746–1899*. Lewiston, N.Y.: Edwin Mellen Press, 2006.

Anderson, Benedict. *Imagined Communities: Reflections on the Origin and Spread of Nationalism*. London: Verso, 1983.

Bayor, Ronald H., ed. *Race and Ethnicity in America: A Concise History*. New York: Columbia University Press, 2003.

Bennett, Susan. *Theatre Audiences: A Theory of Production and Reception*. 2nd ed. New York: Routledge, 1990.

Berkowitz, Joel. *Shakespeare on the American Yiddish Stage*. Iowa City: University of Iowa Press, 2002.

———. "'A True Jewish Jew': Three Yiddish Shylocks." *Theatre Survey* 37, no. 1 (May 1996): 75–98.

———, ed. *The Yiddish Theatre: New Approaches*. Oxford: Littman Library of Jewish Civilization, 2003.

Bharucha, Rustom. *Theatre and the World: Performance and the Politics of Culture*. London: Routledge, 1993.

Bliss, William D. P., and Rudolph M. Binder, eds. *The New Encyclopedia of Social Reform*. New York: Funk and Wagnalls, 1908.

Bonfiglio, Thomas Paul. *Race and the Rise of Standard American*. New York: Mouton de Gruyter, 2002.

Bourdieu, Pierre. *Distinction: A Social Critique of the Judgement of Taste*. Translated by Richard Nice. Cambridge: Harvard University Press, 1984.

———. *The Field of Cultural Production: Essays on Art and Literature*. Edited by Randal Johnson. New York: Columbia University Press, 1993.

Brooks, Daphne, and Roshanak Kheshti. "The Social Space of Sound." *Theatre Survey* 52, no. 2 (2011): 329–34.

Brown, Stephen J. "The Uses of Shakespeare in America: A Study in Class Domination." In *Shakespeare: Pattern of Excelling Nature*, edited by David Bevington and Jay L. Halio, 230–38.

Newark: University of Delaware Press, 1978.

Calvo, Clara, and Coppélia Kahn. *Celebrating Shakespeare: Commemoration and Cultural Memory*. Cambridge: Cambridge University Press, 2015.

Carlson, Marvin. "The Development of the American Theatre Program." In *The American Stage*, edited by Ron Engle and Tice L. Miller, 101–14. Cambridge: Cambridge University Press, 1993.

———. *The Italian Shakespearians: Performances by Ristori, Salvini, and Rossi in England and America*. London: Associated University Press, 1985.

———. *Places of Performance: A Semiotics of Theatre Architecture*. Ithaca: Cornell University Press, 1989.

———. *Speaking in Tongues: Languages at Play in the Theatre*. Ann Arbor: University of Michigan Press, 2006.

Carson, Mina. *Settlement Folk: Social Thought and the American Settlement Movement, 1885–1930*. Chicago: University of Chicago Press, 1990.

Cartelli, Thomas. *Repositioning Shakespeare: National Formations, Postcolonial Appropriations*. New York: Routledge, 1999.

Ceccarelli, Leah. "Polysemy: Multiple Meanings in Rhetorical Criticism." *Quarterly Journal of Speech* 84, no. 4 (1998): 395–415.

Certeau, Michel de. *The Practice of Everyday Life*. Translated by Steven Rendall. Berkeley: University of California Press, 1988.

Chansky, Dorothy. *Composing Ourselves: The Little Theatre Movement and the American Audience*. Carbondale: Southern Illinois University Press, 2004.

Charland, Maurice. "Constitutive Rhetoric: The Case of the Peuple Québécois." *Quarterly Journal of Speech* 72, no. 2 (1987): 133–50.

Cima, Gay Gibson. "Minstrelsy and Mental Metempsychosis: Mid-Nineteenth Century American Women's Performance Criticism." In *The Sage Handbook of Performance Studies*, edited by D. Soyini Madison and

Judith Hamera, 106–23. Thousand Oaks, Calif.: Sage, 2006.

Clark, David Merriett. "John Corbin: Dramatic Critic." Ph.D. diss., University of Nebraska–Lincoln, 1976.

Clinton, Bill. Foreword to *Shakespeare in America: An Anthology from the Revolution to Now*. New York: Library Classics of the United States, 2013.

Courtney, Krystna Kujawinska, and John M. Mercer, eds. *The Globalization of Shakespeare in the Nineteenth Century*. Lewiston, N.Y.: Edwin Mellen Press, 2003.

Davis, Allen F. *Spearheads for Reform: The Social Settlements and the Progressive Movement, 1890–1914*. New Brunswick, N.J.: Rutgers University Press, 1994.

DeChaine, D. Robert, ed. *Border Rhetorics: Citizenship and Identity on the US–Mexico Frontier*. Tuscaloosa: University of Alabama Press, 2012.

Diner, Steven J. *A Very Different Age: Americans of the Progressive Era*. New York: Hill and Wang, 1998.

Dionne, Craig, and Parmita Kapadia. "Introduction: Native Shakespeares; Indigenous Appropriations on a Global Stage." In *Native Shakespeares: Indigenous Appropriations on a Global Stage*, edited by Craig Dionne and Parmita Kapadia, 1–15. Burlington, Vt.: Ashgate, 2008.

Dominguez, Lorenzo. "Editor's Epilogue and Author Biography." In *How the Other Half Lives: Studies Among the Tenements of New York*, by Jacob Riis, edited by Lorenzo Dominguez, 243–57. New York: Chelenzo, 2012.

Dowling, Robert M. *Slumming in New York: From the Waterfront to Mythic Harlem*. Urbana-Champaign: University of Illinois Press, 2007.

Du Bois, W. E. B. *The Souls of Black Folk*. New York: Dover Editions, 1994.

Educational Theatre for Children and Young People. [New York], 1908.

Epp, Michael. "The Imprint of Affect: Humor, Character, and National Identity in American Studies." *Journal of American Studies* 44 (2010): 47–65.

Erdman, Harley. *Staging the Jew: The Performance of an American Ethnicity*. New Brunswick, N.J.: Rutgers University Press, 1997.

Ferrara, Eric. *The Bowery: A History of Grit, Graft and Grandeur*. London: History Press, 2011.

Fisher, Laura R. "Writing Immigrant Aid: The Settlement House and the Problem of Representation." *MELUS* 37, no. 2 (2012): 83–107.

Fox, Richard Wightman, and T. J. Jackson Lears. Introduction to *The Culture of Consumption: Critical Essays in American History, 1880–1908*, edited by Richard Wightman Fox and T. J. Jackson Lears, vii–xvii. New York: Pantheon Books, 1983.

Freud, Sigmund. *The Uncanny*. Translated by David McLintock. New York: Penguin Books, 2003.

Gandal, Keith. *Virtues of the Vicious: Jacob Riis, Stephen Crane, and the Spectacle of the Slum*. Oxford: Oxford University Press, 1997.

Gay, Ruth. "Inventing a Yiddish Theater in America." In *The Jewish King Lear: A Comedy in America*, by Jacob Gordin, translated by Ruth Gay, 73–106. New Haven: Yale University Press, 2007.

Gerstle, Gary. *American Crucible: Race and Nation in the Twentieth Century*. Princeton: Princeton University Press, 2001.

Goldstein, Eric L. *The Price of Whiteness: Jews, Race, and American Identity*. Princeton: Princeton University Press, 2006.

Guglielmo, Thomas A. *White on Arrival: Italians, Race, Color, and Power in Chicago, 1890–1945*. Oxford: Oxford University Press, 2004.

Gustafson, Sandra M. "Eloquent Shakespeare." In Kahn, Nathans, and Godfrey, *Shakespearean Educations*, 71–91.

Haenni, Sabine. *The Immigrant Scene: Ethnic Amusements in New York, 1880–1920*. Minneapolis: University of Minnesota Press, 2008.

———. "Visual and Theatrical Culture, Immigrant Fiction, and the Immigrant Subject in Abraham Cahan's *Yekl*."

American Literature 71, no. 3 (1999): 493–527.

Hall, Stuart, ed. *Representation: Cultural Representations and Signifying Practices.* London: Sage, 2001.

———. "Signification, Representation, Ideology: Althusser and the Post-Structuralist Debates." *Critical Studies in Mass Communication* 2, no. 2 (1985): 91–114.

Hart, James D. *The Oxford Companion to American Literature.* 6th ed. New York: Oxford University Press, 1995.

Hecht, Stuart J. "Social and Artistic Integration: The Emergence of Hull-House Theatre." In "Insurgency in American Theatre," special issue, *Theatre Journal* 34, no. 2 (1982): 172–82.

Herring, Scott. *Queering the Underworld: Slumming, Literature, and the Undoing of Lesbian and Gay History.* Chicago: University of Chicago Press, 2007.

Herts, Alice Minnie. *The Children's Educational Theatre.* New York: Harper and Brothers, 1911.

Heskes, Irene. "Music as Social History: American Yiddish Theater Music, 1882–1920." In "Music of the American Theater," special issue, *American Music* 2, no. 4 (1984): 73–87.

Hill, Errol. *Shakespeare in Sable: A History of Black Shakespearean Actors.* Amherst: University of Massachusetts Press, 1984.

Hill, Howard C. "The Americanization Movement." *American Journal of Sociology* 24, no. 6 (1919): 609–42.

Holland, Peter. Foreword to Courtney and Mercer, *Globalization of Shakespeare in the Nineteenth Century,* i–iv.

Howe, Irving. *World of Our Fathers: The Journey of the East European Jews to America and the Life They Found and Made.* New York: Galahad Books, 1976.

Huang, Alexander C. Y. *Chinese Shakespeares: Two Centuries of Cultural Exchange.* New York: Columbia University Press, 2009.

Jackson, Shannon. *Lines of Activity: Performance, Historiography, Hull-House*

Domesticity. Ann Arbor: University of Michigan Press, 2000.

Jacobson, Matthew Frye. *Whiteness of a Different Color: European Immigrants and the Alchemy of Race.* Cambridge, MA: Harvard University Press, 1998.

Johnson, Randal. "Editor's Introduction: Pierre Bourdieu on Art, Literature and Culture." In Bourdieu, *Field of Cultural Production,* 1–25.

Kahn, Coppélia. "Caliban at the Stadium: Shakespeare and the Making of Americans." *Massachusetts Review* 41, no. 2 (2000): 265–84.

Kahn, Coppélia, and Heather S. Nathans. Introduction to *Shakespearean Educations: Power, Citizenship, and Performance,* edited by Coppélia Kahn, Heather S. Nathans, and Mimi Godfrey. Newark: University of Delaware Press, 2011, 22.

Kahn, Coppélia, Heather S. Nathans, and Mimi Godfrey, eds. *Shakespearean Educations: Power, Citizenship, and Performance.* Newark: University of Delaware Press, 2011.

Kaplan, Amy. *The Social Construction of American Realism.* Chicago: University of Chicago Press, 1988.

Kennedy, Dennis, ed. *Foreign Shakespeare: Contemporary Performance.* Cambridge: Cambridge University Press, 1993.

———. "Introduction: Shakespeare Without His Language." In *Foreign Shakespeare: Contemporary Performance,* ed. Dennis Kennedy, 1–18. Cambridge: Cambridge University Press, 1993.

Kessler, David. "Reminiscences of the Yiddish Theatre." In *Memoirs of the Yiddish Stage,* edited by Joseph C. Landis, 3–54. Flushing: Queens College Press, 1984.

Klier, John. "'Exit, Pursued by a Bear': Russian Administrators and the Ban on Yiddish Theatre in Imperial Russia." In Berkowitz, *Yiddish Theatre,* 159–74.

Knowles, Ric. *Reading the Material Theatre.* Cambridge: Cambridge University Press, 2004.

Koegel, John. *Music in German Immigrant Theater: New York City, 1840–1940.* Rochester: University of Rochester Press, 2009.

Leviatin, David. "Introduction: Framing the Poor—the Irresistibility of How the Other Half Lives." In *How the Other Half Lives*, 2nd ed., by Jacob Riis, edited by David Leviatin, 1–50. Boston: Bedford St. Martins, 2011.

Levine, Lawrence W. *Highbrow/Lowbrow: The Emergence of Cultural Hierarchy in America.* Cambridge: Harvard University Press, 1988.

Lhamon, W. T., Jr. *Raising Cain: Blackface Performance from Jim Crow to Hip Hop.* Cambridge: Harvard University Press, 1998.

Lott, Eric. *Love and Theft: Blackface Minstrelsy and the American Working Class.* Oxford: Oxford University Press, 1993.

Lubove, Roy. *The Progressives and the Slums: Tenement House Reform in New York City, 1890–1917.* Pittsburgh: University of Pittsburgh Press, 1964.

MacDonald, Joyce Green. "Acting Black: 'Othello,' 'Othello' Burlesques, and the Performance of Blackness." *Theatre Journal* 46, no. 2 (1994): 231–49.

Macdonald, Robert R. Foreword to *Gotham Comes of Age: New York Through the Lens of the Byron Company, 1892–1942*, by Peter Simons, 7. Rohnert Park, Calif.: Pomegranate Communications, 1999.

Maffi, Mario. *Gateway to the Promised Land: Ethnic Cultures on New York's Lower East Side.* New York: New York University Press, 1995.

Marcus, Jacob Radner. *United States Jewry, 1776–1985.* Vol. 4. Detroit: Wayne State University Press, 1993.

Massai, Sonia. "Defining Local Shakespeares." In *World-Wide Shakespeares: Local Appropriations in Film and Performance*, edited by Sonia Massai, 3–11. New York: Routledge, 2005.

McGaw, Charles J. "William Winter as Dramatic Critic." *Educational Theatre Journal* 4, no. 2 (1952): 115–21.

McGee, Michael Calvin. "A Materialist's Conception of Rhetoric." In *Explorations in Rhetoric: Studies in Honor of Douglas Ehninger*, edited by Ray E. McKerrow, 23–48. Glenview, Ill.: Scott Foresman, 1982.

Michaels, Walter Benn. "Race into Culture: A Critical Genealogy of Cultural Identity." *Critical Inquiry* 18, no. 4 (1992): 655–85.

Miller, Tice L. "Alan Dale: The Hearst Critic." *Educational Theatre Journal* 26, no. 1 (1974): 69–80.

———. *Bohemians and Critics: American Theatre Criticism in the Nineteenth Century.* Metuchen, N.J.: Scarecrow Press, 1981.

Moon, Krystyn. *Yellowface: Creating the Chinese in American Popular Music and Performance, 1850s–1920s.* New Brunswick: Rutgers University Press, 2006.

Mott, Frank Luther. *American Journalism: A History of Newspapers in the United States Through 250 Years, 1690–1940.* New York: MacMillan Company, 1941.

———. *A History of American Magazines, 1885–1905.* Cambridge: Harvard University Press, 1957.

Ngai, Mae M. "Race, Nation, and Citizenship in Late Nineteenth-Century America, 1878–1900." In Bayor, *Race and Ethnicity in America*, 96–130.

Ono, Kent A. "Borders That Travel: Matters of the Figural Border." In DeChaine, *Border Rhetorics*, 19–32.

Ono, Kent A., and John M. Sloop. *Shifting Borders: Rhetoric, Immigration, and California's Proposition 187.* Philadelphia: Temple University Press, 2002.

Painter, Nell Irvin. *The History of White People.* New York: Norton, 2010.

Paolucci, Anne. Preface to *The Italian-American Immigrant Theatre of New York City, 1746–1899*, by Emelise Aleandri, i–iv. Lewiston, N.Y.: Edwin Mellen Press, 2006.

Pennington, Michael. *Hamlet: A User's Guide.* New York: Limelight Editions, 1996.

Pittenger, Mark. "A World of Difference: Constructing the 'Underclass' in Progressive America." *American Quarterly* 49, no. 1 (1997): 26–65.

Pollock, Della. "Introduction: Making History Go." In *Exceptional Spaces: Essays in Performance and History*, edited by Della Pollock, 1–45. Chapel Hill: University of North Carolina Press, 1998.

Pratt, Mary Louise. "Arts of the Contact Zone." *Profession*, 1991, 33–40.

———. *Imperial Eyes: Travel Writing and Transculturation*. 2nd ed. New York: Routledge, 1992.

Ray, Angela G. *The Lyceum and Public Culture in the Nineteenth-Century United States*. East Lansing: Michigan State University Press, 2005.

Recchiuti, John Louis. *Civic Engagement: Social Science and Progressive-Era Reform in New York City*. Philadelphia: University of Pennsylvania Press, 2007.

Rice, T. D. "Otello: A Burlesque Opera." In *Jim Crow, American: Selected Songs and Plays*, by T. D. Rice, edited by W. T. Lhamon Jr., 110–58. Cambridge, MA: Belknap Press, 2009.

Riis, Jacob. *How the Other Half Lives*. Edited by David Leviatin. 2nd ed. Boston: Bedford St. Martins, 2011.

———. *How the Other Half Lives: Studies Among the Tenements of New York*. Edited by Lorenzo Dominguez. New York: Chelenzo, 2012.

———. *The Making of an American*. New York: Macmillan, 1901. Accessed 18 March 2018, www.bartleby.com/207/.

Roediger, David. *The Wages of Whiteness: Race and the Making of the American Working Class*. New York: Verso, 1991.

Rogin, Michael. *Blackface, White Noise: Jewish Immigrants in the Hollywood Melting Pot*. Berkeley: University of California Press, 1996.

Romeyn, Esther. *Street Scenes: Staging the Self in Immigrant New York, 1880–1924*. Minneapolis: University of Minnesota Press, 2008.

Rosenwaike, Ira. *Population History of New York City*. Syracuse: Syracuse University Press, 1972.

Sandrow, Nahma. "Romanticism and the Yiddish Theatre." In Berkowitz, *Yiddish Theatre*, 47–59.

———. *Vagabond Stars: A World History of Yiddish Theatre*. Syracuse, N.Y.: Syracuse University Press, 1996.

Scheil, Katherine West. *She Hath Been Reading: Women and Shakespeare Clubs in America*. Ithaca, N.Y.: Cornell University Press, 2012.

Schudson, Michael. *Discovering the News: A Social History of American Newspapers*. New York: Basic Books, 1978.

Scobey, David. *Empire City: The Making and Meaning of the New York City Landscape*. Philadelphia: Temple University Press, 2002.

Shakespeare, William. *The Merchant of Venice*. Edited by John Drakakis. London: Arden Shakespeare, 2010.

———. *The Tempest*. Edited by Virginia Mason Vaughan and Alden T. Vaughan. London: Arden Shakespeare, 2005.

Shapiro, James, ed. *Shakespeare in America: An Anthology from the Revolution to Now*. New York: Library Classics of the United States, 2013.

Shattuck, Charles. *Shakespeare on the American Stage: From the Hallams to Edwin Booth*. Washington, D.C.: Folger Shakespeare Library, 1976.

Smith, Barbara Herrnstein. "Contingencies of Value." *Critical Inquiry* 10, no. 1 (1983): 1–35.

Smith, Charles Sprague. *Working with the People*. New York: A. Wessels, 1904.

———. *Working with the People*. Repr. ed. New York: Funk and Wagnalls, 1908.

Sorin, Gerald. *A Time for Building: The Third Migration, 1880–1920*. Baltimore: Johns Hopkins University Press, 1995.

Spiegelberg, Frederick. *Souvenir Book of the Fair in Aid of the Educational Alliance and Hebrew Technical Institute*. New York: DeLeeuw and Oppenheimer, 1895.

Sturgess, Kim C. *Shakespeare and the American Nation*. Cambridge: Cambridge University Press, 2004.

Taylor, Diana. *The Archive and the Repertoire: Performing Cultural Memory in the Americas*. Durham: Duke University Press, 2003.

Taylor, Gary. *Reinventing Shakespeare: A Cultural History from the Restoration to the Present.* Oxford: Oxford University Press, 1991.

Thomashefsky, Bores. *Mayn lebens-geshikte.* Amherst, Mass.: National Yiddish Book Center, 1999.

Thompson, Ayanna. *Passing Strange: Shakespeare, Race, and Contemporary America.* Oxford: Oxford University Press, 2011.

Toll, Robert C. *Blacking Up: The Minstrel Show in Nineteenth-Century America.* New York: Oxford University Press, 1974.

Topp, Michael Miller. "Racial and Ethnic Identity in the United States, 1873–1877." In Bayor, *Race and Ethnicity in America,* 63–95.

Twigg, Reginald. "The Performative Dimension of Surveillance: Jacob Riis' *How the Other Half Lives.*" *Text and Performance Quarterly* 12, no. 4 (1992): 305–28.

Vaughan, Alden T., and Virginia Mason Vaughan. *Shakespeare in America.* Oxford: Oxford University Press, 2012.

Vaughan, Virginia Mason. "Shakespeare in the Gilded Age." In *Shakespeare in the Nineteenth Century,* edited by Gail Marshall, 332–47. Cambridge: Cambridge University Press, 2012.

Warnke, Bettina. "Reforming the New York Yiddish Theatre: The Cultural Politics of Immigrant Intellectuals and the Yiddish Press." Ph.D. diss., Columbia University, 2001.

Wild, Mark. "Americanization Movement." In *Encyclopedia of American Urban History,* edited by David R. Goldfield, vol. 1, 29–30. Thousand Oaks, Calif.: Sage, 2007.

Williams, Raymond. *Culture and Society, 1780–1950.* Garden City, N.Y.: Anchor Books, 1960.

———. *Marxism and Literature.* Oxford: Oxford University Press, 1977.

Williams, Simon. *1586–1914.* Vol. 1 of *Shakespeare on the German Stage.* Cambridge: Cambridge University Press, 1990.

Wilson, Christopher P. *The Labor of Words: Literary Professionalism in the Progressive Era.* Athens: University of Georgia Press, 1985.

Winter, William. *Shakespeare on the Stage.* Vol. 1. New York: Moffat, 1911.

Wolitz, Seth L. "*Shulamis* and *Bar Kokhba:* Renewed Jewish Role Models in Goldfaden and Halkin." In Berkowitz, *Yiddish Theatre,* 87–104.

Wolter, Jürgen C., ed. *The Dawning of American Drama: American Dramatic Criticism, 1746–1915.* Westport, Conn.: Greenwood Press, 1993.

Zarefsky, David. "Presidential Rhetoric and the Power of Definition." *Presidential Studies Quarterly* 34, no. 3 (2004): 607–19.

Page numbers in italics refer to figures.

Charities, 54, 99
See also *Charities and the Commons*
Charities and the Commons, 53–54
Chase, George C., 43–44
Children's Educational Theatre, The 37–40,
42–44, 45
Chinese American theatre, 59, 93, 111–12
Choy Ting Quoy, 160
Church Street Colored Theatre, 114
class
lower, 180n4
middle, 23, 25, 50, 108–9, 119, 121–22, 124, 131
upper, 16, 22, 36, 45, 95, 98
Columbia Theatre, 142
community building, 16, 61, 78, 91, 176n6
Conried, Henrich, 66, 103
contact zones, 171n8
Cooper, James Fenimore, 10, 48, 131
Cooper Union, 19, 30–31, 34, 49, 58
Cooper Union People's Institute. *See* People's
Institute
Corbin, John, 95–112, 120–30, 133–34, 42, 45
"How the Other Half Laughs," 95–96, 98,
106–8, 110–11, 122, 124, 129–30, 133
Crosman, Henrietta, 100
culture, term/category, 22, 93, 168–9, 179n60
Cushman, Charlotte, 113

Dale, Alan, 81, 98, 101–2, 127–28, 150
Daly, Augustin, 48, 55, 101, 143–47, 145–46, 153,
156–57, 159, 160–62, 164–66
Daly's Theatre, 101, 143, 160
Darrach, Marshall, 30–31
Davenport, Edward Loomis, 112, 160
Dawison, Bogumil 138–39, 160, 162
daytshmerish, 104, 181n19
*Di arbeyter tsaytung (The Workman's Newspa-
per),* 81
Di idishe velt (The Jewish World), 137, 155
Di yidishe gazeten (The Jewish Gazette), 136,
141, 177n19
Doesticks, Q. K. Philander. *See* Thompson,
Mortimer Q.
Dos abend blat (The Evening News), 140, 164
Douglass, Frederick, 158–59
drama criticism, 16, 94–99, 111, 148, 178n44
See also English-language criticism; Shake-
speare, William: reviews of; theatre
criticism
Dramatic Mirror, 98, 130, 133
Drew, John, 100

Educational Alliance, the, 20, 26, 28–29, 37, 40,
42–46, 50–52, 55, 58–59, 60, 88–89, 96
Educational Theatre for Children and Young
People, 38
Ellis Island, 167
English-language criticism, 94, 96, 104–7, 110,
119–21, 135, 164
See also drama criticism; Shakespeare,
William: reviews of; theatre criticism
ethnicity(/ethnic), 7, 20–21, 24, 47, 56, 59, 61,
116, 126, 128, 168, 182n42
extra-illustrated editions, 159, 161–62, 164–66

Farfariello, 68, 74, 135
focused gathering, 62, 66, 81
Folger Shakespeare Library, 1–3, 5, 15, 17, 144,
157, 159, 161, 166
Folger, Henry Clay, 1
Forrest, Edwin, 65–66, 110, 112–13, 160, 162
Forum, 98, 100, 180n4
Forverts (Forward), 51–52, 81, 127, 142–43, 148, 164
Four Hundred Club, the, 86–87, 94, 138
Frohman, Daniel, 55, 64
Fry, Emma Sheridan, 37, 53, 55, 170
Furness, Horace Howard, 48
Fyles, Franklin, 98, 112–13, 126

Garnier, Philippe, 160–62
Gentile America, 143
geography, social implications of, 6, 10–11,
20–21, 60, 104–5, 109–10, 117, 123, 125–26,
138–39, 142, 162
German theatre, 5, 67, 82, 93, 95, 104–5
Germania Assembly Rooms, 73
Germanness, 103
gesture, 40, 125, 128, 132, 134, 149, 152
Goffman, Erving, 62
Goodwin, Nat, 101
Gordin, Jacob, 67, 74, 88
Grand Theatre, 52
Greet, Ben, 1, 19, 28, 31–32, 34, 101
Griggs, Edward Howard, 30

Haenni, Sabine, 10, 25, 56, 59, 61, 66–68, 85,
103–4, 108–9, 119, 121
Hamlet, 4–5, 8–9, 30, 52, 57–59, 65–68, 72, 74,
81–83, 86–87, 103, 107, 115, 121–23, 125,
127–28, 130–31, 133, 138
Hamlet (character), 3, 8, 37, 49, 65–66, 70–71,
79–80, 82, 102, 122, 127–28, 133, 150
Hapgood, Hutchins, 73, 98, 104, 106, 133